How I Changed My Mind II:
Overcoming Self-Abuse Through Psychedelics, Psychology, Philosophy, and Diet

By

Neil Holmes

Copyright © 2025 Neil Holmes

ISBN: 978-1-918038-16-3

All rights reserved, including the right to reproduce this book, or portions thereof in any form. No part of this text may be reproduced, transmitted, downloaded, decompiled, reverse engineered, or stored, in any form or introduced into any information storage and retrieval system, in any form or by any means, whether electronic or mechanical without the express written permission of the author.

Dedication

This dedication goes to those who have played an essential role in my life, having me for the way I am and for being there at those critical moments in my life: Mum, Jayne, Nan, Jude, Pam, Malcolm, Riss, Paul, John B, Sylvia, Jasmin, Hannah, Silke, Andreas, Jens, Debra, David, Daniela, Kirsten, Hugh, John G and Justine.

Disclaimer

This book details the author's personal experiences with and opinions on psychedelics, philosophy, nutrition, psychology and other subjects. The author is not a healthcare provider.

The author and publisher provide this book and its contents on an "as is' basis, making no representations or guarantees concerning it or its contents. The author and publisher disclaim all such representations and warranties, including warranties of merchantability and healthcare for a particular purpose. Additionally, the author and publisher do not represent or warrant that the information accessible through this book is accurate, complete, or current.

The Food and Drug Administration or any other similar agency has not evaluated the statements made about products and services. They are not intended to diagnose, treat, cure, or prevent any condition or disease. Please consult with your physician or healthcare specialist regarding the suggestions and recommendations made in this book.

Except as explicitly stated in this book, neither the author nor the publisher, authors, contributors, or other representatives will be liable for damages arising out of or in connection with the use of this book. This medium contains a comprehensive limitation of liability that applies to all damages of any kind, including (without limitation) compensatory, direct, indirect, or consequential damages; loss of data, income, or profit; loss of or property damage; and claims by third parties.

This book is not intended as a substitute for consultation with a licensed healthcare practitioner, such as your physician. Before starting any healthcare programme or making lifestyle changes, consult your physician or another licensed healthcare practitioner.

As such, using this book implies your acceptance of this disclaimer.

Table of Contents

Preface 11
Introduction 13
A Psychological, Philosophical and Nutritional Overview Towards Well-Being 21
    Psychology 21
    Philosophy 24
    Health 26
Why This Book Is Written Differently 28
    Reflection on the First Book 28
    Motivation for the Second Book 28
    References 30
    Diverse Opinions 31
The Year 2019 33
    Therapeutic Session No 6 33
    Interpreting the Nothingness 35
    The Questions of Identity and Purpose 36
    Post-Session Awareness 36
    A Trip to the Lake District 37
    The Beginning of a Turnaround 37
    Discovering Alan Watts 38
The Year 2020 40
    Discovering The Game of Life 40
    Seeking Alternatives 40
    Working Through Alan Watts' Material 41

Embracing the Kybalion 42
The Challenges of February 2020 43
Breaking the Cycle of Despair 44
A Low Point in June 45
A New Perspective 47
Visualising a Path Forward 49
Enrolling on a Psychology Course 51
The Year 2021 - University 54
Introduction to Distance Learning 54
Modules 1 & 2 55
Modules 3 & 4 55
Breakdown and Flashbacks 56
Modules 5 & 6 and Coping with an Unexpected Loss 57
Modules 7 & 8 and Therapy Session with Magic Mushrooms 59
Navigating Challenges 61
The Final Project 62
Dialectical Behaviour Therapy 64
University Course Expectations 68
Thank You 69
My Non-University Reading Material While Studying 70
Realising the Issue 71
Breakdowns 72
The Onset of a Breakdown 72
Embracing Nothingness 73
Possible Steps to Recovery 75

A New Beginning 78
Taking Responsibility 81
Living in the Now 81
Embracing the Future 82
Phase Three – 2022: The Re-Programming 84
Discovering My Narcissism 86
Their World 89
Philosophy 93
The Role of Philosophy in Modern Life 94
Stoicism 94
Philosophical Contrasts: Hedonism 95
Personal Experience with Stoicism 96
Toxic Positivity 98
Three Stoic Principles 100
Further reading 103
Philosophy and Psychology 104
Our Systemic and Biased Lifelong Education 107
Seeking Universal Laws 111
The Year 2023 113
The Next Step: The Carnivore Diet Revelation 114
Commercial Foods and Potentially Commercially Related Illnesses 115
Overcoming Health Issues 117
The Possible Impact of Commercial Foods on Psychology. 118
Questioning the Psychologists' Perspective 119
The Personal Impact of Chemical-Free Living 119

Emerging Awareness and Gratitude 120
Existential Therapy and Logotherapy 122
The Gatekeeper Concept 123
Understanding Meaninglessness 125
Personal Responsibility and Freedom 126
Death, Freedom, Isolation, and Meaninglessness - A Review 127
Viktor Frankl's Influence 128
Death 132
The Taboo of Death 132
Personal Preparation and Acceptance 133
Living With Acceptance 133
Ancient Texts on Death 134
Facing the Past 135
Responsibility and Reconciliation 136
Daily Acceptance of Death 136
Proximity of Death 137
The Journey 138
Realising the Present Moment 138
Working Through Issues 139
Acceptance and Responsibility 139
Moving Forward 140
The Afterlife and Previous Lives 140
Acceptance of Universal Laws 141
Freedom 143
Misconceptions of Freedom 143

The Universe and Ethics 144
Reflecting on Responsibility 145
Relationships and Communication 146
Practicing Discipline 147
The Cycle of Self-Harm 148
Personal Journey and Transformation 148
Isolation 151
 Therapy vs. Medication 153
 A Shift in Career and Life Priorities 153
 Embracing Isolation as a Strength 155
 Consequences of External Expectations 156
 Recognising The Societal Game 157
 Challenging the Standard-Provided Scripts 159
 Choosing Our Paths 161
 Playing the Game 161
Meaninglessness 162
 The Elusiveness of Meaning 162
 The Fluidity of Self 164
 The Search for the Natural Self 166
 The Fear of Meaninglessness 167
 Accepting Meaninglessness 168
 Observing Meaninglessness 168
 Fictional Society 169
 Defining Our Philosophies 170
 Understanding Life Choices 171

- The Fate of Those Unaware 171
- Self-Commitment 172
- External Reflection 173
- The Freedom of Meaninglessness 174
- The Depths of The Game 176
- Living Authentically 177

Happiness 179
- Reflecting on Happiness 179
- Embracing Contentment 179
- Living Life Actively 180
- The Concept of Eudaimonia 181

Control 183
- The Illusion of Control 183
- Ultimate Responsibility 184
- Cultural Interpretations of Luck 184
- Facing the Meaninglessness of Control 186
- Questioning Everything 187
- Turning to Philosophy 189
- An Experiment 191
- Universal Laws and Systems 192
- Reflections on the Past 195

Adler 198
- Personal Reflections on Adler's Theory 198
- A Full Circle: Returning to the Present 199
- Transforming Relationships: From Enemies to Comrades . 200

Building Trust: A New Approach 200
Core and Character 201
Further Work to the End of 2023 202
   Taking a Break and Shifting Focus 202
   Exploring Jung's Archetypes 202
Dietary Change: A Radical Shift 204
   Challenging Conventional Wisdom 204
   Questioning the High-Carbohydrate Diet 204
   The Confusion of Modern Diets 205
   Understanding Macronutrients 206
   My Experience 207
   The Benefits of the Carnivore Diet 207
   A Little Further Down the Rabbit Hole and Transitioning to the Carnivore Diet 210
Exploring Different Diets: From Lion to Carnivore 212
   The Lion Diet: A Strict Approach 212
   The Carnivore Diet: A Softer Approach 212
   The Ketovore Diet: A Balanced Middle Ground 213
   Observations on Weight and Health 214
   Rethinking Conventional Wisdom 214
Results After Three Months on the Carnivore Diet 215
   Physical Health Improvements 215
   Mental Health Improvements 217
   The Broader Impact of the Carnivore Diet 217
The Bulgarian Clinic: A New Approach to Health 219
   Discovering a Unique Healing Method 219

The Importance of Professional Guidance 219
A Diabetic Specialist's Dilemma 221
The Reality Behind Dietary Advice 221
A Broader Issue in the Medical Field 221
Finding Meaning Amidst Deception 222
A Reflection on the Impact of the Standard American Diet (SAD) Diet 222
A Question of What Might Have Been 223
Experiments and Observations 224
My Food Experiments 225
Experiment One: The Return of Narcissistic Tendencies ...225
The Chemicals: A Deeper Dive 226
Experiment Two: Reverting to a High-Carbohydrate Diet..227
Taking Responsibility for Our Health 229
The Environmental Impact of Eating Meat 231
A Quick Response to Side Effects 235
Why the Carnivore Diet? 236
The Carnivore Community: A Growing Movement 237
Famine Foods or Medicine? 238
Oxalates 238
Histamine 239
Lectin 239
Salicylates 239
The Broader Implications 240
Fruits and Vegetables as Medicine: Occasional Consumption for Health Benefits 241

Mushrooms 241
Onions 242
Coffee 242
Garlic 242
Ginger 242
Herbs 243
Further Questions 244
  The Impact of Processed Chemicals on Our Health 244
  Macros 246
  Recommended Reading and Resources 247
  Nutrition and Physical Degeneration 249
  Pottinger's Cats 250
Further Reading 251
Fasting: A Powerful Tool for Health 254
  Recommended Reading and Resources 257
Insulin: The Double-Edged Sword of Health 259
  The Concept of 'Diabetes III' 260
Sport and Fitness 262
  A New Approach to Fitness 263
  The Role of Technology 264
  Our Only Guaranteed Goal in Life: Death 265
An Overview of My Highs and Lows 266
  The Highs 266
  The Lows 267
  The Fine Line of No Return 269

- Understanding Luck 270
- The Rest of 2023: Discovering Alfred Adler 272
  - Adler's Five Stages of Problem Behaviour in Children 272
  - Binge Eating: A Surprising Discovery 274
  - A New Part of My Philosophy 275
  - The Game of Life 276
  - Rules, Roles, and Participants 276
  - Reflections on What I Did and Didn't Do Through These Last Years 279
- Finally, The End 286
  - Psychedelics 287
  - Nutrition 289
  - Philosophy 292
  - Psychology 293
  - Where Am I Today? 297
- Thank You 302

Preface

I decided to include this section because, upon reflection, I realised how I wrote this book and how it evolved through the editing process fell short of what I had initially envisioned. That's the dilemma: I feel it loses its spontaneity if I keep reworking it. Although I am not a philosopher, my philosophical thoughts and ideas continue to evolve and expand with each revision, making this feel like an ongoing work in progress.

Please be patient if you think I am wrong, have overlooked something, or could have expressed myself more clearly.

The book's release was delayed by around 24 months longer than expected, and I'm okay with that. It allowed me more time to reflect on my thoughts, which I neglected when writing my previous book. It has also helped me confirm that I have found what I have been searching for all my life.

The very last section was entirely unplanned. Throughout 2024 and 2025, I encountered many conflicting views on psychology and therapy, as well as their achievements and areas where I think they fall short. I've noted my reflections, although they're not fully developed here. I feel increasingly convinced that we, as therapists and psychologists, are not always offering the kind of support people genuinely need for their mental health challenges.

I haven't delved deeper into this topic because it's not central to this book, and I'm unsure how to explore it beyond my approach to working with clients.

Finally, the contents of this book are open to discussion. I would love to hear your thoughts on whether you agree, disagree, or believe I've overlooked something important. This is by no means a definitive word on the subject. I am still learning, both through my own experiences and from others and constantly refining how I support my clients in letting go of their past as swiftly and gently as possible. It's a journey that continues.

Please enjoy the book, take what resonates with you, and feel free to leave the rest.

With love and best wishes,

Neil

The privilege of a lifetime is to become who you truly are.
Carl Jung

Introduction

Thank you for investing your time and money in this second book, where I delve into unresolved mental issues that I didn't realise were still hampering me after releasing my first book under the same name (without the 'II' and without 'I'). This time, I explore not the first seven years of my life but rather the intense self-inflicted abuse stemming from a lack of self-worth and other self-harming actions I did to myself throughout my life based on those first years.

Although I used psychedelics a couple of times during this journey, I soon realised they only helped me progress to a certain point in understanding aspects of my past. The rest was up to me. I drew on various psychological techniques and philosophical thoughts and ideas to provide tools and structures for restructuring parts of my everyday life, regardless of the external circumstances that could arise.

What did all this teach me? It taught me to let go. Once we let go, external influences such as fear, guilt, shame, inner conflict, anger, and sadness lose power over us. With a more neutral mind, we can focus on what we deem relevant and essential, which gives us more options based on our environment for what we want from our short life.

Near the end of this journey, I significantly changed my diet, switching from a carbohydrate-heavy diet (Standard American Diet – SAD) to a ketogenic diet and then to a Carnivore diet. The impact was so profound that I am convinced it addressed my remaining mental issues that would have been impossible to deal with without making that nutritional change. Even now, more than a year later, I adhere to the Carnivore/ketogenic diet. Whenever I revert to my old eating habits, my health issues, narcissistic tendencies and other inhibitive thoughts return with a vengeance.

We all have a certain level of egoism that isn't a threat to ourselves or others; it's essential for survival, integration, and effective communication with the outside world. However, the deep-rooted, constantly assessing, obsessing, and manipulative narcissism that plagued me influenced my thoughts and behaviour for as long as I can remember.

What is also important to remember is that, given the vast array of psychological, philosophical, and nutritional options, I kept it simple by experimenting with various techniques and methods as I encountered them. Although I've tried hundreds of different tools and strategies over the years, I know I haven't tried them all. It's about finding what works, mainly through trial and error. This is our responsibility because no one else will help us as rigorously as we can.

Contrary to what is commonly thought in commercial medicine, there isn't a one-size-fits-all approach to addressing past issues. It's multifaceted and much more complex than simply administering medication with the hope that it will solve the problem while generating substantial revenue for the pharmaceutical company. One thing I haven't done in this book is to mention the tools that didn't work for me, as I hoped you would choose what appeals to you based on your history and research and decide on their effectiveness yourself.

I chose not to visit a therapist because I wanted to find out what was suitable for me and not to re-enter society as it expects us to, all dosed up on drugs to the nines, playing the role of a zombie waiting to come off them only to deal with the problem as it was before, plus the permanent/temporary potential damage the drugs could cause. Not only that, but I have also always been suspicious of therapists regarding what they do or do not offer a client, but at the time, I didn't know why. I aimed to understand my place here and feel more comfortable as an outsider among others who share my thoughts.

As you will read, I have exceeded my expectations in dealing with my past and my place in this world, and I am convinced that not visiting a therapist was the right choice for me, my personality, and my view of what is essential for the rest of my life. And I have never taken a commercial pharmaceutical tablet to numb something, no matter how painful it was for me.

A crucial yet daunting aspect of releasing the past is delving into our minds' deepest, darkest corners to find and recognise what is bothering us, to accept and embrace those outdated reactive fears. When we can thank them for their fantastic job protecting us all these years and then let them go, we set ourselves free, giving ourselves a new foundation to rebuild our lives.

By recognising those problems, we couldn't find answers to our questions; we take them for what they were, and when we do, we can acknowledge that the past is still part of us, which gives us new strength and qualities that help us make the most of what lies ahead. We still trip up, run against the wall and experience pain, but this time, we know how to take it for what it is, pick ourselves up, dust ourselves down and carry on. No one is going to do that for us except ourselves.

Doing something terrible at some point doesn't necessarily make us bad. We all have the potential for such actions, but our programming determines if we act on them. Everyone is driven by an inner positive intention, even if it initially doesn't seem that way. Like a computer, changing the programming changes our performance. We can 'reneuronise' our minds to let those old patterns fade by replacing them with more open and neutral ways of thinking and behaving that represent who we indeed are, which aligns with our ethics and inner values when interacting with the external world.

We never forget the past, which is a good thing, no matter how intense it may have been. Those worked-through memories allow us to review them at any time, learn from our mistakes, and take action that aligns with our values. Yet, our experiences, weaknesses, and behavioural patterns make us human and remind us we are all fallible. Nobody is perfect. Not only that, but those problematic moments and mistakes (such as a maths problem), once worked through and understood, give us unique qualities that those who haven't experienced such an experience as we have can never achieve. That's what makes us unique. Ultimately, who can you be honest with if not yourself?

Only when you want to work through and change your opinion on past troubles do you take full responsibility for yourself and your outcomes. An expert can guide and point you in the right direction, but that's all. You are responsible for your overall wellbeing and managing your triggers. Nobody can work through your feelings of hurt, pain, or shame without experiencing something challenging along the way.

While you work through your past issues, you may be surprised by the varying intensities you encounter as you remove each issue individually. However, having trusted people around you to talk to is essential during moments of confusion, doubt, and hopelessness. One way of considering this is that these moments of painful realisation signal the weakening of the foundation that has held us back for so long.

Yet, once that ill-built foundation crumbles, there's also no turning back. You need to confront and work through what you start to understand about yourself, no matter how much you dislike it. Only then can you build the foundation that aligns with your ethics and values.

If you don't want to face what you've buried deep within you and don't want to change the personality and the defensive trigger networks you've created, put this book back on the shelf and find something else to distract you. It won't help you, no matter what you do. You have to want to change.

If, however, you think medication is better, or you prefer the support of people who have been encouraged to accommodate your triggers and needs, giving some sense of deceptive wellbeing, that's your choice. Whatever you decide, you have to live with the consequences. Not only that, whatever you choose, you will lose something in the process. Which do you prefer to lose?

Should you embark on a journey to address your behaviour-related past, don't give up, no matter what challenges arise. These hurdles need to be overcome. Once you give up, it wins; it leaves you stuck in limbo and probably leaves you feeling like a failure. You are closer to releasing those past issues than you think.

How do we know we are making progress once we embark on such a journey? You may notice that triggers have changed, becoming less sensitive or giving rise to new problems, or you are responding more relaxed and in control, gaining a fuller understanding by taking responsibility for your thoughts and actions as they are.

Your life may change in ways you never considered or hoped for, which is great because life reveals something you never knew existed and couldn't have believed you could experience. It's better to wonder how to respond differently than you have in mind than to remain stuck in that old vicious circle that brings you nowhere except another round of inner punishment. Keep asking questions and seeking that mental shift until you feel more at peace with every step.

You will naturally stop with investigations at some point, which is where you need to be. You may also start up again and investigate something because something bothers you. This is acceptable because it's a part of life. Nothing goes smoothly. Part of the skill is picking yourself up, dusting yourself down and moving on, even if you need to invest some time to understand what happened.

Another step forward is that you may not feel inferior or superior to others, but instead accept yourself and them as they are. We are on the right path as we reach a state of neutrality in our thoughts and beliefs about what is happening around us. This doesn't make us cold but allows us to reflect more objectively on what is happening around us without adversely affecting our minds and bodies.

What worked for me was tackling one past issue at a time that presented itself first or felt like the most pressing one to address. If new setbacks arise, you've likely progressed to the next pressing problem because you've understood the previously pressing problem, not that you're back to square one. It's up to you to keep moving forward until each vital issue is resolved.

You may be shocked by what you encounter. If a challenging issue takes time to resolve, continue to ask questions, review the information, and consider different perspectives. These issues took years to develop into the massive beasts they have evolved into today, so don't expect to fix them overnight. If it feels endless and no solution seems apparent, remember that you know how to deal with it; you just haven't discovered the solution yet. With perseverance, it will come. Not only that, keep your mind open to all eventualities, even those that society may consider incorrect or otherwise.

Once you've released enough of your past (or an essential aspect of it), you can start living life as it is. There won't be any euphoria, celebrations, or recognition; life will continue as before, but you will do it differently, automatically and mostly without much effort. The only change is that you've accepted yourself and your life for what they are. Your life now belongs to you, not the restrictive fantasies you were bound to through what happened to you from someone who messed up themselves and used you as their scapegoat.

One thing to be aware of is that during this journey, you may experience euphoria and a range of other emotions. Enjoy it as it occurs because you may still be on your journey to free yourself from your past. So, if another problem arises, greet it with open arms and deal with it accordingly. It (as well as the others) protected you this far, but now it is out of date and needs to be released.

Ultimately, you are your first-line psychologist, doctor, nutritionist and philosopher. You are responsible for your mental and physical health, not society, not industry and not the government. They don't care. Democracy is a capitalistic land where business success comes before you, regardless of the industry. We are just pawns in their game of profit, being passed from one to the other.

Before you can feel comfortable around others, you must feel comfortable with yourself. You are the only person you are with for every second, minute, hour, day, year, and decade of your life. You guide yourself when you die, just as you did when you were born. Because of this, love yourself for who and what you are. You are the love you radiate and recognise within yourself that matches your inner identity. You are unique, as we all are. That uniqueness makes you human and unique.

You are here to live the life you want within the current system. Listen to others, but remember that your final decision always impacts you in one way or another. There will be beautiful moments and terrible challenges along the way, so make the most of what you have to deal with. As easy as it sounds, the skill is picking ourselves up, dusting ourselves off, and getting on with what we have to deal with this moment. The moment is now. You are not here to be a martyr to someone else's opinions or desires because they couldn't cope with it and wanted to offload it onto you. Don't let them do this with you. To think this way isn't selfish; this is self-respect.

You know how to love and set boundaries; you've just forgotten due to all the other distractions in your life. Reset them by whatever means allows you to live in the moment. That is all there is: the present. The past is a memory, albeit an unreliable one, and the future is only a fantasy.

I couldn't do this when I started writing the first book. After releasing this book and releasing my past, I can do most of it most of the time, and it's an immensely freeing and gratifying feeling. I occasionally forget and get caught up in things, but now I know how to get back on track and reclaim my life. I hope you do, too.

The unexamined life is not worth living.
Socrates

A Psychological, Philosophical and Nutritional Overview Towards Well-Being

This chapter provides a brief account of my transformative journey through various psychological therapies and philosophical explorations. It encapsulates my quest for personal growth, change, and a deeper meaning in life. Through various therapeutic and philosophical lenses, I examine the intricate process of self-understanding and comprehending the world around us. Each section reveals how these approaches have shaped my perspectives, addressed my fears, and ultimately guided me towards a more fulfilling and authentic existence.

Psychology

Dialectical Behaviour Therapy: As I have mentioned, I have used many various psychological tools. However, this was one of the essential psychological tools that started the ball rolling. It provided me with enough new ideas to help release me from most of my intense daily narcissistic thinking and behavioural patterns. This significant change enabled me to make further progress, considering more unique tools and perspectives on problems where nothing had previously helped me. I am deeply grateful for this initial breakthrough, as it marked the beginning of my journey toward personal growth and a deeper search for meaning.

Transition to Existential Therapy: Building on the foundation of Dialectical Behaviour Therapy, I felt ready to delve deeper into understanding myself and my existence. This led me to existential therapy, which helped me clear up several questions that other sessions hadn't previously addressed adequately, but helped to change my perspectives in four critical areas: death, freedom, isolation, and meaninglessness. Confronting these profound topics compelled me to examine myself deeply, an essential step in my ongoing journey of personal growth. The intense nature of existential therapy revealed why some of my biggest fears existed and allowed me to address them directly, driving significant change in my life.

As a guide, at worst, some of these new perceptions took me several weeks to several months to work through, helping me adjust my thinking and gain a deeper understanding of myself.

What I like about this development is that it is a great reminder that nothing is fixed in stone; everything is in constant flux, and no two people think alike. We constantly experience an ever-changing perspective based on the ever-changing roles we play in an ever-changing life's ever-changing moments. Nothing stays still long enough to be the same thing twice.

However, existential therapy can be a demanding experience. It requires a willingness to confront some of the most challenging aspects of human existence, which can be daunting, to put it mildly.

Adlerian Psychology: Embracing life's fluid nature, I turned to Adlerian psychology, which deepened my understanding of existentialism and guided my thoughts in a new direction. Adler posits that we are not defined by our past but by our current thoughts and desires about our environment. This perspective was crucial for my growth, encouraging me to focus on who I wanted to become rather than being constrained by my past, as in Freudian psychology.

Jung's Archetypes: Continuing my journey of self-discovery, I delved into Jung's work on archetypes. This exploration unlocked parts of myself that previous work hadn't touched, allowing me to clear away more metaphorical debris and finally see the floor for what it is, where I had stood disillusioned each day. It also answered existential questions that had become more pressing since I started exploring existential therapy.

One critical insight was recognising how brief our time on this planet is and how we squander our precious, non-renewable resource, time, which is wasted on mental fantasies based on events from the past and imagined futures that are unlikely to occur. Sure, it's lovely to dream, and it's essential to plan, but living in one of these non-existent worlds for most of our time isn't healthy.

This realisation opened a mental door, filling my mind with light and illuminating the darkest corners of my psyche. I saw that I had been living in a mental prison of my design, trapped by my thoughts for all those years. For the first time, I saw a way out through the door, and not only that, but the door had never been locked or closed; it had stood open all along. Like a life-long confined animal, it took me a couple of days to muster the courage to leave that self-created prison cell of fifty-odd years, but when I did…

I will pause here because I decided to stop documenting my experiences after this profound impact and take a break from it all. I felt calm and relaxed in my newly perceived world, and delving into further details seemed unnecessary. While I still read about psychology and love the subject, I now only consider and implement new tools or perspectives if they support my new persona.

However, my interest in philosophy deepened. I began exploring its theories and practical applications more thoroughly, and I find them fascinating. Inspired by this passion, I started a philosophy group in my city, seeking diverse perspectives to expand my understanding. The group continues to operate and grow, welcoming new members throughout the year. The more I engaged with philosophy, the more I understood Socrates' assertion that the only thing he knew was that he knew nothing.

Philosophy

Philosophy explores fundamental questions about existence, knowledge, values, reason, mind, and language. It is an ancient discipline that seeks to understand the world and our place in it through critical thinking, rigorous analysis, and systematic reasoning, which was once considered the study of the mind.

Philosophy encourages us to explore profound and often abstract concepts, such as the nature of reality, the foundation of morality, and the limits of human understanding. We do this when sitting with a therapist and answering their questions. By challenging assumptions and exploring different perspectives, philosophy provides a framework for examining life's most essential questions, fostering intellectual growth, and guiding our actions and beliefs.

Stoicism: I first turned to Stoicism because it is practical, easy to understand, and straightforward to implement in everyday life. Making it into a routine or habit took more time. Unlike some philosophical doctrines that can be abstract and complex, Stoicism offers clear and actionable advice. Its teachings focus on living a virtuous and fulfilling life by cultivating wisdom, courage, justice, and temperance. As with anything in life, all one needs is a bit of commitment when undertaking something new, and Stoicism is no exception.

When I began exploring Stoicism, I delved into the (secondhand) works of Zeno of Citium, the founder of this philosophy. Zeno's teachings, as presented by Marcus Aurelius, Seneca, Epictetus, and others, resonated with me because they offered theoretical musings and practical guidelines relevant to today's society despite being written long ago. I also reviewed several other popular Hellenic philosophies, including Platonism, Pyrrhonism, Pythagorism, and Cynicism, to deepen my understanding. This comparative study helped me appreciate the distinctiveness of Stoic thought and reinforced its practicality.

This hands-on approach to philosophy provided a solid foundation for my search for meaning. It provided tools to navigate life's complexities and address daily challenges more effectively. For example, the Stoic practice of reflecting on what is within our control versus what is not has helped me manage stress and maintain composure in difficult situations. The emphasis on living in harmony with nature and accepting one's fate fostered a sense of inner peace and resilience.

Incorporating Stoicism with Existentialism: At this time, I also considered newer philosophies, such as existentialism, absurdism, and nihilism, and felt that they perfectly complemented Zeno's Stoicism, along with Pythagorism and other Greek philosophies I have not mentioned. Combining them has given me a core structure that continues to evolve as I incorporate new insights. This lifelong learning journey and continual growth are something I embrace wholeheartedly.

Philosophy is inherently part of our life journey, shaped by family, friends, media, and other external influences. Many of us have, at some point, inadvertently copied or adopted parts of these and other philosophies; yet, when asked, we may be aware of some aspects but not all of them. However, our philosophy has never been fixed; it changes with our experiences, reflections and the environment that affects us. It often takes a significant event to realise our unconscious inherited beliefs may no longer serve us, prompting a search for our own 'truth'.

As Adler observed, we choose who we want to be each morning by either carrying over our thoughts from the previous day or starting anew with something fresh, determining our day's personality. Our lifestyles reflect the philosophy we've consciously developed over time. We are not defined by others' perceptions but by our experiences, emotions, needs, and desires. I've learnt that it's perfectly fine to think differently and prioritise what may not appeal to the majority, but embracing open-mindedness makes us uniquely individual, engaging, and accessible.

Health

I have included a brief section on health and fitness, detailing my struggles and how I could never fully appreciate it for what it truly is. Since my teenage years, I have longed to immerse myself in it, yet I repeatedly hindered my progress due to weak and poorly chosen inner values and beliefs about myself. Today, I cherish my daily workout sessions and relish every moment of the proper foods I eat.

Dietary Changes: One crucial aspect that has significantly influenced me is altering my carbohydrate intake to alternate between the Ketovore (not the ketogenic diet) and Carnivore diets once I understood the impact these (and other) eating styles could have on us. The Carnivore diet has helped eradicate the last remnants of my narcissism and resolved a host of physical health issues, which I will discuss in more detail later.

Food Experiments: Once I had my health under control through what I ate, I started to intentionally and unintentionally experiment with different foods that helped me determine some things that triggered my narcissistic behaviour patterns. This was a pretty scary realisation that certain foods and chemicals found in foods (such as vegetables and nuts) and food-like processed products created a mental imbalance within me, altering my thought processes enough to become a different and more unpleasant person than I am.

Fortunately, as you will later read, I was able to eliminate those unwanted traits quickly and regain control over my thinking by simply avoiding such foods and food-like products altogether.

Additionally, after following the Carnivore diet for a while, I intentionally began testing different foods individually to determine their impact on me. I have included some to demonstrate my sensitivity to certain plant toxins and food chemicals, whether added or naturally occurring. This, however, doesn't mean this is a potential risk for everyone; some of us may not react to certain plants and chemicals, and we need to test one plant or food-like product at a time to find out what issues they could cause us. Then again, some of us may be more sensitive than others. Remember, we don't live in a one-size-fits-all world, even though we are encouraged to think this way.

Personal Responsibility for Health: We are all unique, so we must take full responsibility for ourselves and our health. Our mental and physical health are closely linked, such that when we react to something we have consumed as food or a food-like product, an issue affecting mental health can be seen physically and vice versa. This is the way I dealt with my past and my health. I am aware I may have been able to do it quicker, but it turned out fine in the end.

What is important to remember is that no one is there to help you, not even those we pay (well, maybe a minority of people), because ultimately, we make the final decision on what is asked of us. If something goes wrong, as it appears internationally with mental and physical health, then only we are to blame for the circumstances we are in.

Life is a series of natural and spontaneous changes. Don't resist them; that only creates sorrow. Let reality be reality. Let things flow naturally forward in whatever way they like.
Lao Tzu

Why This Book Is Written Differently

I chuckle as I write this, but I have no choice but to write this book in a style different from the one I had initially planned. After some deliberation, I am grateful to have written this book in a more modular format than as a chronological diary of events, as I did for the first book. Let me explain why.

Reflection on the First Book

My first book was formatted more as a diary of events for those who have read it. It started with my experiences regarding microdosing and progressed to the intense and powerful therapy sessions I had carried out. My opinion about the first book is that it is not easy to read, partly due to how I wrote it and my perceptions of what I went through. The problem was that when I had finished writing the first book, I thought I had dealt with my past, but I hadn't.

Motivation for the Second Book

I decided to write this second book because once I understood that I had more inner work to do, I felt I was deceiving those who had read the first book, expecting that I had picked myself up and was getting on with life. I could have left interested readers thinking this was all the self-therapy work I had to do, but I would have been lying. When comparing their progress with mine, this could have become a problem for those still struggling with themselves. This second book addresses the issues and concerns I had caused myself.

After I released my first book and realised that I needed to take this journey further, I took extensive notes in diary format for 2020, 2021, and half of 2022. Around June 2022, I had made significant progress, felt good, and was getting on with my life – my seemingly impossible dream was coming true. I needed that break from constantly assessing myself, as it had become somewhat of an obsession. With hindsight, it was the right thing to do because it was also becoming increasingly difficult to identify inner issues to work on.

At this time, I had also reached a point where I wanted to pursue other interests in life, so I took up a new hobby (astronomy) and started socialising (a little more) again. I felt that I had reduced my lifelong inner screaming voices to two, and one was reduced to (mostly) a whisper. The other one I started to hear was my authentic inner voice. The other one I had reduced in volume was my uncontrollable narcissistic voice (it took me a bit longer to discover it was the remaining narcissistic part of me, though).

In January 2023, I revisited my notes to update the book's final section, which had been absent for several months, in preparation for its release three months later. I opened the notes on the computer and quickly realised that I had nearly lost them all! I had nothing except for my notes in 2020 and a little bit for 2021. At first, I was in a bit of a panic, but when I reviewed the remaining notes, I realised how superficial my thinking and communication style had been, which helped me accept that this had been my style for most of my life. After some thought, I decided that was a good thing to happen because I had the chance to convey these experiences differently, and I hope to do so in greater depth.

Writing this book in a modular form, based on a general timeline of events (with some diary format remaining), gives each section a better separation and a more precise flow from one to the next. It provides a straightforward overview describing what helped and how it affected me. You may recognise that I have sometimes struggled to convey this experience because what one goes through internally isn't always easy to put on paper. I appreciate your patience if some of my descriptions are unclear.

Because of this, I hope this second book provides more explicit guidance and support for those on similar journeys. By presenting my experiences in a more structured and modular way, I aim to offer insights and practical advice that can be more easily understood and applied. I encourage readers to reflect on their experiences and consider the approaches discussed here.

Remember, your life journey is unique, and I hope this book serves as a helpful companion on your journey of self-discovery.

References

I included numerous first-hand references in my first book, anticipating their necessity. However, some readers who contacted me were unsure how to interpret them. Consequently, in this book, I have referred to specialist works authored by experts who can convey the message more effectively, along with some direct research references. I have also organised these references into a more readable format directly related to each section in each chapter, which, I acknowledge, is unconventional. There is a reason, and I will address this later.

When discussing topics within this book, I have read and understood the articles, and although I do not reference all of them directly, they are available. Given the abundance of excellent reading material available, I have not had the opportunity to read or understand every relevant paper. Therefore, I have refrained from commenting on material with which I am not entirely familiar. Research papers are included where I have consulted specific papers.

To use the references effectively, you can find them directly within each chapter where they are relevant. For more in-depth research, you can also use tools like Google Scholar to locate additional supplementary material or start with the reading material I provided to help you get an overview before diving deeper into what affected me the most. This approach ensures that you can easily access and understand the context of each reference.

Naturally, I use references from non-industry-sponsored sources to avoid highlighting something potentially misleading unless it is to highlight the difference between the two types of scientific research methods.

Diverse Opinions

You may disagree with my approach to mental health, dietary choices, and other topics I discuss, and you have every right to do so. There are multiple ways to approach these issues, and I am aware of them. For example, with my clients, I have applied what I have learnt and worked more specifically with them than I did with myself, which has had a significant impact. However, this is my approach to dealing with it as effectively as possible, given the resources I had at the time, and your life choices are ultimately your responsibility.

Suppose you sit with me in a session. In that case, I work differently and more effectively to help you address your past by showing you various ways of approaching what happened philosophically and psychologically.

I encourage you to critically evaluate the provided references and any additional sources you find and to form your own opinions based on the evidence presented. Please continue to ask questions and try to identify where we differ. If you wish, please let me know; however, the activity is intended for you to see what you need to do, not to assist me. I have found what I have been looking for, yet I am always open to new and old ideas; we may have overlooked trying them out.

Your journey is yours. The experiences of others help you discover what could work for you, and with each step, you can find what works for you and discard the rest.

Let's buckle in, delve deeper, and continue from where I left off in my first book without further ado.

To live is to suffer; to survive is to find some meaning in the suffering.
Friedrich Nietzsche

The Year 2019

When the first book was released, I felt tremendous euphoric. I was motivated to tackle whatever came next and thought that the intense work I had endured was starting to pay off. The only problem was that as time passed, I began to recognise that I wasn't doing anything constructive with my time. I was wasting it by doing nothing, feeling directionless and lethargic again. It reached the point where I didn't know what to do or how to break out of that ever-increasing, despondent, and stagnant cycle.

Therapeutic Session No 6

After considering what to do about that feeling of directionlessness and despair, I returned to the mushrooms for a 6th therapeutic session. Not knowing what to ask, I let the Universe decide what I should focus on and was curious about the outcome. It was my first time taking this approach, and my only worry was that I felt I was taking a risk because I couldn't find any experience, guidance, or tips from other psychonauts who had done something similar.

If you've read the first book, you'll know that I went into great detail about the setting, preparing the question, and the environment to help you understand what I went through. I will not mention any of that this time unless it's relevant. Instead, I want to focus on what I learned from the sessions.

About an hour into the session, I unexpectedly and repeatedly started to ask myself, 'Who am I?' as I felt the psychedelics pulling some information out of the darkest corners of my mind. I relived a personality that I thought was (a part of) me. After a while, I said, 'No, that isn't me. It's a façade. Who am I?' Over the next few hours, I went through many different personalities I had tried to emulate at some point. Each time, I concluded that they weren't the real me and rejected them one after another.

After about seven hours of trying out different personalities and rejecting them all, I noticed the psychedelic effects wearing off and realised this session was coming to an end. I felt sad that I hadn't been able to discover who I am, and felt that nothing was left. Preparing to stand up, I had the urge to lie down again, and without warning, I saw who or rather, what, I am. Or so I eventually interpreted it.

I envisioned myself as a wooden fence, each panel 5 to 10 cm wide and standing about waist-high. The wooden boards were old and weathered, with most paintwork worn away. Aside from some irregularities in its form, it remained stable and appeared to serve its primary function(s).

Nevertheless, I felt something lift from me, but I still don't know what it was, even after much reflection. Had I understood this symbolism correctly, that all my false masks and personalities had been stripped away, leaving my bare and beaten self still standing upright? Had I correctly understood that no matter how much gloss we put on our lives, we are only as solid and accurate as the foundation underneath? This is one interpretation I have considered regarding that symbolism. If I'm interpreting this correctly, I'm not entirely sure.

Once this phase passed, I decided to take a shower. But, as always, the mushrooms knew best. When I tried to stand up, I felt compelled to lie down again. As my head hit the pillow, a wave of intense nausea overcame me. With no other choice, I curled up and hugged my aching stomach. While rocking in pain, a new question emerged, repeating itself: 'Why are you here?' I was back searching in that nothingness, unable to find an answer.

During this uncomfortable time, several images flashed by that didn't make sense. A few minutes later, it all went blank, and there was absolutely nothing (this makes sense to me!). About an hour later, the pain in my stomach subsided, and I remained in bed, absolutely exhausted.

Then, it was nothing more than a flash, maybe a millisecond, which made me think intensely about what I had experienced. I saw and recognised the nothingness for what it is! But how do you see nothingness yet conclude that it embodies our meaning and time here?

Interpreting the Nothingness

Does it mean that I have nothing in my life? Does it mean I have nothing holding me back? Does it mean that nothingness means everything? Does everything mean nothing? Does it mean I have nothing of worth in my life and am nothing? Or conversely, does it imply that the nothingness in my life is the only thing I have that has meaning? Does it have a different meaning, and if so, what is it?

I suppose the bare fence I saw earlier symbolised the nothingness surrounding us. Once, it was a tree, a fallen trunk, a plank, and then it became a fence, but only temporarily. After that, it returns to its baseness of nothingness again. But doesn't a fence have a purpose and a function because it (I) created one (for myself) based on my environment, or is it that no matter what happens and what we perceive ourselves to be, the nothingness remains as it is, for eternity?

Have I found the basis of who I am through this?

If we have found a role that we have consciously chosen to give us meaning and purpose, it doesn't mean it has meaning and purpose from another person's perspective; it has meaning and purpose only for ourselves, for as long as we choose to need it. Is this an individual act that we are responsible for if we want to set ourselves free?

The Questions of Identity and Purpose

The two questions, 'Who am I?' and 'Why am I here?' are strongly related. How? Our current thoughts define us in that moment until we think of something else, such that we constantly adopt new thought identities, not just mentally but physically as well. This means that if we let go of those limiting identities and take on the ones we desire with full commitment, then we are that person, even if only for a brief moment. Over time, we can practice being that person until it becomes second nature.

Later in the book, I elaborate on the fact that we all possess an extensive range of abstract process labels assigned to us by others or that we have adopted ourselves. Some abstract process labels include sympathetic, busy, gay, cold-hearted, psychologist, intelligent, engineer, weird, different, depressed, borderline, father, etc. Often, we are unaware of many of these abstract labels until someone points them out based on their interpretation of what they mean. Unfortunately, if we aren't careful, we tend to conform to these labels by adjusting our personality to match our own or others' interpretations, making them part of our perceived identity, which they aren't.

This poses a risk as we may become so bound by these abstract process labels that we can never discover our true potential. If we allow these process restrictions to take hold, we lose control of ourselves and thus become players in a game dictated by others for their use. And that is a great shame.

Post-Session Awareness

One thing I like about the magic mushrooms is that immediately after a session, I am more aware of and in tune with my surroundings (this usually lasts from a few days to several weeks with me) because a part of the brain (my (alter) ego) either switches off or is so zapped and confused that it leaves me alone. Either way, it's an excellent opportunity to take advantage of this window and get ahead.

Inspired, I decided to fast. It lasted seven days, enabling me to lose just over 5 kg (11 lb). It was a small triumph that I had reached my lowest weight since coming to Germany. Why am I mentioning this? Because when this part of my brain isn't working, I can control my eating. I have no temptations or weaknesses and can avoid carbs and other food-like temptations.

A Trip to the Lake District

Shortly after the fast, my wife and I flew to the UK to hike in the Lake District. We love this beautiful corner of the world and have enjoyed some great walks together. Those who have been there will know what I mean. The scenery is stunning, and the locals are warm, friendly, and welcoming.

After the holiday, I felt motivated, relaxed, and full of hope, waiting for the next stage of my life to begin.

Did you notice the operative word? I 'waited'. Finally, I had found what I had been looking for!

By August, I felt my life starting to fray at the edges again. I had found no direction or focus and was beginning to lose hope for the future. I thought my old ways were returning, and I was isolating myself again. Not only that, but my weight had also increased by a couple of kilos again. What had happened? What had gone wrong? I spent weeks churning this over with no answer in mind.

The Beginning of a Turnaround

I consider this phase the beginning of my life turnaround because it marked the start of my flashbacks and the gradual remembrance of things I had said and done wrong to those around me, ultimately causing hurt. These brief thoughts and memories disturbed me as I saw myself for the first time as I genuinely was. Naturally, I could think of this time of sinking deeper into oblivion, and I was. I'm speaking from hindsight here. I consider it a turnaround because I started facing the darkest parts of my life for what they were. That hurt, and pain eventually turned to heal and release.

Initially, the flashbacks were sporadic, but soon they came in waves, with one memory following another. At first, they were disheartening, and it took me a while to learn how to work through them. Was I beginning to wake up from a long, deep, hypnotic sleep I had been in since early childhood?

Interestingly, occasionally, I also recalled things I had done right. These rare thoughts helped remind me that I was not entirely the worthless person I believed myself to be. This realisation allowed me to take responsibility for my large and small mistakes, which will remain with me for the rest of my life. These memories inspired me to reflect on what I had done wrong and consider how I could have acted differently if given the chance again. This critical and progressive step helped me develop a structure to navigate some of the darker moments that would inevitably arise as time ticked by.

Discovering Alan Watts

On the last day of the year, I discovered Alan Watts. I don't recall how I came across his work, but it had a profound impact on me, influencing the turnaround that still affects me today. I heard his article about life as a game that should not be taken seriously. Life is not to be taken seriously? Really? Reflecting on this, I realised I couldn't have taken the last fifty-odd years more seriously if I had tried! That seriousness controlled every thought and decision with such intensity. You would probably have avoided me if you had met me because I would have projected that seriousness, all-knowing attitude, and despondence onto you, too.

Yes, I was that bad.

That New Year's evening, I told my wife what I had listened to (we celebrated a quiet New Year that year). She asked a brilliant question: how do we play the Game of Life?

Life isn't about finding yourself. It's about creating yourself.
George Bernard Shaw

The Year 2020

2020 was pivotal for me, marked by a profound breakdown, self-discovery, and personal growth. As the world grappled with unrelated, unprecedented challenges, I was on an unexpected journey of introspection and transformation. This chapter chronicles the highs and lows, the breakthroughs and setbacks, and the invaluable lessons learned. It was a year that began with uncertainty but ultimately led to a deeper understanding of myself and the path I wanted to forge ahead. With reflection on the quote above, I still wasn't ready to create myself as I still didn't know who I was. Join me as I delve into the experiences that shaped my year 2020 and set the stage for a new chapter in my life.

Discovering The Game of Life

Good old Google came into action just after the bells rang out for the New Year, and I found a super informative book called *The Game of Life and How to Play It* by Florence Scovell Shinn. I read it from cover to cover on that first day of the year. Each day after that, I did my best to follow the Universal rules she had discussed in the book, some of which I still follow today.

Seeking Alternatives

Many might wonder why I didn't turn to one of the many and varied religions when faced with such challenges. Following someone else's interpretation of ancient texts, which are often based on translations and revisions made for a different time and have incorporated deletions and inclusions of other beliefs and cultures that are no longer relevant today, is not my style. I approach these texts critically, accepting opinions only after careful consideration and examination. This feels like blind subservience, and that's not my approach. I am desperately trying to escape the destructive and limiting beliefs and opinions that I have unquestioningly dedicated my life to for the last fifty-odd years. I didn't and don't want to bind myself to something even the various flavours of religions still can't agree upon.

If I had, I would have merely set aside my inner insecurities and mistakes, continually living with their consequences, not mine. At the same time, the religion would attempt to reframe them in a way that bound me to its blame game through guilt and shame against myself. I had had enough of that from my father without relying on an institution that has another one next to it, disagreeing with its fundamental aspects. If they can't harmonise themselves, how can I find the one?

I am here to listen to the messages and lessons that come my way, regardless of their source. I am not here to focus on who the best messenger is or which is the best fictional blame system to dedicate oneself to while discreetly praying to either the sun, moon or Saturn god. I want to be responsible for what I discover, interpret, and apply to my life, aligning with my ethics. Not to adjust it to someone else's moral standards.

However, I appreciate that we all have our preferred routes. If someone is willing to give up their autonomy to someone else, is content with the consequences, and finds what they are looking for, that is great. It is their responsible decision to do whatever they like as long as it harms no one else, and they are content to live with the respective implications of their choices for the rest of their lives (every decision has an implication somewhere). They are free to choose the life path they want to follow. Please don't expect me to dance to that tune.

Working Through Alan Watts' Material

One aspect of working through Alan Watts' material presented a challenge to me. I don't like the word 'god' because it has become more of a marketing and manipulation tool than what it should represent. I prefer the words "Soma" and "Universe" interchangeably. My wife suggested I swap the word 'god' for one of my preferred terms while reading his material, and it made the text much easier to digest. This approach helped me understand how Watts (and others) metaphorically interpreted the Bible, and suddenly, those stories began to make sense, and I could see how they could help me understand my life differently.

This was a great start, but after a while, I wanted the original material in its proper context rather than something copied and pasted from two thousand years ago to help me advance my thinking further.

Embracing the Kybalion

I came across the Kybalion, and after reading it, I began to live by the simplicity of the seven principles' duality (and still do). Although the principles are easy to understand word for word, it took me a while to grasp what they collectively meant. These seven principles highlighted that my life theme for the moment is survival, which helps me find the right balance in being who I am (isn't this the case for everyone?).

When I took the time to reflect on my life again, with a different perspective gained from what I had learnt about myself, it became apparent that I had survived a great deal. I survived my father's unfatherly physical aggression, just as I survived his intense and manipulative verbal abuse during my first seven years. I also survived the self-isolation and self-punishment dictated by my irrational fears and severe lack of self-worth and isolation because I wholly believed what he had said to me in those early years.

I survived those incorrect assumptions about how others perceived and judged me. I also survived the misinterpretation of my physical disabilities along with the deluded personality I had created for myself, which made my life more challenging, as if I didn't have enough to deal with already. That's a lot to have survived, starting from being a tiny, defenceless baby in the hands of the wrong person!

Around this time, I also began meditating. However, about a year later, I realised I wasn't meditating. Instead, I was sitting on the floor with my eyes closed, thinking things through while believing I was meditating. Later, I discovered a great tool to enhance this reflection method, which I still use today, albeit with slight variations, and I will discuss it later. Nevertheless, this practice helped me organise my thoughts better. Unbeknownst to me, it also laid the foundation for what would happen the following year.

The Challenges of February 2020

In February, I hit a low point because all the work and effort I had put into my life, based on the advice from the book *The Game of Life*, weren't yielding the expected results. One key aspect I struggled with was being the person I wanted to be, a central message in the book. Essentially, it states that we are what we believe we are, regardless of how we view (delude) ourselves. Suppose any contradictory thoughts occur while practising this fantastic technique. In that case, those misleading thoughts prevent us from becoming what we want to be because we cannot fully commit to it, and we may start to misinterpret what we want to think we are.

This also leads to another misinterpretation: we have found what we have been searching for, put ourselves above others, and become something else altogether. In reality, we become this unknown and unplanned thing and get on with our lives accordingly, doing our daily activities as though nothing had happened, thinking we are respecting life and those around us with love and admiration for those we meet when we are the ego's interpretation of what we think we aren't.

Yet, if we get it right, it is a wonderful experience to navigate life without distracting thoughts or actions that could harm us in some way. We still maintain our boundaries without judgment, and we know how to respond more effectively in moments that might otherwise hinder us. It took me a long time to realise that.

What is worth noting here is that if we appreciate the more 'minor' things that come our way, we become more perceptive to the immense wealth around us, which money cannot buy.

Breaking the Cycle of Despair

Sadly, once we fall into a deep hole of despair, it seems impossible to find a way out because that's all we experience. Breaking that pattern is extremely difficult and often seems impossible if we are unaware of the available resources.

Many of us haven't been taught how to think or act differently, and as a result, we remain stuck in a cycle of despair. We tend to learn from previous generations that the only options are to fight against it or punish ourselves while trying to keep from sinking further into the proverbial quicksand.

Without inner resources and support to react differently, what chance do we have of seeing the precipice, let alone glancing beyond it? And therein lies the challenge: where to look for those inner resources to escape that mental situation we can't escape.

It took me until the year 2023 for that penny to drop.

Back to 2020. This feeling of failure dragged me down because I still hadn't understood why I wasn't receiving the promises I demanded from the Universe in the way I thought I had understood the book I had read.

Naturally, when one approach doesn't seem to work (it does if done correctly), I turned to the teachings of the Diamond Approach, developed by A.H. Almaas. It opened my eyes to how much further I needed to go to find myself, and I started to work through this material steadily. My wife and I had planned to go on one of their courses in November. Sadly, the coronavirus became a global issue, and the upcoming restrictions prevented us from attending.

A Low Point in June

I hit another low in June. I was still getting my knickers in a twist about the Universal frequencies and how to reach them because I didn't know what to recognise or what to change within me to achieve them. In this case, even though I thought I was a person of a specific calibre of what I wanted to be, it wasn't who I was; I was still a confused person full of doubt and misaligned hope.

I felt lost. What was I doing wrong? Was I making it more complicated than it needed to be (yes)? Was I not thinking clearly enough about the person I wanted to be (probably yes), and could I overpower those doubtful thoughts with inspirational thoughts alone (at this moment, no)? And what do the frequencies feel like within me to know I have reached them (Hmm, this took a long time to understand, but when we stop thinking about it and get on with life with an open mind within the environment surrounding us, we are there or are at least approaching the optimal frequency)?

One day in June, I started crying during a fitness routine. I had been struggling with increasingly intense flashbacks over the past few days. I retreated to my bed, consumed by the thought that I could never escape my childhood. Deaf in one ear, burdened with my manky leg, and plagued by other childhood memories of my father, I couldn't shake the feeling of worthlessness.

These memories reminded me of my deluded past and the misleading beliefs on which I had built my foundation for many years. Each emotionally charged flashback lasted only a few seconds, yet its impact lingered for weeks. I recalled the regular hospital visits with Mum when I was a child, while wearing specially made shoes with a calliper strapped to my manky leg. Even then, I knew I was different from the other schoolchildren, but didn't understand why. I had to contend with my deafness and inner doubts stemming from my father's abuse, although at the time, I couldn't recognise it for what it was. As a child, I had many questions that I asked myself. Still, then one reached a point where I gave up asking, erecting a defensive barrier that focused less on what was happening around me and more on stopping the thoughts about myself and how I was starting to perceive the world within me.

The closest analogy I can think of to describe how I felt is like a spider trapped in a bathtub. No matter how hard it tries to escape, it can't climb up the steep, smooth sides nor clamber high enough to see the horizon to determine whether the effort would be worth it.

Through those uncontrollable, continual cycles of flashbacks, it was followed by the devastating realisation of the things I had once said and done. I felt so low, helpless, and lost. They were intense enough to cause me immense pain and shame. The behaviour I had developed was always sufficient to make good contact and then break it, with enough humiliation for me to fall into the trap of repeated self-mental flagellation. For example, when talking to others, once I had made contact, I gradually lost control of what I said and operated without any verbal or thought filter.

Ultimately, I was controlling what I was saying because of its consequential effect, forcing me to live the life I thought I deserved. I was an expert at this self-punishment, although, at the time, I didn't realise it. I thought it was normal; everyone seemed to be doing this or had gone through it somehow.

I'm sure we've all met someone whose company isn't always pleasant to others, even when they're nearby. Yet, once I had found out what their qualities were (or, instead, their weaknesses), I used this information to help me degrade them to help me feel better than they did (yes, the further development of my narcissistic trait – unknown at the time). I must have been highly entertaining for a short while, and then I was someone to avoid altogether.

Can you imagine first reaching middle age and realising how cruel you had been to others for most of your life? That helped me understand why people avoided me. This realisation knocked me for six. I was devastated.

For my whole life, I wanted to do things I enjoyed, but, in most cases, I wouldn't let myself do them; otherwise, I would have been living a free life. That was forbidden because I thought I didn't deserve such pleasures – I was meant to suffer and be unloved in some way.

However, one small pleasure I have always had is reading. It provided me with escapism into other worlds and lives by allowing me to experience life through fictional characters. I discovered reading later than the average child (Enid Blyton's books first got me hooked – Famous Five, Secret Seven, etc. – thanks, Mum!). Once I did, I have always had (and still have) at least one book on the go. Reading doesn't involve anyone else. I can't hurt anyone when reading (except when I should be doing something else, I suppose!).

A New Perspective

I mentioned earlier that I felt like a spider trapped in a porcelain bathtub, unable to see the horizon, and I want to continue with this metaphor. Something happened mentally as I assessed all these memories one after another, and I finally came to understand something. This caused that slippery-sided circular porcelain tub to shrink enough for me to glimpse the horizon. All I could see was an infinite and blinding white landscape, whichever way I looked. That was it: just whiteness. Nothing else.

Now that I could see the never-ending horizon in all directions, what was next? Somehow, I had to get out of this porcelain bathtub first.

Over time, the more I realised that I was damaging myself with my thoughts and that no one else was involved, the more that mental and circular porcelain bathtub shrank (or I grew, I'm not sure which). This change allowed me to jump up, grab the edge and eventually clamber out to escape. Free, at last, but which way should I go when every direction had an infinite whiteness? There needs to be something to focus on in this life, shouldn't there? Isn't that why we are here?

Had I escaped one prison only to start again and escape the next layer of nothingness I had built, only to find that it wasn't and never was there? Were the breakthroughs I kept experiencing akin to peeling back the metaphorical emotional layers of an onion, revealing a created fantasy and delusion built on that enlightened nothingness that had been covered for all those years? Did this mean I would have to continuously deal with the most pressing problem that didn't exist before to address the next issue that didn't exist until I had worked through them all? I suppose so. How many layers are there, and when will I know I've finished?

Reflecting on this metaphor gradually led me to consider that another layer of historical problems will always emerge beneath the surface, and that the journey of self-discovery never truly ends. I suppose only death is the ultimate, conscious understanding we gain about ourselves.

Isn't it remarkable that the only two things we can't or don't talk about are the two guaranteed experiences in our lives: birth and death? Everything else we discuss consists of superficial individual experiences, opinions, thoughts and inner fantasies about interpreting reality as we progress through life towards death.

Visualising a Path Forward

In my mind's eye, I saw a vast expanse of whiteness as a crowd of people headed in one direction. I considered following them, but stopped myself when I realised that I had always been an outsider, doing what I believed was best for my positive intentions. I may not have always been right, but my choices ultimately led me to where I am today, given the resources and experiences I had at the time. So why not continue to trust my instincts, as I believe this is one thing I did that was, and is, right for me?

In my visualisation, as long as I continued moving in a direction other than following the masses, it would help me determine and adapt to my new, ever-changing, positive intentions. If I need to retrace steps to get back on track with my life and work towards what is important to me, then so be it.

That's okay with me because, even if I have to revisit most of the past fifty-odd years to learn from those poor life decisions, allowing me to progress towards what is essential, finally, is to be me. The detour will have been worth every step.

Not only that, but why rush? What's a few extra days, weeks, months, or even years of adjustment compared to all the years I have already messed up? After all, if I'm still moving in a direction that I believe is forward and that I'm content with, while allowing me to learn about myself, then I'm still progressing. Even if I still do something wrong, I am aware of it, and what one does with that understanding is essential. Not the punishment. That benefits others.

This turned out to be an excellent idea! We must remember that no path leads to anything worthwhile except death, except the commitment to what we dedicate our lives to.

Sometimes, we refuse to leave a chosen path that no longer serves us because we think we know what that path has to offer and feel obliged to remain loyal. Instead, we should be open to leaving that expired path behind as we constantly pass new potential junctions every day. There's nothing worse than realising we should have changed paths earlier, but we remain on the same one that's empty and devoid of what we need, regardless of what it is. Oh, what an uneducated Ego can do to us!

Looking back, I realise I have been and jumped on disastrous paths. However, I finally managed to get where I am today by leaping onto another. Not every path was wrong, but I have made and stuck with some lousy path choices. Reflecting on what I said and did and considering where I could have ended up, I couldn't be in a better place today. I am grateful for that experience. Even those disastrous paths I chose have unlocked inner strengths within me that I would never have discovered on my own.

Because of this, I have a chance at a new life, a new direction, and a vast range of new experiences that will carry me to my end goal in a way that differs from most people. Let's not wallow in those mistakes. Learn from them, change our self-perceptions, and move on. All we can do when we have that option again is respond differently. That is our free will.

Around August, the Coronavirus Pandemic took a back seat, allowing many to get out and enjoy life again. We took a lovely holiday to the charming village of Wernigerode in Germany. Besides the Lakes in the UK, this is our regular and reasonably local haunt. We love the friendly small town, the beautiful countryside and the surrounding areas. It's the perfect place to escape the hustle and bustle of daily city life and home and to allow my inner challenges to enjoy some of the more relaxed atmosphere in this beautiful area.

A few days before we set off for our much-anticipated break in Wernigerode, I shared a conversation I had with my wife earlier that week, which I had with a friend. During our chat, my friend and I reminisced about our past studies, and I confessed that, given the choice, I would have preferred to pursue a degree in psychology rather than engineering. Psychology has always fascinated me as a means to understand my own experiences. However, I also feared it would open a Pandora's Box of unresolved issues that would have overwhelmed me. Although I wasn't aware of it at the time, I was already overwhelmed with myself in my twenties. That decision to study psychology would have been too much for me, and I would not have managed to complete the studies. I am aware of that now.

The concern was the vulnerability that came with sharing my deepest fears. The thought that someone could understand every aspect of me was terrifying, leaving me feeling exposed and fearful. I carried a deep shame about my past, and the idea that psychologists could see through me, perhaps even control me, filled me with such fear and paranoia.

If only I had known in my younger years that the power to release that burden lay within myself. I had spent so many hours searching externally that I am sure, with the money I had wasted, I had increased Britain's GDP by a couple of per cent each year. Despite my desperation for a solution, I don't think I was ready back then to let go of the patterns of behaviour that were causing me so much pain. I still had to suffer in some way, and that was deserved. Yes, I know how delusional that is.

Enrolling on a Psychology Course

When I shared this conversation with my wife, she suggested studying psychology might be a great idea. She also mentioned that she wouldn't be surprised if the coronavirus panic surged again in the latter part of the year. She was correct; it did!

I found a long-distance one-year master's course in psychology at Brunel University in London, UK, and applied for a September start date. However, before I could begin the master's, I needed a copy of my bachelor's degree to prove my previous studies. I couldn't locate my original certificate and had to request a copy from my old university, which typically takes a couple of weeks to arrive by post.

During the enrolment process for the Brunel course, the representative asked about my knowledge of statistics, as it is a crucial part of the curriculum. I fibbed and said it was fine. The truth was, I had skipped those lectures during my engineering studies, believing I would never need the subject. Up until this point in my life, I had been right.

While waiting for the university to send me a copy of my certificate, I found an old, unused statistics book on my bookshelf and thought some reading wouldn't do any harm. Why waste time? In Wernigerode, the weather was stunning, the walks were refreshing, and I spent my free time reading up on statistics. Learning something new and different from psychological techniques was a great feeling.

Anyway, my old university took about ten weeks to send me a copy of my certificate, which meant I missed Brunel's September start date. A Brunel representative informed me that I could join the next available start date in January (online distance learning), which I did.

After we returned from holiday, I continued working through the statistics material until I understood it reasonably well. This was also a fantastic distraction from my other issues because I felt motivated and had a direction in my life, and the learning kept me busy. I even read up on bits of practical psychology, thinking it would help me with the course (it didn't). I felt I had cracked the last part of whatever held me back.

Since the rest of the year passed without any flashbacks or issues, there is little else to add to the end of 2020. In retrospect, it seems fitting to label 2020 as 'Preparation for 2021,' 'Teaser Year for 2021,' or, my personal favourite, 'The Lull before the Storm.' Why? During 2020, I discovered that I was not who I thought I was and was content with that. I thought that was enough to move forward and start a new life.

With optimism and a new goal ahead of me, I believed I was back on track with my life and that nothing could go wrong. To put it in perspective, for the four years leading up to the end of 2020, I thought I had ventured down the rabbit hole and emerged relatively unscathed.

I hadn't.

In other words, I had only been peeking inside the burrow compared to what happened next. In 2021, I was unceremoniously dragged through that rabbit hole with no chance of escape until I faced, understood, and released what I needed to work through to reach the next phase of my life. Everything I had learned up to this point would be the foundation to carry me through the coming year.

Out of suffering have emerged the strongest souls; the most massive characters are seared with scars.
Khalil Gibran

The Year 2021 – University

This chapter explores the transformative journey I undertook during my 2021 master's degree in psychology. The distance learning course began in January and was marked by excitement and apprehension. Unlike my university days in the nineties, this new learning mode presented unique challenges, particularly in building connections with absent peers and lecturers.

The following sections provide an in-depth exploration of the modules, the personal hurdles I encountered, and their impact on me. The complexity of inferential statistics and the emotional upheaval of studying the differences in healthy and unhealthy child development and upbringing triggered a breakdown in each module, which brought trials and revelations along the way.

Introduction to Distance Learning

On January 4th, 2021, I began a year-long master's degree in psychology at a relatively early age, in my early fifties. Having not engaged in such intensive study for a considerable time, I naturally felt a mixture of nerves and curiosity about what lay ahead. The sensation of renewed energy and curiosity was invigorating.

This was my first experience with distance learning that lasted more than a few days. One intriguing aspect of the year was my perception of my fellow students and lecturers. Unlike my university days in the 1990s, when I physically met and interacted with people, all my impressions were faceless here.

I had to use other indicators to help me remember which person I was supposed to be. Interestingly, the relationships and rapport felt more detached than those experienced in person on campus.

This detachment was noticeable before my initial issues arose, such that this perception, no matter how well I related to the other students, persisted throughout the year. Although this did not impact my studies, I believe this is a curious experience worth sharing.

Modules 1 & 2

The first two modules I covered were descriptive statistics and neurological psychology. Thanks to my preparatory reading, I progressed smoothly through descriptive statistics, emphasising mathematical form. In contrast, neurological psychology felt like learning a new language, filled with Latin and Greek terminology. I barely passed this module, which served as a stern warning about the intensity and complexity of the upcoming modules.

Modules 3 & 4

We studied inferential statistics and child development from conception to old age in March. Unlike descriptive statistics, inferential statistics conclude from data gathered through interviews or conversations. This approach offers freedom and flexibility, similar to epidemiological studies, allowing for open interpretations that support various opinions, albeit tentatively.

However, its scientific validity is often debated due to the potential for data manipulation, as seen in controversial nutritional studies, such as Ancel Keys' 'Seven Countries Study', for example. While inferential statistics can generate research ideas, their wide tolerances, the free selection of included and excluded data, and the potential for causal relationships often lead to subjective interpretations.

Nonetheless, I found the inferential statistics reports insightful that were related to research papers on various forms of child abuse and how the victims felt and dealt with their history by reassuring me that my diverse thoughts were not unique, and this helped to broaden my understanding, challenging and sometimes changing my perspectives.

The second module, Child Development, provided a profound and poignant insight into my childhood and its lasting impact. The initial part detailed a child's development in a stable environment, highlighting what I had missed. The latter part, focusing on unstable environments, felt like reading my biography, which rattled my inner stability immensely. I needed a few days to regain my composure before continuing with the module, to prepare myself for the next six weeks of intense work.

Breakdown and Flashbacks

I managed three weeks before the subject details of childhood abuse overwhelmed me. One day, while trying to process the day's material, I found myself unable to focus, with my mind racing with various forms of anxiety. As I sat at my desk, I began to hyperventilate, a sensation I had never experienced before. Seeking relief, I went to the living room, repeatedly telling myself I couldn't go to the hospital, though I didn't understand why I thought I needed to go at the time (I still don't know what the reason was for having that thought).

When my wife returned home, my condition rapidly worsened. She found me in distress and tried to calm me. As she held me, I broke down completely. The sobbing escalated into uncontrollable screaming and wailing. I then experienced vivid and painful visual flashbacks to my early childhood.

In one flashback, I was eight months old, with my father's face close to mine, filled with rage. He grabbed me by the ear and picked me up while threatening me verbally and physically, thus causing excruciating pain in and around my ear that I was feeling as an adult at that moment. The memory of my ear nerve snapping intensified my screams.

Another flashback followed quickly after that, where my father spat in my face as he snarled something at me while crushing my foot with his hands. As I felt intense pain in my foot, my adult body was writhing in agony.

These flashbacks revealed the source of my lifelong limp, my deafness in my right ear and the start of the severe verbal abuse I endured for the next six and a half years. It was a harrowing experience that fundamentally changed my view of the world of distrust, self-image and inner value issues.

Following this breakdown, my wife contacted my course tutor, who would become a crucial support for me for the rest of the course, and informed her of what had happened and that I wouldn't be attending for the next few days. I wanted to continue, but I had to reduce my study load by focusing only on essential readings and assignments as I was dealing with mental turmoil. This course provided a lifeline, helping me confront and work through my past and keeping me distracted, at least for some of the time.

Despite the difficulties, I passed the child development module but narrowly failed the inferential statistics module. This failure was understandable because I didn't understand the concept of inferential data at the time, which I now accept.

Modules 5 & 6 and Coping with an Unexpected Loss

The third batch of modules I managed to pass might be surprising to some, given that I was still finding my footing from that breakdown and that my father had died during this period. If you have read the previous book, you will know I visited him to address some lingering childhood issues. When I heard from a cousin that he had passed away, my first thought was relief that I had already confronted him and dealt with that part of my life and not that he was dead. A wave of relaxation came over me, knowing he couldn't hurt anyone again. His passing was the best thing he ever did for the family.

Unexpectedly, I went through a mass of emotions: disappointment that he didn't take the chance to apologise when we met and that he hadn't kept a simple promise he made a few years ago, even though I knew he wouldn't follow through on it. He was a disappointment in every way. It hurt because, no matter what, I am still a part of him. He was my father, and I felt let down. I felt disappointed because he didn't meet my expectations. Perhaps I shouldn't have set any hopes and expectations in the first place.

My course tutor told me I was grieving, which initially surprised me. However, her words helped me to focus on dealing with it. Another turmoil I experienced was not wanting people to attend his funeral to pay their respects because they did not know the kind of person he was and the pain he had caused to others (selfish of me, I know). Perhaps he had changed, but that idea didn't occur to him.

My cousin, bless her, organised a pauper's funeral for him. Neither my sister nor I wanted to arrange his funeral. We both felt our time wasn't worth investing in someone so despicable. The whole family agreed to his pauper's burial. No one knows when and where he was cremated, nor where his remains were dumped. I cannot describe the smile that crossed my face when my cousin told me that! One less beast on this planet.

About a week after his estimated funeral, I forgot about him, settled down again, and continued my studies. By the end of this module, I had even begun working on some of the module's voluntary assignments and was getting back into the swing of things. Privately, I was also delving deeper into spirituality and related Eastern texts.

Modules 7 & 8 and Therapy Session with Magic Mushrooms

I felt much better, although my thoughts were still scattered. I decided to do a psychedelic therapy session two days before these two modules started. I had learned a lot about myself, but I was still hitting some brick walls in progressing from what happened to me last March. I decided to use magic mushrooms to get some clarification I couldn't find.

That turned out to be an understatement!

As I progressed through this session, the mushrooms showed me the causes of my issues and their knock-on effects. The memories were so intense that I had to ask them to stop showing them after several hours. Thankfully, the mushrooms heard me and stopped showing me. As a result, the rest of the session was a blur, but the release was tremendous.

After the session, I was in an intense daze, unlike any previous euphoria or uncertainty I had experienced. It felt like I had experienced several severe yet beneficial 'wake-up slaps across the face with a cricket bat'. I was emotionally and mentally empty, with no more beliefs or opinions to lean on. Everything I thought I knew was turned upside down, such that my previous life suddenly seemed like an absurd dream.

The next day, a Saturday, I sat at home in a daze, trying to find something to anchor myself to, but nothing was left. Everything was gone. I began to comprehend what had happened and concluded that this empty slate wasn't bad, but rather refreshing. The problem was, I didn't know what to do with this clean slate, even though the proverbial ruins of my old self still surrounded me. I asked myself, 'What do I want, and who am I? ' Back to square one.

When using NLP techniques to eliminate a behaviour, a replacement with a new behaviour is required to prevent the old one from returning. Given the total emptiness I was experiencing, I felt driven to find a more suitable replacement to avoid the old ways from returning. A second question came up while searching, and that was if I didn't see a replacement behaviour and given that I had used the mushrooms, would my natural and freed personality rise and replace the old distorted one, or would the old one return?

I later discovered that the answer is that if the core of the problem is eliminated, which affects our personality and causes us to behave in a certain way, a new and more natural personality will arise of its own accord. If a side effect is not addressed with a replacement, it will likely recur.

The next day, I began to grasp what had happened to me. Although I knew I had broken that last stubborn bond, my thoughts were still everywhere in a vast space of nothingness where every misleading thought and decision used to be. I explained to my course tutor what I had gone through, how it had impacted me, and how I envisioned my future. After writing the email, I reviewed it for clarity and readability and sent it off.

Two days later, when the last two modules had started, I reread my email and was horrified by what I had written! It was a jumble, lacking comprehension and structure. It read like a desperate person who had just suffered a breakdown. I do not know how she let me stay on the course. I wrote back and apologised. Thankfully, she reassured me and encouraged me to continue the course, offering me a way out if needed. What she was thinking on the other side of that screen, I prefer not to know!

My narcissism was non-existent throughout the last two modules, thus allowing me to enjoy these subjects immensely. I immersed myself in the subjects, did all the practice assignments, and even had ideas for my final psychology project.

But nothing runs smoothly for long…

The greatest weapon against stress is our ability to choose one thought over another.
William James

Navigating Challenges

Navigating the complexities of life while studying is often fraught with unexpected hurdles and miscommunications that can test a student's reasoning. These challenges can spark intense emotional reactions and require deep introspection to understand and manage personal responses effectively. In the face of sudden changes and inconsistencies, the journey becomes more about academic achievement than personal growth through resilience.

At the start of the academic year, the university informed us that we would have two weeks free before commencing our final project, which I had intended to use for a break. However, midway through the last two modules, the university altered its schedule. The final project lectures began in the penultimate week of the final modules' assignment period and overlapped with the two holiday weeks.

I flipped!

My Karen-like narcissistic tendencies resurfaced with a vengeance. At home, I shouted and screamed, throwing a full-blown tantrum. I emailed the project and course leaders a curt email, but it didn't change anything (sorry!). The decision was final, and we had to accept it. Out of stubbornness, I chose not to attend the lectures while finishing the last parts of the assignments (thankfully, they were recorded, and I returned to them later once I had picked up my many teddy bears from the floor).

Interestingly, this massive tantrum helped me recognise that I have a natural inner voice. I realised I could pay attention to my destructive voice while simultaneously hearing my calm inner voice. It was as if I had two distinct personalities, like Jekyll and Hyde. This raised the question of how many voices had been screaming in my head when I was at my worst for all of those years.

Whenever my destructive inner voice took control, another voice would try to rationalise the situation. Gradually, my inner Gatekeeper (ego) was learning to influence my thinking. It might sound like I was losing my mind, but the following year, I realised this was perfectly rational.

After submitting the final assignments for the last two modules, I took a well-deserved holiday with my wife. However, instead of relaxing, I stewed over the university's inconsistency. I refused to watch the recorded lectures or contact the staff. I was furious. The course planner stated that the project would start on a specific date, and I intended to stick to it!

The Final Project

After returning from our holiday, I felt no benefit from the break. In hindsight, I should have swallowed my pride and reviewed the lectures and materials as they were released. However, my inner stubbornness was too strong to overcome. I later discovered the reason behind that mental meltdown.

I began reading my emails on the official start date and found that I had been assigned a supervisor. When I explained my project idea, she rejected it. Although I understood her reasoning for needing to select another idea, it made me feel the time pressure was mounting because most other students were already further ahead with their projects.

The transition from fuming to acceptance took me about the first five weeks allotted for the project, plus the two weeks on holiday and the additional two weeks when the university started the final project earlier than the allotted start date. During this time, my calmer inner voice reflected on my actions and sought ways to alleviate the mental distress I was causing myself. My internal Gatekeeper was gradually learning to manage those frustrating thoughts.

Eventually, I chose the Stroop test for my project, which proved to be a fascinating subject. This involves stating the colour of the text rather than the colour the word describes. For example, if the word says 'BLUE' but is written in green, the correct answer is green. It turned out to be an interesting project that I eventually came to enjoy.

After settling on a project, I formulated a hypothesis, adjusted my scope to fit the project's time constraints, and submitted it to the ethics department for review. This process took about three weeks, and I started to panic about running out of time. This anxiety triggered my inner antagonist, urging me to drop the course. However, my Gatekeeper kept convincing me to persevere. After much internal dialogue, I continued the course and deleted the 'I quit!' form I had filled out.

While waiting for ethics approval, I began writing the final report, leaving the results and statistical calculations for later. The Stroop test is well-known in the psychological world, with extensive reports and information available. Once I received final approval, I sent the experiment to potential participants before Christmas. Although I didn't reach the statistically required minimum number of participants, I gathered enough data to identify trends, which I reflected in the report. I was buzzing and started to enjoy it.

About three weeks before the deadline, I had a narcissistic wobble. Even though I had plenty of time and was well ahead of schedule, I wrote to the course tutor to request an extension or to consider dropping out of the course. This was another attempt at self-sabotage. I realised there was a part of me I still had little to no control over, especially considering how well the project was going. The other voice within me remained silent in these moments, just as it had since childhood when I had decided to stop asking specific questions about myself. If so, what source had I been using all my life to find a way out of this mess? Has it been communicating to me differently than I wasn't (and still am not) aware of?

I replied to the tutor, asking her to ignore the previous email and admitted to self-sabotaging. This realisation was something new; that I was engaging in self-sabotage. It was something I had been searching for a long time.

At the same time, I approached a different psychology professor by 'asking for a friend', inquiring about suitable therapy for such behavioural conditions. I was recommended Dialectical Behaviour Therapy (DBT).

Dialectical Behaviour Therapy

I purchased an eBook called *Dialectical Behaviour Therapy Skills Workbook* by Matthew McKay, Jeffrey Wood, and Jeffrey Brantley to begin working through DBT techniques. This marked the beginning of my next life phase, which I call the 'Re-programming Phase'.

After downloading the eBook, I read it from cover to cover, completing every exercise before the New Year arrived. I didn't even touch my final project once. I had already written it up; all it needed was a thorough review. I also had some project questions for my supervisor after the New Year. I still had plenty of time to make the necessary corrections before submission after talking to her, so I felt justified in taking a short break.

Over the following days, as I worked through each exercise, I felt my inner antagonistic (my still unrecognised narcissistic) voice relax and quiet. It seemed to settle down, or perhaps my Gatekeeper (Ego), I'm not sure which, was finally learning new ways to respond to various triggering situations.

It's hard to believe I was throwing a hissy fit a few weeks ago because I thought I didn't have enough time, and now I'm ignoring my report for some intense exercises.

One of the first things I learned was that walking away from a confrontational situation is often the best course of action. Previously, I never walked away from such situations; I would engage verbally with more than enough aggression to prove I was right.

One evening at home, a minor discussion with my wife escalated into a minor argument. I decided to test this technique by walking away instead of arguing further.

After walking away, I initially felt like I had succumbed to a defeatist strategy. However, I soon realised that 'losing face' was acceptable if it helped to keep the peace. Later in the evening, I felt intrigued by the unfamiliar sensation of remaining relaxed and calm, allowing us to enjoy our time together without any post-argument tension.

I concluded that I had protected myself and my wife from the intense strife I usually caused. This experience led me to change my opinion about walking away from conflicts, recognising that I hadn't 'lost face' but instead that it was a strength. My wife appreciated that the argument hadn't escalated and felt better that I had chosen to walk away.

The first battle point was not awarded to my inner antagonist; instead, I had taken the first step in reducing its power over me.

On the evening of December 24th (Christmas Eve), I felt I had turned a significant corner and was finally on the right path. It was one of the best Christmases I could remember; even as a child, I had never felt good enough to deserve Christmas. I knew I still had more to learn, and this was just the beginning of finding my true self.

By the time I finished the DBT book around the end of the year, I felt more in control of my thoughts and emotions. My inner Gatekeeper seemed better equipped to manage my internal antagonist, and I had many new tools to respond to various situations. I didn't expect perfection, but one has to begin somewhere, and I knew I still had a long way to go.

On New Year's Day, in the early morning hours, I decided that my assignment was now the utmost priority and needed to be finished promptly. Finally, I felt my inner antagonist was under enough control to submit my assignment on time without further issues. I felt motivated and thoroughly enjoyed the remaining time improving what I had written, searching for more information, and solving statistical problems I hadn't cracked earlier.

Shortly after the New Year, from the first day the university reopened, my supervisor disappeared altogether, despite the looming deadline. The university couldn't provide an answer, nor could it indicate how it would handle the situation, which left me wondering what was happening and who to contact for help with my unanswered questions. Two days before the deadline, someone from the IT department contacted me and suggested I request an extension for the final psychology project. And that was it. Not a word from the psychology department.

I was nearly finished, except for some unresolved questions. Why should I apply for an extension when the university didn't even know where its staff were or who to replace them with in case of absence? Okay, I appreciate people can fall ill at short notice, but this wasn't the case. Why should students bear the brunt of the delay by missing their deadline for something beyond their control? Nowadays, I don't care. That was the University's problem and their way of dealing with it. I took responsibility for deciding how to respond under the circumstances.

However, it's worth mentioning that I didn't lose control of my emotions this time. I didn't get flustered or have a hissy fit! I dealt with it professionally and calmly. I didn't take their offer for an extension and turned to external help to answer most of my project questions. Afterwards, I felt my final project assignment was sufficient to pass comfortably. At last, I was in control of my thoughts and actions. I had taken control of the situation. It felt good.

Because I had failed a module earlier in the year, the highest I could achieve was an overall pass. If I had redone the inference statistics paper I had failed earlier that year, I think the highest I could have gotten would have been a merit. I can't remember exactly. I wasn't too bothered about coming out with just a pass because, as a bonus, I had no intention of becoming a research scientist or a psychologist. As a bonus, I had resolved a significant portion of my remaining psychological issues!

After I had submitted that assignment to the university, I recognised that my antagonist had failed to prove how worthless I thought I was, and it no longer had such a hold on my life. I felt that a part of that antagonist left me. Bye-bye!

Mission completed.

The students who didn't request an extension received their grades in March, and I had passed my degree. I was elated. It also reconfirmed that I was worth and clever enough to do whatever I wanted to do with my life and that I wasn't as thick as two short planks as I had once believed. Then, I felt another part of that sabotaging inner antagonist leave me, giving me a feeling of inner freedom.

That was lovely. This is an understatement of how I felt on this day.

March was also another significant turning point in my personal life. However, first, I would like to close my discussion about my time at university, how my messed-up perceptions misled me in some areas, and the apparent changes I managed to recognise within myself.

University Course Expectations

Before starting this course, I expected to learn practical psychological techniques. There were none. It was all theoretical and statistical in preparation for psychological research, which I enjoyed despite being sidetracked by my issues. The lack of practical application was my fault, as I had not read the course material closely enough and had not asked the right questions during the interview. This behaviour was typical for me, jumping in with little to no idea what would happen. Fortunately, the course reading material often referred to many therapy models and techniques that I had investigated and tried out throughout the course.

Throughout that year, I tried almost every technique I encountered. I also asked the lecturing staff for tips if I was unsure about some techniques or where to turn next. They always pointed me in the right direction, for which I am thankful. And why shouldn't I ask? I had some of the best psychological specialists surrounding me at the time.

Had I started this study before my first-ever therapy session with the magic mushrooms, I would have been immensely disappointed due to the lack of practical applications of psychology. If that had been my primary goal, other courses at other institutions might have been a better fit for me. However, as I mentioned earlier, the course provided everything I was looking for in helping me sort myself out and prove something to myself, which were crucial aspects that kept me going until the end.

Previously, I would have heavily criticised the university for its approach towards the final project. However, with hindsight, I recognise that mistakes happen, and things can get overlooked in any industry. I am sure the university and its respective department have reviewed what went wrong and made the necessary changes to minimise the chances of it happening again.

Ultimately, that's their problem, not mine; even though I have an opinion, it's just that. Perhaps it was intentional to show students that plans don't always work as expected, serving as a lesson in dealing with spontaneous changes. I don't know. Yet, I must also respect that possibility. I know I am terrible at organising things and often make mistakes, so how can I overly criticise someone else's business decisions when I don't have all the information to understand what happened?

Suppose I had been highly vocal about what happened. In that case, I don't think the university would have necessarily suffered because most potential students reading such public reviews know that nothing runs smoothly all the time, even if the industry likes us to believe otherwise. To put it nicely, if I had written something biased and derogatory, the reviewers would have considered me a challenging student based on my old, direct criticism style, especially if I had been the outlier compared to most students who provided more balanced feedback.

Each university, both internationally and nationally, has an overall rating carried out externally. Based on its previous year's scoring for the psychology department, I would say Brunel's rating was fair.

Ultimately, once students return to the real world, they must make the most of their lives with the tools they have formally and informally acquired while at a learning institute and with what life throws their way, not the other way around.

Thank You

As for the course tutor who supported me when I was struggling, she excelled and went above and beyond the call of duty.

To this course tutor: I am grateful for your support, guidance, and patience throughout the year, especially when I struggled with myself, and for recognising how my history has impacted me. Without your help, working through this course would have made finding my way out of my inner labyrinth even more difficult. If I had no one to talk to, I probably would have followed through on one of those erratic moments when I convinced myself to quit. I would never have known what I could do if that had happened. Thank you!

My Non-University Reading Material While Studying

Before I bring this section to a close, I would like to share the private, non-course-related reading material that helped me through that year. I had started a few more books but found that they weren't helpful (or I wasn't ready for them), and I haven't included them in the list. I have put an asterisk next to the names I found most helpful. You may recognise that most of the books I read are spirituality-oriented:

- Alan Watts – All his works.
- Rob Brezny – *Pronoia*
- Jon Kabat-Zinn – *Wherever You Go, There You Are*
- Eckhart Tolle – *Stillness Speaks*
- Eckhart Tolle – *A New Earth*
- Eckhart Tolle – *The Power of Now*
- Vadim Zeland – *Transurfing 1-5*
- Vadim Zeland – *Princess Itfut*
- Vadim Zeland – *Tufti the Princess*
- Neville Goddard – *All works*
- Thomas A. Harris – *I'm Okay, You're Okay*
- Dawson Church – *Mind to Matter*
- Bob Marshall – *The Perennial Way*
- Todd Watson – *Buddha in a Teacup*
- Johann Hari – *Chasing the Scream*
- Nellie Bly – *Ten Days in a Mad House*
- Stephen Gilligan – *Generative Trance*

- Mihaly Csikszentmihalyi – *Flow*
- Steven Kotler: *Stealing Fire*
- Mark Flaherty – *Shedding the Layers*
- Joseph Murphy – *The Power of Your Subconscious Mind*
- Richard Rosen – *The Yoga of Breath*
- Sam Harris – *Waking Up*

Realising the Issue

Before I continue writing about what happened in March 2022, I want to discuss how that breakdown affected me.

If reading this section is too much, please skip it and proceed to the next section.

Sometimes, you have to lose yourself to find yourself.
Jenna Blum

Breakdowns

This chapter has been the most challenging to write because discussing breakdowns related to past experiences is always a delicate subject that can cut close to the nerve. It's essential to remember that breakdowns can affect us in different ways. Some readers may think what I went through wasn't a breakdown but something else entirely. After all, the word is just an abstract label open to interpretation, and you are right. Either way, should someone want to name it differently, whatever it was, it was the start that changed my life permanently. Although it took me to the proverbial hell and back to get here, it was worth it.

What I have written here reflects my understanding of the impact of that breakdown and its effect on me. I have also included my recovery process because I believe it can be more challenging to pick oneself up and continue with a completely new life without any inhibitions, symbols, anchors, or old beliefs than to remain in that state of despair, surrounded by those delusional expectations and hopes. Whether we have plenty of support around us or are alone in such moments, ultimately, we have to find out what works for us individually. No two experiences and paths forward are the same, and no one can pick us up except ourselves.

The Onset of a Breakdown

When we begin to break down, we feel as though we no longer have anywhere to go, having run out of energy, hope, and ideas as we desperately try to hold onto the delicate foundation we have built over the years.

Hitting rock bottom is a lonely place to be. It is seemingly more desolate than any of the worst emotions and fears we have felt at any other point in our past. The energy and strength one needed to hold that frail structure together as it begins to crumble before our desperate eyes. It starts to weaken and crumble gradually. Yet, we either chose to ignore it because of another problem that needed immediate attention or thought we somehow had it under control, hoping it would correct itself without too much morale-sapping intervention.

All those façades start to crumble once we realise that we have nothing left to give in keeping it together and that nothing is left within us to convince ourselves that our lives are under some form of control. Those things we had used in the past to convince ourselves were nothing more than delusional psychological tricks given to us as though that was all we needed. In reality, we were barely surviving, not living. And yet, here we are, slumped and exhausted, with our thoughts and emotions shredded beyond recognition. We have nothing left to give.

Embracing Nothingness

What happened?

This time, there are no delusional answers; the old hopes and aspirations have crumbled away. All the shame, guilt, and anger of being 'weak,' 'depressed,' 'a failure,' 'sad,' and 'putting on a brave face until it gets better' or using some other unhelpful phrase as a prop means nothing anymore. All those motivational lies we once told ourselves to drive us on have dissolved into nothing. We've stopped comparing ourselves to external expectations that never existed except as delusional fantasies within our misdirected minds.

All the effort we invested in this delicate balancing act becomes nothing. All that created pride, promises, and the other tricks we used to convince ourselves to keep holding it together finally became worthless. We clung to all those external beliefs and false encouragements to avoid disappointing our and others' expectations. In that deal, we forget our inner and authentic selves that have returned with such a vengeance; it knocks us for six, but we don't know what it is now because experiencing our genuine authenticity is such a foreign sensation. In that absolute realisation, our body is limp wherever we are, our mind dazed and thinking of nothing coherent. In its place, we see and feel the emptiness, the nothingness around us, just as we feel it within us, and that is what we are – just ourselves in a world of nothingness.

We have hit rock bottom, and anyone who sees us will know that the pretence we convince ourselves of every day, hour, and minute of our lives doesn't work anymore. What others think about us doesn't matter because there is nothing more to lose. That mask of pleasing others and the delusions we clung to in portraying that mask have fallen. There was nothing behind it except emptiness. The desperation and hope in that vast lostness have gone. All we have is ourselves and the nothingness around us.

It was all a show. Now the show is over. This is us, as we are, as we always were, but hidden away for all that time, only now living it in its purest form.

Once we have a breakdown, there is no more will within us to convince others that we are okay because we no longer remember what being okay means. There is no more will to convince ourselves that the delusion we have been trying to live with is no longer under perceived control.

When we are there, and all those delusions are gone, all we can do is welcome the embrace of the nothingness surrounding us once we recognise it.

To begin with, this nothingness is unbelievably foreign when we realise that our illusion was just that, an illusion. That is one unfamiliar sensation, but this nothingness was always there. Only we couldn't recognise it, and if we could, we didn't know what to do with it because this was something we had never been told about. This nothingness has been enveloping, protecting and hugging us all along, and we have been putting things in the way for all these years.

Nothing is more humbling than being forced to open our sensations to this expanse of nothingness. Nothing is more numbing than the helplessness of not knowing how to embrace the nothingness that has always been by our side, ready to be there for us. Nothing is more humbling than realising how alone we feel after all the effort we invested in avoiding nothingness for so long, all that wasted time dedicated to things that were never there and can never be lived again. Nothingness is always present and will remain after we die as we become a part of it, allowing others to turn to it.

We may be still and silent when nothingness is introduced, but we may also rock our bodies, cry, or scream. We have finally become aware of the absolute silence that nothingness has always enveloped us. Perhaps that primal cry is an inner release from finally letting go of the last of those fictions and delusions.

Perhaps it is what we have always been searching for, but we don't know what we have been looking for because we have been brought up to think it has to mean something rather than the tranquillity of nothingness, which is, in fact, the ultimate reality. As soon as we have nothing, we have everything. All that noise that has surrounded us for most of our lives was a distraction from the ultimate peace that has enveloped us since the day we were born. Yet, the silence can be pretty deafening within this absolute tranquillity of nothingness.

Possible Steps to Recovery

How do we pick ourselves up after what we have just gone through? We have done it before, but this time it's different. This time, there are no inner reserves of delusion to lead us astray. We know how we have done it before, but no type of carrot-and-stick motivates us this time to continue.

But what can we do?

We may think there's nothing more to live for when that nothingness envelops us without resistance. We might think that all those we love are better off without us. We might believe we were hindering the lives of others by abusing their free time when they were 'constantly' helping us out. We may have even thought that we are a burden and a heavy weight around the necks of others. Or maybe we thought something else similar, but how wrong we are.

Instead, we might ask what we have done 'wrong.' We tried everything to push the inevitable breakdown away instead of embracing it. Why do we do that? Is it because we were told to, or because they didn't understand the power of nothingness either? Is it a systemic expectation we are brought up to follow without questioning? Didn't our parents tell us because they didn't know either?

Accepting this nothingness and allowing it to envelop us removes that fear, replacing it with a new type of serenity, as it embraces us without judgment, expectations, or demands. That nothingness has finally broken all our fictional bounds and set us free to be ourselves.

Indeed, there has to be something within the nothingness, right? If that isn't the case, then it would mean we have lived a lie for all these years, convincing ourselves that the expectations of others were more important than our true inner thoughts and intentions. Yet nothingness remains as nothing, waiting to offer us everything once we accept its immensity. Everything is nothing, and nothing has 'no thing' to bind us to because there is nothing there anyway. It was all fiction.

Those first moments of recognising that nothingness has always embraced us can be confusing and overwhelming initially.

We may realise that our lives suddenly make no sense because of this. It never has and never will, except for the sense we give it.

Our reason for being here is meaningless; we stare at that clearly for the first time and see, feel, and hear nothing. And if we open ourselves up to it, it is so tranquil. Whichever way we turn, it is there, and although initially, we may have feared it, it is the only thing that has never threatened us in any shape or form.

Even though we have never been told what nothingness is, we are attracted to it and want to accept it because nothingness cannot hurt us. It protects us. There is no judgment, expectation, or emotion. That is forgiveness. That is our release. That is our self. That is acceptance. That is love.

As we sit there, dazed after everything around us has broken down, we may gradually become aware of our surroundings and realise what has happened. We may remain there, wherever we are. We may go to bed for a while. We may feel we cannot return to the societal and fictitious expectations we once dedicated our lives to because they no longer hold value, meaning, or enticement. Yet, we don't know how to continue from this point on because we can't go back once we have experienced it. That's also a problem.

We may think of the time before it happened; what was it all for? What a waste of valuable time I've lost. All that moralistic and mechanistic advice that told us how to behave for the benefit of others, that we should think and act in specific ways to feel we belonged, all that self-sacrifice without considering its meaning.

In this moment of realisation that life can't carry on like this anymore, maybe someone holds us close. Still, there is no consolation because our body has lost all sensation related to those once-considered fictitious goals we were encouraged to have. We are numb. Most of those around us don't understand what we're experiencing because they've never been where we are today. And even if some people have and do understand, we sense it, but we still don't know what to do. We are alone, but we are not alone. Some others know where you are and what you must do with this peaceful nothingness. They have always been there, but we thought they were different. They're not. You're not. You're free. Only you don't realise it yet.

Possibly, a doctor prescribes some medication to shut out the peaceful power of nothingness for a while, or maybe we turn to alcohol to temporarily numb the vastness of nothingness until we know what to do with it if we get around to it. Perhaps someone will recommend a prepared religion to tear us from that nothingness and replace it with a limited, unquestionable, one-sided, fictitious façade of distraction. Maybe someone will try to take over our lives in another way, ripping us out of that tranquillity and back into chaos.

Maybe the other option is to quit life altogether and become a part of that nothingness. But to do that, we must compare ourselves to something within our fictional system to adjust ourselves accordingly to a fictional societal label that doesn't exist before we can carry out that ultimate deed.

Either way, it doesn't matter because we all return to that peaceful nothingness at some point.

A New Beginning

After a breakdown, we are no longer who we once were, so why resist the change? All that has shifted is our perspective of ourselves and our surroundings; we are merely responding to this newfound awareness of ourselves, the world, and others around us.

Now that we understand our unique differences, isn't embracing our individuality better than conforming to the masses who strive for sameness, blandness and conformity? By setting our own rules for what we consider a fulfilling and meaningful life, we acknowledge that while our problems may not disappear, our relationship with them can undergo a transformation. Once we understand this, this is part of what liberates us.

Since we cannot alter how others perceive us, why should we consider their judgments when we choose to live by our standards rather than someone else's exaggerated morals? No two people have the exact expectations, and it is impossible to please everyone without losing a part of ourselves. Regardless of our actions, someone will inevitably be offended. So, let them be offended as we live on our terms of freedom, peace and love.

We may lose those who no longer understand us. Conversely, this new state of tranquillity within this nothingness will attract those who resonate with us, allowing us to connect with like-minded individuals. While we must remain vigilant against manipulators, this was also necessary.

Additionally, when we are in a tranquillity with nothingness, there are no rules except the Universal laws of Nature, of which we are a part.

Once we have experienced it and may still not recognise it for what it is, there is no return to our previous life, no matter how hard we might want to try. And that is a blessing. Once we stand tall again, we no longer view things the same way. Those old thoughts never truly existed, just as no absolute right or wrong exists, and we begin to recognise that now.

The breakdown reveals that we were trying to fit into a fictional society that wasn't necessarily designed for us, Universalists of nothingness. And that's perfectly fine.

Our society doesn't care what we do as long as we provide what it demands, which requires immense effort and blind acceptance. The breakdown shows us that nothing and no one cared or could care enough about what we do, think, or are. Everybody has problems, often trying to elevate themselves by bringing us down in moments of their inner need. They distract themselves because they don't understand that there is no inherent reason to be here.

The breakdown reveals that we are solely responsible for our freedom and meaningfulness and that what others think or say holds no significance in a world of nothingness. There is no 'us'; there is no 'self'. We are what we are when we think and do it. Everything else is a delusion. We are free from conflicting opinions and judgments, both our own and those of others. We are ethically free to pursue what we want, when and how we want, within our environmental constraints. Free from the societal prison of the 'eat, work, entertain, sleep' cycle, we can do what is important to us, not what others expect.

The more we learn to act and play the game according to our rules, the less effort, thought, and involvement we require to remain within it. However, the system is designed to be incomplete, to confuse us, to corner us within, keeping us caged like an animal with the hope that we lose our responsibility and Universal freedom.

Yet, we must still navigate this societal realm to survive, occasionally playing a part in the societal game to keep us out of it. We still need to earn money to exchange for necessities like food and clothing, especially if we cannot directly barter with others. To earn it, we must sacrifice our most limited resource: time, so we must choose how we wish to make that sacrifice.

When we embrace this other option, we can say, 'This is who I am.' We can declare, 'This is all I have because this is all that matters to me,' as long as it supports what is needed to be who we are. Once we recognise the universal beauty surrounding us, we can enjoy it for what it is, not what we are told to want.

Nobody knows our whole story. They never will, no matter how close they are to us. Let them consider what they like because they will form their opinions anyway. By living according to our ethical standards, we attract those who resonate with us, respecting each other's individuality, interests, and boundaries. Those who think and feel similarly will naturally be drawn to us.

And that frequency that attracts us to the universe and towards others is authenticity.

There is no right or wrong way to live—there is simply life and living it in a way that is important to us. That is our way.

Yet, we must remember that we cannot change the past, but we can learn from it and let that understanding grow within us. We can choose what is meaningful to us and adjust ourselves accordingly by getting on with it, because the act of doing is what defines us.

Taking Responsibility

One thing we can do is take responsibility for what happened, even if it wasn't our fault. We can learn from it and thank the defensive system we created, which initially began to build up in complexity, for serving us. Then, we can let it go, allowing our resourceful inner self to emerge free from those bounds while still holding those lessons learnt should they be needed sometime in the future.

Why? Because that old defence system tried its best to protect us with the limited and outdated resources we had at the time. Yet, that robust protection scheme kept us from living life to the fullest.

However, once we can let go without judgment and accept what happened, that's forgiveness in its purest form. It's a forgiveness filled with nothingness, as nothing holds us to push or pull us in any direction. This absolute love for oneself makes us stable, unshakeable, and undefeatable.

Remember, we can still maintain our boundaries as part of our protection system, which is perfectly fine. Some people cannot forgive and wish to hurt others to justify their inner weaknesses, losses, or desires.

Living in the Now

Living in the present is the only time our lives genuinely exist. Constantly reliving past moments or obsessively planning the future is futile, as these times no longer exist or haven't arrived yet. Spending so much time there is mostly a waste of time that could be spent in the present. There is no other time to live than now, when we are free from the mental games we once played. Living in the now involves occasional planning for the future, then letting it go to focus on each step we take in the present. It means savouring the moments of our journeys. This is the peace within the nothingness that protects us.

We could worry about and fear the future, but that wastes time and energy because what we plan to deal with that fear rarely happens, and ultimately, we can never control the moment when it comes. We may think we can, but we can't. We have no control over anything except what we think, say, and do. All we can do is influence it a little if we're lucky.

Some may not understand or agree with what I said, which is fine. It's your life, and you can do with it as you please. Regardless of our interpretation, this understanding offers us a fresh start, free from the old limiting beliefs that once hindered us—unless we hold onto them. Although we can't start life from the beginning, our experiences give us the advantage of knowing how to approach things differently from this moment on.

Embracing the Future

Discovering the incredible power of nothingness and the meaninglessness of life has helped free me and many others from our fears; it can take time and effort to get there, but the journey becomes more beautiful. At times, it can still be daunting to recognise how vast this nothingness is, especially when encountering new aspects of life we haven't considered. Yet, when we reach these unexplored parts, it should encourage us to take even more responsibility for ourselves, leading us to the next step of a fearless and unrestricted life.

The wonderful thing is that this part of the journey never ends. The deeper we immerse ourselves in this nothingness, the more we grow and understand who we are, what we are doing, and how we are constantly feeding the other at the detriment of ourselves.

We are no longer caged animals performing societal tricks for deluded rewards that encourage more societal tricks and false recognition. Instead, we live freely, roaming this beautiful planet and doing what has meaning to us. Although we still have limits and boundaries within a societal system, we can choose how to navigate it best.

This remarkable year brings us to the end of 2021.

The wound is the place where the Light enters you.
Rumi

Phase Three – 2022: The Re-Programming

Before delving into this year's events, I would like to mention that after the breakdown I experienced in March 2021, it took about fifteen months of questioning and reflection to reach a point where I could start living my life again rather than remaining a hermit that I had become. This duration is a valuable measure of the time I needed to heal. As we will read, this new phase marked significant changes that led me to cross an old threshold and enter an astonishing new era.

Here is how 2022 unfolded, but first, starting at Christmas 2021

My first authentic taste of inner freedom came at Christmas 2021. It was my first step beyond my old, destructive beliefs, offering an exciting glimpse into a new and unknown world. As I continued to release that past emotional baggage, new and promising sensations emerged. I felt like my efforts were finally paying off, and I was starting to make real progress. This release allowed me to enjoy time with my wife and take advantage of the seasonal break, savouring every moment.

The following enlightening experience occurred ten days later, at the beginning of the New Year. Something within me (I can't recall precisely what it was) made me say, 'Yeah, I don't need that anymore,' and I let it go. The feeling was so good that I had to remind myself that while this was a significant step forward, I still had a way to go.

Throughout the years of working through my past, I have learned to stay calm about my progress. I have lost count of the times I thought I had cracked it and felt jubilant, only to find that I had only removed another layer of inner issues, allowing the next one to surface. After so many disappointments, I was cautious not to be lulled into a false sense of security.

The next six months were still a bit of a roller-coaster ride as I recalled the great things I had done and the depressing mistakes I had made. Thankfully, the painful memories were becoming less intense and less frequent. Some occasional memories hit hard, but I now have the experience to handle them, even when challenging ones took a little longer to navigate.

From the end of June onwards, I experienced no more painful memories. However, the good memories continued to surface, which was refreshing and helped to further boost my ever-improving mood.

In July, I decided to take a break from self-assessment, as I was finding fewer mental issues to work on and felt that I was creating problems unnecessarily. Instead, I immersed myself in other activities and made the most of my free time. This decision was the right thing to do, and the rest of the year went smoothly.

I want to highlight some key points that significantly impacted me this year and how I addressed them, which are more effectively presented individually rather than in a diary format.

We are what we pretend to be, so we must be careful about what we pretend to be.
Kurt Vonnegut

Discovering My Narcissism

In March 2022, a year after my breakdown, I discovered that I still harboured strong narcissistic tendencies. As I began to piece together the more apparent aspects of my behaviour, I realised the profound impact it had on my relationships and what others were having on me. Many of these relationships were rooted in outdated and toxic patterns that served my narcissistic needs rather than fostering genuine connections around me.

Through researching narcissism, I began to identify similar behavioural patterns within myself. This was a startling revelation, as I had believed I had dealt with this issue years ago. Acknowledging that I still had more work to do, I committed to learning new, healthier ways to interact with others. By adopting neutral responses to narcissistic triggers, I saw remarkable improvements in my behaviour and overall well-being. This built further on the work I did through dialectical behaviour therapy.

This journey not only transformed my relationships but also opened my eyes to the complexities of human interactions. I began to see people and their behaviours in a new light, fostering a deeper understanding and empathy. This process has been a remarkable eye-opener, helping me move towards more genuine and meaningful connections.

Over time, I recognised that I no longer needed to engage in these toxic two-way narcissistic dynamics, and consequently, I ended such relationships that were so. While some might think I was only looking out for myself, I understood that relationships often evolve or devolve due to changes in personality, situations, or other reasons. Moreover, I noticed that instead of mutual narcissistic toxicity, I was bearing the brunt of it. Experiencing this firsthand made me realise how I was hurting others along with the pain, and I struggled with an immense amount of embarrassment, realising what I had inflicted on them.

After decades of this behaviour and only recently realising it, I want to apologise to those receiving my toxic rants. Now that I have experienced it firsthand, I understand how difficult it was for others to be around me and why many people tried to avoid me.

What I'm about to say might seem unusual if you haven't experienced such a shift in perception. However, it's how I began to see myself and others; it was an eye-opening and incredible experience.

One of the benefits of working through the past and understanding it for what it was (or wasn't) is that I started seeing people and their behaviours differently. It wasn't that their behaviours were changing; it was that my projections of their behaviours were changing.

Without repeating myself too much and going back to the delusional theme at hand, it was when I was searching for information on narcissism and how to handle such toxic relationships that I began to recognise how similar those behaviour patterns were within myself. Once I was aware of them, it became clear that I still had narcissistic issues. This was shocking because I thought I had dealt with them years ago. If you have read my previous book, you might recall that I once believed I was a narcissist, sociopath, and psychopath. My narcissistic mind had convinced me otherwise. I was gullible (perhaps I still am).

Through reading about narcissism, I learnt how narcissists operate and the tricks they use to get what they want. Recognising my narcissistic tendencies, I started responding neutrally whenever a similar issue arose. Although it didn't work every time, this yielded fantastic results in learning to behave differently and to stay calm.

My primary method was to identify a narcissistic pattern within myself. Once I understood it, I thanked it (it had a function and had tried to protect me based on a survival model I had used as a child that had become a complex mess over the years), let it go, and considered a more appropriate behaviour for future occurrences. I selected several potential solutions, tested them, and refined the most effective ones until I was familiar with them. Then, I applied it in real life. If it didn't work, I reviewed other alternatives until I found a successful one. This hit-and-miss technique worked well overall. It wasn't perfect, but it was a great start.

Is this how a narcissist works in being something they are not? Yes and no. They do this, and non-narcissistic people do this too – we train our egos on how to behave appropriately in given situations when we are children, which we improve on as we age. The process is the same; we start learning how to do it later, and the learning phase can be a bit more intense for adults. Still, we have much more experience to work on as adults in improving our ego behaviour than we did as children. This is why we sometimes feel overwhelmed when adulting in new situations – we must relearn some behavioural pattern for a particular problem we haven't encountered before, or that the old pattern is no longer valid.

Here, I cover specific narcissistic patterns that I had developed over the years and used from an early age up until recently, with an explanation of how I was and how I think I have changed.

Narcissists typically have little to no self-esteem (they often exhibit an over-inflated sense of self-importance), so their behaviour patterns focus on self-justification. One primary technique is subtly making others feel worse by understanding how to exploit our weaknesses, thereby increasing their sense of superiority and control, as they are adept at reading us to identify our shortcomings. This temporary fix of self-inflation lasts only briefly (from minutes to a day or two) until something deflates their inner bubble, forcing them to restart their cycle of sapping strength from someone again.

Narcissists might use indirect insults disguised as compliments or ghost us to make us feel guilty, hoping we will grovel back for their perceived levels of devotion. If questioned about something they did that bothered us, they deny any wrongdoing and distract us with other comments that we may have misunderstood the situation. If they admit a mistake, it's usually for a selfish reason, and their apology might be worded to place the blame on us instead of themselves.

They often display exaggerated emotions and overly affectionate behaviours in the hope that we will forget the last problem they gave us because they think we depend on their stroking (they know how to compliment and praise us precisely as we need it). If they want something from us, they usually prepare us by either softening us up with compliments or throwing indirect comments to make us feel guilty for doing something for their benefit. If that doesn't work and we avoid them for some reason, they might also use loyal minions to influence our responses again through praise or criticism; however, they will deny using them later if questioned.

This, however, is just the tip of the iceberg!

Their World

Narcissists view people in their lives in binary terms: yes or no, are we helpful or unhelpful to them? They value us for what we can offer them, and the less we have, the lower their value is regarding us. It's not the value of a good friend because we are not friends to them; we are a resource and nothing more. They play the friend to get access to that resource.

If we try to escape their control, they strive to win us back, and when they have, they will punish us in some way (usually emotionally) for leaving their circle of resources without their permission. Even if we ask to be left alone, they ignore our request and do their best to portray us in a bad light because of it.

When they know we know that they have wronged us, have pushed us too far or want something from us that we realise is taking the Mikey, narcissists usually ghost us for a while (ghosting is ignoring us completely), hoping we feel guilty enough so they can manipulate us to feed their needs again. While explaining why they forgive us for our behaviour, even though we have a problem with them, they tend to fantasise about our reactions while trying to manipulate us into some guilt trip, ready for the subsequent demand they want from us.

Another strategy a narcissist uses is that when they realise they have been caught, they try to cover their tracks with lies and manipulations, often blaming others but never themselves. If we pay attention to what they are saying, we can recognise that their logic is unbelievable and not worth following through. If backed into a corner, they might respond aggressively by shouting and screaming to wear us down into submission.

Think of Pavlov's dogs and how he trained them to salivate at the sound of a bell, signalling that they were about to be fed. Pavlov's experiment demonstrated how conditioning works, a concept that applies to many aspects of our lives. This includes the narcissist's strategy when they try to condition us into putting up with their mental abuse. This strategy can be very successful for a narcissist for those who are unaware of what is being done to them.

When a narcissist repeats a slightly negative pattern that gradually worsens over time, combined with ghosting, love bombing, triangulation and other techniques, we can become conditioned to their gradual change in behaviour. The narcissist, however, pays careful attention to where our limits are and will try to touch them as much as possible without us realising what they are doing. Through careful observation, they determine our level of punishable acceptance based on our behaviour, such that they will continuously test it until it eventually becomes too much for us. Then the ghosting begins again...

A couple of years ago, a narcissistic friend repeatedly did something I disliked despite my requests for them to stop. After many empty promises and apologies, such that I was doing all the work to keep the relationship healthy and balanced, I realised the friendship wasn't for me (this was becoming more apparent as I was working through this material on how narcissists tick. Because of the way I was manipulated and how terrible I felt about myself after meeting up, gradually over time, before meeting up with this person, I required mental preparation before the meeting, scripting my conversations to protect my privacy.

After meeting up, I needed to go through exhausting self-debriefs with myself (and talking to my wife to calm down) to work through the anger and frustration that had built up while being with them for that short period. It reached a point where, before I decided to end the friendship, the debriefs would take several days for me to move on and forget about them. However, you don't really forget about them, even once we have ended communication with them. Those memories of manipulation occasionally come flooding back.

Narcissists rehearse specific responses to manipulate others, helping them to convey false emotions convincingly. This realisation was painful for me, as I saw how my constant lying and manipulations had driven people away just as that narcissist was treating me in my life. It's a sad state to be in, unable to enjoy others' company because of the need for short-term self-worth boosts through degrading others.

Narcissists are never relaxed around others, constantly plotting and scrutinising their behaviour to conceal their guilt and shame. This is exhausting work. Unlike psychopaths, narcissists experience guilt and shame for their actions once they realise, or suspect, that others have recognised their manipulative behaviour.

They are perpetually monitoring our behaviour and responses to maintain control over us. If a narcissist apologises, expect a long, illogical explanation aimed at portraying themselves in a better light while making us feel guilty for accusing them, even though they know we are correct, and they have wronged us. It's another version of love-bombing or stroking.

When a narcissist needs help, they expect quick, high-quality assistance from us. If our help doesn't meet their expectations, they offer subtle criticism. One note, however, is that you should not expect the same level of support in return.

This is just a glimpse of what a narcissist can do to us if we let them.

Later, I will describe how I dealt with my remaining narcissistic tendencies by changing my diet in 2023. Until then, I discovered that specific philosophical tools, predominantly Stoicism, helped me manage my behaviour further, but I couldn't eliminate it.

Philosophy is a battle against the bewitchment of our intelligence through language.
Ludwig Wittgenstein

Philosophy

Philosophy, derived from the Greek words 'philo' (love) and 'sophia' (wisdom), is the pursuit of knowledge and understanding about the fundamental nature of reality, existence, and human experience. It seeks to explore and answer profound questions about life, morality, reason, and the universe. Philosophy is not merely an academic discipline but a way of thinking critically and systematically about our world and our place within the system we have created.

Historically, philosophy has been divided into various branches, including metaphysics, which examines the nature of reality; epistemology, the study of knowledge and belief; ethics, which explores the concepts of right and wrong; and logic, the science of valid reasoning. Each branch addresses different aspects of our understanding and challenges us to think deeply and rigorously.

Philosophy encourages open-mindedness and intellectual curiosity, urging individuals to question assumptions, analyse arguments, and consider multiple perspectives. It fosters critical thinking, clarity of thought, and the ability to articulate and defend one's beliefs. Throughout the ages, philosophical inquiry has influenced numerous fields, including science, politics, art, and religion, thereby shaping the intellectual and cultural development of societies.

In essence, philosophy is a timeless endeavour that inspires and challenges us, urging us to seek wisdom and understanding in our ever-changing world. It was once our psychology until religion came along and banned it as such.

The Role of Philosophy in Modern Life

Despite these challenges, philosophy remains essential for understanding our thoughts and the lives we lead. Once we know our life philosophies, we can determine how far to push and combine them for optimal mental and physical health and well-being. Philosophy encourages critical thinking, enabling us to navigate the complexities of contemporary society with greater clarity and purpose. By engaging in various philosophical ideas, we cultivate a deeper awareness of our values, beliefs, and motivations, which in turn help us make more informed decisions. Not only that, but this intellectual rigour enhances our cognitive abilities and fosters empathy and understanding towards others, promoting a more compassionate and just society.

Stoicism

When Greece was the world's philosophical centre, it was home to towering figures such as Plato, Socrates, Pythagoras, Diogenes, and Epicurus, to name a few. Philosophy wasn't just a subject to discuss, but a way of life that was deeply reflected upon and hotly debated. At any given time, various philosophical models jostled for superiority and recognition. Many theories faded because their creators or teachers failed to attract enough students to sustain them.

One enduring philosophy that emerged during this vibrant period is Stoicism, founded by Zeno of Citium. This philosophy continues to influence Western thought profoundly today. Through rigorous debate and lived experience, Zeno explored philosophies such as Cynicism, Epicureanism, and Pythagoreanism, gradually shaping his unique outlook. While the modern interpretation of 'Stoic' often implies emotionlessness and detachment, this is a misconception. The term 'Stoic' originates from the Greek word 'stoa,' meaning 'porch,' referring to the Stoa Poikile in Athens, where Zeno and his followers would gather to discuss and develop their ideas.

Stoicism's core emphasises the importance of virtue, wisdom, and rationality. It teaches that individuals should strive to maintain inner tranquillity by mastering their reactions to external events beyond their control. This does not mean suppressing emotions but rather understanding and managing them in a balanced way. Zeno's philosophy also highlighted the interconnectedness of all people, advocating for cosmopolitanism—the idea that we are all citizens of the world, bound by a shared humanity. This principle encouraged Stoics to act justly and compassionately towards others, fostering a universal sense of brotherhood and unity.

Philosophical Contrasts: Hedonism

Today's prevailing philosophy, hedonism, centres on indulging all the senses and seeking pleasure and enjoyment, often at significant cost to our lives and health. While it aims to increase pleasure and reduce pain, this pursuit can blur the distinction between the two over time. Hedonism can be categorised into two types: enlightened hedonism, which necessitates effort and thoughtful decision-making, and unenlightened hedonism, which pursues short-term pleasures without considering the consequences.

Enlightened hedonism advocates for a more balanced approach to pleasure, encouraging individuals to consider the long-term consequences of their actions and decisions. This form of hedonism advocates for a thoughtful engagement with life's pleasures, recognising that some degree of effort and self-control is essential for sustainable happiness. For instance, engaging in regular exercise or maintaining a healthy diet may not provide immediate gratification, but can lead to greater overall well-being and contentment in the long run.

In contrast, unenlightened hedonism often results in reckless pursuit of immediate gratification, with little regard for future repercussions. This approach can lead to a cycle of dependency on fleeting pleasures, such as excessive consumption of alcohol, unhealthy food, or other vices that provide a temporary high but ultimately harm one's physical and mental health. The allure of instant pleasure can be so compelling that it overshadows the long-term negative consequences, creating a dissonance between what is truly beneficial and what feels suitable for that moment.

The societal implications of hedonism are profound. A culture steeped in the pursuit of pleasure can lead to widespread issues such as addiction, mental health crises, and a general decline in overall life satisfaction. The relentless chase for pleasure can overshadow meaningful pursuits and relationships, fostering a sense of emptiness and dissatisfaction. Moreover, the environmental and economic impacts of a hedonistic lifestyle are significant, as the constant demand for more can lead to overconsumption and waste, straining the planet's resources.

However, it is essential to note that the pursuit of pleasure is not inherently harmful. When approached with mindfulness and balance, hedonism can contribute to a fulfilling and enjoyable life. The unchecked and thoughtless pursuit of pleasure poses risks. By adopting an enlightened hedonistic approach, individuals can enjoy life's pleasures while also considering their long-term well-being and the broader impact of their actions.

Personal Experience with Stoicism

In April, I stumbled across Stoicism and quickly learned that it was a great way to gain control over myself and address the remnants of my narcissistic traits. Stoicism helps me structure my day, thoughts, aims, and ambitions, and address the little things that still bother me. The techniques the Stoics espouse are straightforward to learn and implement, offering powerful ways of thinking to maintain emotional and physical balance.

I haven't adhered to just one Hellenic philosophy but have instead followed Zeno's thinking by incorporating elements from Pythagoras, Socrates, Hellenistic principles, and modern philosophers. This eclectic approach helps me accept my current thoughts and actions by embracing Descartes' idea, 'I think, therefore I am,' in a different and personal way. Drawing from various philosophical traditions, I can create a more comprehensive and adaptable framework for personal growth and self-improvement.

Stoicism, in particular, offers practical strategies for managing emotions and developing resilience. Techniques such as negative visualisation, the dichotomy of control, and mindfulness practice enable me to confront challenges calmly and rationally. By focusing on what is within my control and accepting what is not, I can navigate life's complexities with greater ease and composure.

Modern philosophers also provide valuable insights, allowing me to integrate contemporary perspectives with classical wisdom. This holistic method not only helps me address my narcissistic traits but also fosters a more profound sense of self awareness and personal integrity. Through this ongoing philosophical exploration and integration journey, I continually learn to live a more balanced, thoughtful, and fulfilling life.

The truth will set you free, but first, it will make you miserable.
James A. Garfield

Toxic Positivity

Firstly, it is essential to understand that Stoicism is not about positive thinking or 'toxic positivity'. A positively toxic person will often impose overly optimistic, chirpy thoughts on others as a quick fix for any problem they may be enduring or as a way of blocking what they try to avoid themselves. I used to do this, believing I was being helpful and clever, but in reality, I was upsetting people and causing them to avoid me. My intention was positive, but the outcome was anything but.

When I engaged in toxic positivity, I was essentially a cocky arse, preaching that my life was perfect as though I was some walking guru while using it to block the issues I was avoiding to face myself. Most could see through this façade, although I couldn't. This behaviour alienated others and prevented me from addressing my problems, as I deluded myself into thinking I was making a positive impact in the world.

Examples of toxic positivity include statements like: 'You did that well,' 'You look good every day!', 'It is what it is,' 'We only have good vibes here,' 'Be optimistic,' 'Be grateful for what you have,' 'You are feeling such and such because you are…,' 'All you need to do is…' and 'Everything happens for a reason.' More such phrases can come across as dismissive and insincere.

People who use these phrases may think they are helpful, but in reality, they are gaslighting us. They show no genuine interest in listening to us and want us to leave them alone to avoid conflict. Toxic positivity can also manifest as blind encouragement focused solely on end goals rather than the journey itself.

This might be a short-term, feel-good factor, but it can demotivate and disappoint both sides in the long run, especially for children who grow up expecting constant praise. When positive comments lack authenticity and depth, they fail to provide the support and understanding that individuals genuinely need, leading to feelings of isolation and frustration.

Instead of offering positive praise or reprimand, I've learned to ask people how they achieved something and discuss their approach to it. This helps them understand that the process is essential for well-being and self-value. Empty praise, such as 'Oh, that's great!', provides no meaningful feedback and can be manipulative. Focusing on how they arrived at their current state and the efforts involved can foster a deeper appreciation for personal growth and development rather than just the outcome.

To avoid emotional swings between positive and negative toxicity, it is beneficial to remain as neutral as possible. Constantly dwelling on either positive or negative thinking can be a way to push away opposing thoughts or prevent us from understanding and appreciating the emotions we are feeling for what they truly are. Neutrality enables us to consider both the positive and negative aspects, allowing us to objectively balance the overall information. This balanced approach can lead to more stable and realistic perspectives, enhancing our ability to cope with various situations.

We need at least five related positive thoughts to neutralise a negative thought. However, I know from experience that thinking of one can be challenging when feeling down.

Negative emotions like fear, shame, and guilt are misunderstood tools that try to protect or guide us. Accepting and understanding these powerful emotions and what they are trying to convey can help us let go of those disturbing feelings and replace them with the inner strength and resources we have always had but weren't aware of.

What can Stoicism do for us? It helps us think, prioritise, and live in the moment.

Three Stoic Principles

Incorporating these three Stoic principles, among others, into daily routines can lead to a more mindful and intentional way of living. For instance, I spend a few moments each morning visualising my day and focusing on the most considerable potential difficulties I could experience. I rehearse how I might respond with patience and rationality. This exercise prepares me for the day and reinforces the Stoic value of stability, helping me maintain a balanced perspective regardless of external circumstances.

Moreover, practising gratitude and reflecting on what I can control versus what I cannot has been transformative mentally. I cultivate a sense of inner peace and resilience by focusing on my responses and the actions I take. These daily reflections and practices involve managing challenges, appreciating the present moment, and finding contentment in everyday life. I wish I had known this fifty years ago!

Before bed, for example, I reflect on the day by asking three questions: What have I done? What haven't I done? What could I have done better? This reflection helps me prepare for the next day and keeps me focused on continuous improvement. By taking the time to assess my actions and decisions, I can identify areas for growth and acknowledge my achievements, fostering a balanced sense of self-awareness.

This evening practice is crucial for maintaining a Stoic mindset. It allows me to recognise where I succeeded and fell short without harsh self-judgment. Instead, I view these reflections as opportunities for learning and self-improvement that encourage a proactive approach to personal development, helping me set clear intentions for the following day.

Another Stoic technique I use is neutralising the value of possessions to reduce stress. By seeing objects for what they are, we can avoid attachment and disappointment if we should lose them. This mindset helps maintain emotional equilibrium, preventing us from placing undue importance on material items. Instead of viewing possessions as extensions of our identity or sources of happiness, we can appreciate their utility while remaining detached from the loss of them. This is easier said than done, especially when something has just happened; however, after some reflection, this exercise proves to have great value.

This perspective can also be applied to relationships with people. We can better cope with loss by valuing their contributions to our lives rather than becoming overly attached to them. Cherishing the experiences and lessons shared with loved ones allows us to honour their memory without being overwhelmed by grief. This Stoic approach promotes a balanced and healthy emotional state, fostering resilience in the face of life's inevitable changes.

Dealing with our imminent death can cause fear, but it is the only certainty we all face. Embracing the Stoic acceptance of mortality can alleviate some of this fear. Stoicism encourages us to contemplate death regularly, not as a morbid exercise but as a means to live more fully and intentionally. By recognising that death is a natural part of existence, we can reduce our fear and anxiety, allowing us to focus on living well within the moment more often.

Stoicism teaches us to view death as a transition rather than an end, fostering an inner sense of peace and acceptance. This approach helps us to prioritise what truly matters, enabling us to live with greater purpose and clarity. By accepting the impermanence of life, we can cultivate resilience and gratitude, appreciating each moment as a precious opportunity for growth and development.

Ultimately, the Stoic approach to death emphasises the importance of living a virtuous and meaningful life. By focusing on our actions and values, we can face mortality with acceptance, dignity, and equanimity, and we can find solace in the knowledge that we have lived well and honourably.

Reading works such as the *Tibetan Book of the Dead* and *Egyptian Books of the Dead* can provide valuable perspectives on handling this inevitability. These texts offer insights into diverse cultural perspectives on death and the afterlife, fostering a broader and more accepting understanding of our mortality. By understanding various perspectives on death, we can gain comfort and insight into the collective human experience.

In communication, we have three options: say something nice, say something not so nice, or say nothing. Choosing a neutral or positive response can defuse tension and encourage self-reflection in others. By adopting a neutral or kind approach, we foster understanding and mitigate conflict, creating a more constructive and supportive environment.

Effective communication is a cornerstone of Stoic practice. We can foster healthier interactions and relationships by carefully considering the words we use and their potential impact on others. When we respond positively or remain neutral, we help prevent conflicts from escalating and enable others to feel heard and respected. This mindful approach to communication encourages openness and trust, facilitating more meaningful and productive conversations.

Even with Stoicism, I have frustrating days and make mistakes. This journey is essential for understanding Stoicism, which helps me navigate life's challenges. Embracing the Stoic philosophy does not mean achieving perfection or never experiencing negative emotions. Stoicism teaches us that setbacks and errors are part of the human experience. Rather than viewing these moments as failures, we can see them as opportunities for growth and learning. Each frustrating day and our mistakes are a chance to practice patience, humility, and self-compassion.

Understanding Stoicism also involves recognising the importance of the journey over the destination. Life is a continuous process of growth and self-discovery, and each experience contributes to our development. By staying committed to the principles of Stoicism, we can navigate life's ups and downs with more excellent stability and purpose.

Moreover, Stoicism encourages us to view challenges as integral parts of our path. By reframing obstacles as necessary steps in our journey, we can find meaning and value in our struggles. This mindset fosters resilience and a positive outlook, helping us persevere through adversity with grace and determination.

Stoicism is not about eradicating frustration or mistakes but embracing them as essential components of our journey. This philosophical framework teaches us to navigate life's challenges with wisdom and poise, continually striving for personal growth and inner tranquillity.

Further reading

Numerous resources are available for those interested in exploring this philosophy in greater depth. Here are some recommended books:

- *How to Be a Stoic* by Massimo Pigliucci
- *The Beginner's Guide to Stoicism* by Matthew J van Natta
- *Stoicism and the Art of Happiness* by Donald Robertson
- *The Practicing Stoic* by Ward Farnsworth
- *The Daily Stoic* by Ryan Holiday
- *Meditations* by Marcus Aurelius
- *The Works of Lucius Annaeus Seneca*
- *Enchiridion* by Epictetus
- *That One Should Disdain Hardships* by Musonius Rufus

We must be willing to let go of the life we planned to have and embrace the life that is waiting for us.
Joseph Campbell

Philosophy and Psychology

Earlier, I mentioned that I didn't want to bring up tools that didn't work, as I didn't want to discourage anyone from using them. However, I'm making an exception here because it underscores the importance of being flexible and exploring various options rather than sticking to a few limited ones. With that in mind, let me highlight two examples related to philosophy and psychology.

One powerful collection of tools I didn't use was Cognitive Behavioural Therapy (CBT). I couldn't get along with it; I felt it lacked a clear structure and didn't align with my thinking. It seemed incomplete, and I didn't feel right about where it guided me. I might be mistaken in these views, but sometimes things don't go as expected.

Yet, after reading some articles, I discovered that the earliest form of a CBT-type system was called Rational Emotive Behaviour Therapy (REBT). REBT was developed in the 1950s by Albert Ellis and was predominantly based on Stoicism. Aron Beck then improved the system in the 1970s, and it has since been further enhanced, now commonly known as Cognitive Behavioural Therapy (CBT). I love Stoic philosophical thinking, but I'm not a fan of CBT.

The second approach I explored was existential therapy, which I found highly beneficial. This method addresses four key topics: death, freedom (responsibility), isolation, and meaninglessness. I delve deeper into these subjects in the section on existential therapy. I found Yalom's work particularly useful; his material challenged my thoughts and beliefs, prompting me to examine them thoroughly. It was worth the effort, as it helped me resolve issues with other approaches I hadn't previously addressed.

Existential philosophy is equally fascinating. Although I haven't yet found a comprehensive summary, the subject spans the key philosophers.

The depth of existentialism can be daunting, forcing a different way of thinking that, for me, was liberating. It helped me shed some limiting beliefs and complex ideas, making me more open-minded. For instance, stripping away inherited beliefs to envision myself alone on this planet revealed my self-delusions and avoidance of self-responsibility. A note from 2025: I love philosophical existentialism, but I needed to approach it one step at a time, exploring the thoughts of various philosophers. I still have a long way to go, but their ideas have helped me formulate mine more effectively.

As this clarity emerged (and continues to do so), I realised that my life was, and still is, entirely in my hands. This perspective allows me to question how to align myself with universal laws rather than the short-term, fictional societal norms we've been taught to follow. Our modern, complex systems within contemporary society often seem at odds with these ancient universal laws, causing more harm than good, ultimately benefiting a few.

By trying to understand my true self, I continue to align myself with these universal principles and, if necessary, live on the fringes of society, engaging with the complexities of our system on my terms. This thinking is new and challenging for me to articulate, but we all have a place within this fictional system and a choice about where we prefer to be. I have a roof over my head, food on the table, and inner peace. Everything else is a luxury of the system.

Not only that, but I am aware that I live in a first-world country where standards are much higher and more advanced for most. I understand that thinking and other issues are different for those who have never had or will never have such possibilities offered to them. I am also aware that if I say this, it is because I have experienced enough of those luxuries, and it is easy to compare not having them to someone who has never experienced them, which would sound conceited.

I can say that because I no longer have to fight those past demons, I can breathe and appreciate every moment for what it is, given the life I have lived. That is my perspective, just as someone has their perspective that reflects their life challenges. What I have and haven't written in this book are my perspectives, opinions, and experiences on adapting my interpretation of the world I sense and live in.

The entire educational and professional training system is a highly elaborate filter that weeds out individuals who are too independent, think for themselves, and cannot be submissive, among other qualities, because they're considered dysfunctional to the institutions.

Noam Chomsky

Our Systemic and Biased Lifelong Education

As my perspective has broadened, I've begun to see the world differently, particularly how we are educated and steered towards specific life paths. This isn't intended as a criticism but rather an observation. Our societal system is built on the pillars of capitalism, hedonism, and religion, among other centralised ideologies.

For many years, I believed that our societal system was designed for the benefit of the masses, but I've realised that this isn't the case. Once our working day is done, we're offered convenience, choice, and entertainment—all of which are shaped by our systems, whether through schools, media, family, external influences, or historical learning. This guidance shapes us from wild creatures into state-trained beings, moulding our thoughts, behaviour, identity, purchasing decisions, and even how we perceive ourselves to our neighbours. We then live within these boundaries for the rest of our lives. Like a pet dog, we learn not to bark at what troubles us; if we do, someone is there to help us restrain ourselves.

Reflecting on recent years, I have been sorting out my life issues; I've found that I needed little external paid advice on my journey. My system required self-investment, but it didn't require much money—save for the mushrooms, a few books, and the time I invested in myself rather than spending my hard-earned cash on other distractions.

Therapy and medication, on the other hand, are expensive. I could have spent my savings on sessions where someone listens to me for hours, amassing a fatter bank account without necessarily providing the answers I sought. In contrast, magic mushrooms were inexpensive and incredibly helpful. This doesn't dismiss expensive therapy altogether but highlights the need for resources to help us find answers. Yet, why do I hear so many stories of people leaving therapy sessions with nothing but pain, confusion, and a sense of abandonment? This doesn't mean there aren't good therapists, but less than 50% notice some improvement. Around less than 5% don't need a therapist for any more sessions due to their past being dealt with. This is extremely low.

While I took the long route, I stumbled upon surprising shortcuts. However, these are often dismissed professionally because they don't generate sufficient profit or fit neatly within conventional models that suggest one medical approach suits all. Because I wasn't spending much money, I had the time to invest in myself. It was worth every moment because I now understand so much about myself, those around me, our system, and so on, even if it took a while.

We must remember that I still have my past (we all do), but it no longer bothers me. It is a part of me that has given me new qualities I love about myself, which allow me to live in peace, be myself, and choose what I do with my life rather than have it dictated to me.

I stressed earlier that this isn't a criticism because the system does provide a general structure and services for those who lack the time or inclination to research these matters themselves. Why should the system offer the best to everyone as a standard? That isn't democracy. Democracy allows us to choose what is available, regardless of its quality and higher intention. While this doesn't always benefit the client, it certainly benefits those offering alternatives that give the appearance of action without challenging the systemic model. It's not perfect, but it serves the dreams of the minority more than it addresses the individual needs of the majority.

Navigating this landscape is challenging, with experts constantly marketing new solutions to our problems, albeit packaged in different ways. There isn't a single solution but rather a range of options that may or may not effectively mask the underlying issues. This is why I advocate for personal research: try something, and if it doesn't work, try something else until it does. But first, strip it back to the absolute basics, and once this is understood, build on that. As soon as something doesn't work as we have been informed, scrap it and choose something else. A collection of people do this daily and know precisely what is available and what to avoid. This is one key thing I have learnt over the years.

Fortunately, the media makes it easier to discover what works and what doesn't, with information at our fingertips. Unfortunately, one branch of science is being manipulated to become more of an industry rather than science, especially considering the manipulation of mental and physical issues. The other is doing its best to convey a clear and unbiased message. Our challenge is working out which is which. Progress, therefore, requires us to know what to look for or recognise what might be sold to us under the guise of advancement.

Given that various industries aren't always honest with us, should we close our eyes and hope they are correct, or should we keep searching for what truly works for us? We are, after all, unique individuals, and every path forward in our lives, mental health, and physical well-being is unique, requiring a tailored approach to optimise our use of the system.

We are allowed to do this. It isn't against the law. It's our free choice, but it involves understanding ourselves, which can be hard work and even more challenging when going against the societal flow. We may feel alone, but we are not. We have the freedom to choose what we believe is right for us and to live by it, though it's seldom marketed this way because institutions profit very little when they focus on the individual.

The universe is under no obligation to make sense to you.
Neil deGrasse Tyson

Seeking Universal Laws

When I began contemplating this, a question arose: What are the Universal laws, and how can I reconnect with them? I've been reading about and attempting to practice these laws for some time, but I wasn't making progress.

I eventually discovered that the easiest way to reconnect with these laws is to be at peace with myself, live in the moment, stick to the basics as my foundation, choose my luxuries carefully, and spend as much time outdoors as possible. I aim to follow a few more principles over time, but this is a solid starting point.

Perhaps it could be better phrased that we all have our place within this system and the Universal laws, regardless of our beliefs, life circumstances, or satisfaction with our current position. It is up to us what we do with it. We all have our roots, issues, and challenges. Some individuals may have an easier life due to external factors, such as access to financial resources, education, and guidance from advisors. However, depending on how we use them, we may lose out on something else. I'm not saying external influences shouldn't be used, as they can enhance our time here. However, if we receive or exchange something for nothing, what growth and understanding do we gain from that, other than a superficial ego boost?

If that's the case, why not choose where we want to be instead of simply accepting where we've been placed, or the circumstances we were born into? Our roots can still ground us, but they don't have to anchor us.

Being the centre of the Universe is a limiting belief. What if we moved with the Universal flow instead? Even if it carries us to the fringes of the restrictive 12 Degrees of Freedom (and the 13th

We Forgot), perhaps that's precisely where we're meant to rediscover something different. Something lost.

Who knows, it might be worth it.

It's about not being dependent on what society offers but choosing what we want and finding a way or a compromise to achieve it, since we in the 'developed world' have the luxury of choice. There are no right decisions; instead, there are decisions with varying consequences of intensity and duration, and we need to choose the one that best suits us. Do we want a general system handed to us on a platter, or do we want to determine what is right for us? Only you can decide.

Now that I've shared this perspective on using philosophy and psychology tools interchangeably, we can look ahead to 2023.

Health is the greatest possession. Contentment is the greatest treasure. Confidence is the greatest friend. Non-being is the greatest joy.

Lao Tzu

The Year 2023

In July 2022, I decided to take a break from self-assessment and researching new techniques to try. It was the right decision, and the break was exactly what I needed. I planned to return to this book at the beginning of 2023 to refine my previous observations and document my experiences to complete the project by March 2023.

However, upon reviewing my notes, I discovered I had lost almost all of them, except for a few early pages from 2020 and a substantial portion from 2021. There was far too much missing information to rewrite in diary format again. I was devastated. The mistake was mine, and there was no one else to blame but myself.

At the beginning of this year, 2023, I felt content with the work I had done regarding my past and was moving forward with my life. I was also starting to accept that the last bit of narcissism within me was a part of me because, no matter what I did, I couldn't eliminate it. I wasn't too worried because I had some Stoic tools to help me through the more challenging moments. If I were having a bad day and aware of the potential verbal bursts of toxic emotions I could cause, I would try to avoid people altogether.

Accepting my imperfections marked a significant shift in my self-awareness and personal growth. Embracing my flaws rather than incessantly battling them allowed me to focus my energy on more constructive endeavours. The Stoic principles I had adopted provided a solid foundation for navigating life's difficulties. By practising mindfulness and emotional regulation, I could maintain a sense of equilibrium even when faced with inner turmoil.

I realised that self-improvement isn't about achieving perfection but striving for balance and understanding. There will always be aspects of ourselves that we wish were different, but acknowledging them and learning how to manage them are crucial parts of the journey. My niggling narcissism, once a source of frustration, became a reminder of my humanity and the continuous work required for self-betterment.

On particularly tough days, when I sensed that my emotions might get the better of me, I consciously tried to minimise interactions. This proactive approach helped prevent unnecessary conflicts and preserved my relationships. It wasn't about isolating myself permanently but about recognising when I needed space to regain composure and perspective.

Reflecting on these experiences, I felt a deep sense of gratitude for the progress I had made. The tools and strategies I developed over time were not just theoretical concepts but practical aids that genuinely enhanced my quality of life. As I continued to grow and evolve, I looked forward to applying these lessons in new and meaningful ways, confident that I could face whatever challenges lay ahead with resilience and grace.

The Next Step: The Carnivore Diet Revelation

For me, the ultimate highlight was when I managed to release those remaining narcissistic issues without using any philosophical or psychological tools whatsoever. I discovered that the root cause of these narcissistic tendencies wasn't solely based on trauma but poor nutrition choices. After delving into the mind-opening realm of the Carnivore diet, I was able to release these issues and other physical ailments completely.

Embarking on the Carnivore diet was a transformative experience that exceeded my expectations in countless ways. It has since become my primary method of eating. This dietary shift has significantly improved my mental and physical health. Although it took me several attempts to adapt fully, I never imagined I would achieve the level of psychological and physical freedom that I enjoy today.

The Carnivore diet not only helped me address my narcissistic tendencies but also brought about remarkable changes in my overall well-being. My energy levels soared, and chronic issues that had plagued me for years began to dissipate quickly. It was like a fog had lifted, revealing a clarity and vitality I had never known.

This journey reinforced the profound truth that the more active responsibility we take for ourselves, the more freedom we gain. Taking charge of my diet and health has unlocked a deeper self-awareness and empowerment. The Carnivore diet taught me the importance of listening to my body and understanding its unique needs, leading to a more harmonious and fulfilling existence.

Looking back, I am grateful for the courage to explore this unconventional path. The results have been life-changing, and I am eager to continue this journey of self-discovery and personal growth. The Carnivore diet has become a cornerstone of my lifestyle, and its benefits extend far beyond the physical realm, touching every aspect of my life.

Commercial Foods and Potentially Commercially Related Illnesses

Before we proceed further with the book, let me pose a couple of questions I encourage you to consider. Are the commercial foods available today one of the primary causes of the numerous illnesses that often require some form of commercial medical treatment? If so, what exactly do we mean by 'commercial foods,' and what are 'commercial illnesses'?

Commercial foods refer to the vast array of processed and packaged products that dominate our supermarket shelves. These foods often contain many additives, preservatives, and artificial ingredients designed to enhance flavour, prolong shelf life, and increase market appeal. They typically include sugary snacks, fast food, ready-to-eat meals, and beverages loaded with high-fructose corn syrup. The convenience and taste of these products can be alluring, but their nutritional value is frequently questionable.

On the other hand, commercial illnesses have become prevalent in modern society, primarily due to contemporary lifestyles and dietary choices. These include conditions such as obesity, type 2 diabetes, cardiovascular diseases, and various autoimmune disorders. These conditions often require long-term management with pharmaceuticals and medical interventions, thereby becoming profitable for the healthcare and pharmaceutical industries.

Now, consider the role of essential animal protein and fat in our diet. Foods that go beyond these essential nutritional components often contain additives and artificial substances. Could our departure from whole, natural foods towards heavily processed alternatives contribute to the rise of these chronic illnesses? If our diets were primarily composed of unprocessed animal proteins and fats, would we see a decline in these commercial illnesses?

As we delve deeper into these questions, we must critically examine the relationship between our food choices and their impact on health outcomes. This inquiry isn't just about identifying problems and seeking solutions to improve well-being and a more natural, balanced lifestyle. The goal is to understand how we can reclaim our health by making more informed dietary choices and recognising the impact of commercial foods on our overall health.

Overcoming Health Issues

Overcoming health issues requires some challenging sacrifices, but those sacrifices have proven to be well worth it compared to the mental and physical benefits I am now experiencing. Can you imagine nearly all the health issues I suffered from for most of my life, such as tinnitus, disappeared entirely within less than the experiment I carried out (my tinnitus vanished after three days after a lifetime of issues? The few remaining issues gradually decrease in intensity with each passing day.

The correlation between the removal of commercial foods and my improved health is striking. Commercial foods, laden with additives, preservatives, and artificial ingredients, had long been a staple of my diet, as encouraged by many marketing strategies. The results were transformative when I started a more natural, whole-food-based diet, focusing primarily on essential animal proteins and fats.

These health issues, which I now believe to be commercial illnesses, were likely exacerbated by the artificial chemical substances and low nutritional value of the processed foods I once consumed. By eliminating these foods, I provided my body with the necessary nutrients, enabling it to heal and function optimally.

Reflecting on this experience, it becomes clear that our dietary choices have a profound impact on our health. The dramatic improvement I experienced in just three months underscores the potential harm of commercial foods and the immense benefits of a natural diet. It prompts us to question the long-term effects of our dietary habits and encourages a shift towards more mindful eating practices.

As we progress through this book, let us further explore the impact of diet on health and consider how reclaiming our well-being might be as simple as returning to the basics of nutrition.

The Possible Impact of Commercial Foods on Psychology

An aspect I will cover later that may be contributing to these emotional responses or outbursts is the type of commercial foods we consume. From what I have learned, I now understand that I can switch my narcissistic traits on or off by simply eating or avoiding certain commercial foods. This raises an intriguing question: if my behaviour and mental state can be significantly affected by what I eat, how many others are similarly affected? Furthermore, what other adverse reactions might we experience that could be alleviated by changing our diet?

Unfortunately, it is not only children experiencing such impressive temper tantrums, for example. We are increasingly aware of adults exhibiting these delusional outbursts in public, at work, within their families, and even when alone. Additionally, when I compare my time as a teenager and in my twenties, I recognise that a growing number of young people are either taking more time off sick or are becoming unemployable due to mental or physical illnesses, often diagnosed as depression, anxiety, or more severe mental conditions such as borderline personality disorder or schizophrenia. Still, when we compare what food-like processed products people eat today, surely there must be a link...

Regrettably, when people experience such intense internal turmoil, they often know that their related behaviour is inappropriate, yet they cannot seem to control their more extreme thoughts and responses. From personal experience, when having inner mental and emotional outbursts, it feels like either part of the brain freezes or becomes so hyperactive that the firing neurons are overwhelmingly intense, as if they have reached maximum capacity simultaneously. I am unsure which, but I can feel a difference in my brain's activity. It is disturbing, indeed.

Questioning the Psychologists' Perspective

Most psychologists assert that there is no connection between the foods we consume and delusional attacks, which they like to label. However, how can they determine this when they don't fully understand the chemical concoctions in these foods on our brains, which could cause us to appear mentally ill? They can't.

For instance, we know that certain pesticides can cause Parkinson's disease and have become a known occupational hazard for those who spray crops with these chemicals. This leads me to question how many of the millions suffering from this disease could lead everyday lives without having to rely on pharmaceuticals to manage their condition if these chemicals were not used in the first place.

Wouldn't it be simpler to ban these harmful chemicals altogether and adopt more sensible forms of farming, as we once did? Why are industry profits prioritised over the welfare of the people, and who are the politicians making the decisions that disproportionately affect poorer communities? I know this is the foundation of democracy, but aren't we taking this too far?

The wealthy can afford non-chemicalised fruits, vegetables, and pasture-raised meat (not organic), leaving poorer communities without any choice but to feed industry profits, ultimately resulting in life-changing health risks. This raises the question of whether politicians work for industries rather than the people they are supposed to represent.

More on this later.

The Personal Impact of Chemical-Free Living

When I eliminated all chemicals typically added to commercial farming crops and consumed organic and pasture-raised meat (not organic, as organic meat is high in omega-6), I noticed that all the long-term mental and physical issues disappeared within days to weeks. I have had some problems most of my life, and they disappeared so quickly; it seems those issues I was suffering from were side effects of what I had unwittingly consumed.

An example of this is that MSG causes me to have neurological narcissistic behavioural problems, immense headaches and muscle, joint and bone pain that restricts my movements (that actively bothers me for about 3-5 days after taking a dose of it.

Suppose I didn't know the problem was related to MSG and continued consuming products containing it. I might never break out of that cycle enough to realise what was happening to me, potentially affecting my relationships with others and myself. Nowadays, we rarely receive proper support from GPs; instead, we are quickly and effectively labelled with conditions like narcissism, borderline personality disorder, or depression, to name a few, followed by some pill that causes a range of other issues.

We are then prescribed pharmaceuticals, often several, depending on our symptoms and the related side effects from the medication, in the hope of masking the issues I'm suffering from rather than identifying and addressing their root causes naturally. Once someone is labelled with a mental health condition, it becomes nearly impossible to shed that label, regardless of any changes one makes in their life. How gruesome is that?

In other words, do those who consume such chemicals and processed foods inadvertently impair the effectiveness of our Gatekeeper (Ego) by causing over, under, or erratic firing of our brain's neurons?

Emerging Awareness and Gratitude

Thankfully, a few forward-thinking therapists are beginning to acknowledge a potential connection between diet and mental health. One such expert guided me to eliminate all added chemicals from my diet, for which I am immensely grateful. Dr Georgia Ede's insight provided the final piece to the puzzle of managing my narcissistic traits by addressing these dietary side effects. This shift in perspective has had a profound impact on my well-being.

By removing products with added chemicals from my diet, whether in the form of crop sprays, cattle feed, or found in processed and packaged items, I have noticed significant improvements in my mental clarity, emotional stability, and overall health. This change not only alleviated the symptoms that were often misdiagnosed as inherent personality disorders but also helped me understand the profound effect that food can have on our psychological state. My gratitude towards this therapist cannot be overstated, as her guidance has empowered me to take control of my health in a natural and holistic manner.

This emerging awareness among some therapists is a beacon of hope for many who struggle with similar issues. It highlights the importance of considering dietary factors when diagnosing and treating mental health conditions. As more professionals begin to explore and validate these connections, it could lead to a paradigm shift in how we approach mental health care, prioritising prevention and natural remedies over pharmaceuticals.

In the coming sections, I will delve deeper into how this dietary transformation unfolded and the broader implications it could have for others facing similar challenges. The journey towards understanding the link between diet and mental health is just beginning, and I am eager to share more about this life-changing discovery.

We are what we pretend to be, so we must be careful about what we pretend to be.
Kurt Vonnegut

Existential Therapy and Logotherapy

While existential therapy and logotherapy are rooted in existential philosophy, they differ significantly in their methods and focus. Existential therapy explores profound questions about human existence, including freedom, isolation, meaning, and mortality. It encourages individuals to confront these issues directly, fostering a deeper understanding of themselves and their choices. This approach emphasises personal responsibility and authenticity, guiding individuals to live meaningfully.

During my psychology studies, I encountered the name of Viktor Frankl. I thought that when I had time, I would read about his experiences as a prisoner in the Nazi concentration camps in how he kept internally fighting against their horrendous regime. He survived four camps, and his philosophy carried him through the worst and most threatening moments of his life during those atrocious years. Frankl's system is called logotherapy.

This approach focuses specifically on the search for meaning. It posits that the primary driving force in human life is the pursuit of purpose. Logotherapy employs specific techniques to help individuals discover and pursue personal meaning, often by recognising and embracing life's inherent challenges and suffering. While existential therapy offers a more open-ended exploration of existential themes, logotherapy provides a structured approach focused on meaning and purpose.

However, within the scope of this book, logotherapy and existential therapy share similar approaches, both offering a structured framework that focuses on meaning and purpose.

When I started this experiment, my primary interest was determining whether it would help me with my remaining narcissistic issues. It didn't. Not one bit. But it helped me with my outlook towards life and significantly changed a part of who I am.

The Gatekeeper Concept

Before delving into how existentialism helped me, I would like to introduce a term I encountered while reading about spirituality last year: 'Gatekeeper,' which represents the ego. I prefer this term as it simplifies Freud's abstract concepts, such as consciousness, the subconscious, and the id. Although the Gatekeeper concept can be expanded, I will maintain this perspective throughout the book. The Gatekeeper is a metaphor for the part of our psyche, specifically the Ego, that regulates and monitors the flow of thoughts and emotions, providing a more relatable framework for communicating with the external world.

The gatekeeper reviews incoming information against our experiences and inner beliefs, which we have gathered from childhood and other more intense experiences. Many of us react emotionally to external responses as a form of defence, often without trying to understand both sides of a situation.

The optimal operation of the Gatekeeper involves keeping an open mind, listening neutrally, and considering whether new information can expand or alter our current opinions, which draw on our experiences, should we need them in an emergency. This means holding back our immediate reactions to understand better the other person's stance and reviewing their opinions about our own to form a more comprehensive perspective.

One concern I have grown to understand is that if we don't engage in thoughtful and open-minded discussions, conversations can devolve into unintelligent, childish shouting matches over whose reality or opinion is more valid. Such reactions often stem from an unwillingness to understand others' opinions, preferring to cling to a narrow, deluded worldview. This could happen because someone didn't get their way or feels ignored and unheard.

Alternatively, it might be an innocent lack of skill in debating or discussing ideas that prevents others from understanding a different perspective. Some may struggle to entertain viewpoints that contradict their own, perhaps because they are unsure of their beliefs or fear admitting they are wrong. They might feel compelled to defend their perspective to avoid losing face.

Regardless of the reason, whether insecurity, inexperience, or stubbornness, these are their issues, not ours. Ultimately, such reactions are based on incomplete information. It's essential to recognise that everyone has challenges and biases. While we can strive for open dialogue, we must accept that not everyone will be ready or willing to engage constructively.

Existential therapy led me to explore the realms of nihilism and absurdism, among others, providing me with a more diverse perspective on my life. These philosophical explorations have profoundly influenced my understanding, even as I ponder my stance. I have realised that I am responsible for choosing what holds meaning for me. This does not imply that nihilism or absurdism lacks value in shaping my overall outlook. Instead, acknowledging these philosophies enriches my journey towards a more nuanced and authentic existence, making what is happening around me more varied perspectives of the personal opinions of others. Does that make sense?

It is incredible what an impact it can have on us when we begin to recognise that we have no pre-defined life goal from birth to death. If we did, we wouldn't have moments of doubt, changes in life and career directions, dreams, and ambitions. It's even more astonishing when we realise how many potential rabbit holes surround us that we continuously try to avoid falling into due to the fear of losing our identity or someone else's fantasy that we have been hoodwinked into believing and committing ourselves to.

What could be worse than discovering that we have been living our lives according to other people's opinions for all these years and not knowing what to do about the meaninglessness that remains? Not only that, but we haven't even started to express our opinions. But what if such a task is overwhelming in size? It almost makes us want to ignore our thoughts and views, continuing to live in the delusion we have committed ourselves to, with the hope that maybe, just maybe, we were right in the first place. Who likes admitting to ourselves and others that perhaps we have made a lifelong mistake? And no one likes restarting their life after so many years of struggling with the old one because they know how it works; they know where they stand and how they have had to build their lives around it.

Understanding Meaninglessness

Meaninglessness is everywhere. Once we have food, drink, and shelter (today, we also need clothing), what else do we need to survive in the outside world? Once we have these basics, the rest is our free time, but how many of us remember that? In today's world, we have made our free time so complicated that it seems essential to our survival.

Once we realise that we don't have to limit ourselves to the abstract and undefinable societal upbringing based on opinionated inheritance provided by family, along with institutional beliefs and expectations, we can open ourselves up to the possibility of a simpler, more comfortable, and less stressful life. This realisation offers us more options moving forward, as long as we consider our ethics each time we make a decision.

Understanding this can lead to a profound sense of freedom. By shedding the unnecessary complexities imposed by societal norms, we can focus on what truly matters to us. This allows us to craft a genuine life, free from the constraints of others' expectations. In turn, this can lead to a more fulfilling and authentic existence, where our choices are driven by our values and desires rather than external pressures.

Personal Responsibility and Freedom

How does this work? If we decide to do something and get it wrong, it's our problem. However, if something is chosen for us and it goes awry, we usually don't believe it's our fault, even though we decide to trust or go along with it. Ultimately, those consequences are still our responsibility. Since that's the case, how do we become aware of how alone we are in our decisions and actions?

Each time I needed to strip away another of those old beliefs I had held onto desperately, I faced this challenge. Once I had it, it was quite a shock to realise how much of my own life I had given away to someone or something that was never there for me and never existed except as a fantasy in someone's mind. This awareness only comes once those old beliefs are gone. Today, I view this meaninglessness as an open playground to do what I like within my ethics (not morals, which are too restrictive, inconsistent, and belong to others) and environment.

And what a difference that makes to the quality of my life!

Embracing personal responsibility has been liberating, enabling me to reclaim my autonomy and craft a life that aligns with my values and desires. I am no longer bound by the constraints of outdated beliefs or the expectations of others; I now navigate my choices with a sense of freedom and authenticity. This shift has profoundly enhanced my sense of self and overall well-being, transforming what once seemed like a daunting responsibility into a source of empowerment and joy.

Death, Freedom, Isolation, and Meaninglessness – A Review

I found death fascinating because it helped answer lingering questions I didn't even realise I had. Freedom was a revelation, highlighting how much of my life is my responsibility and how much I had been giving away. The exploration of meaninglessness profoundly transformed my perspective. It allowed me to see life as an open playground where I can create meaning and purpose rather than being bound by societal or inherited expectations.

Isolation confirmed that, unknowingly, I had been in the right place throughout my life. I had been searching for a connection to others, and everything around me that never truly existed in the way I believed. This realisation helped me accept the inherent solitude of human existence and focus on authentic connections and experiences rather than chasing illusions. This insight has brought a more profound sense of peace and acceptance into my life.

The section on meaninglessness proved to be my biggest challenge. As we strip away the beliefs that give us false hope and direction, we realise those fictional crutches never worked and never will. This sacrifice leaves us with consequences we must face. Our dedication to those lifelong delusions determines the consequences we are still dealing with today, and perhaps for the remainder of our lives.

We try to hide from these delusions by playing the pantomime of inconsequence within the cyclic routine of eat, work, entertainment, and sleep, willingly placing our lives in the hands of others. While playing these cyclical roles, we secretly hope or create some prayer or routine, wishing the consequences will disappear or turn in our favour someday. Sadly, when this doesn't happen and as we age, it can leave an unshakable bitter aftertaste that taints our lives further. Nothing is worse than realising that what we have been waiting for doesn't exist and will never arrive, especially when we think it is too late.

Viktor Frankl's Influence

As mentioned earlier, I first read Frankl's book, *A Man's Search for Meaning*, before delving into any other works on existentialism. This book provided several insights that helped me answer questions I hadn't considered. One poignant point was that it is not the physical pain which hurts the most, but the mental agony caused by the injustice and unreasonableness of it all. This helped me understand why I was so filled with conflicting emotions about my father's rejection and his need to show his inner frustration through cowardly violence and continual verbal abuse towards my mother and me.

The most painful part of a beating is the insult it implies. This insight helped me recognise the source of my confusion and emotions, making me realise why I felt so angry and useless due to my father's mistreatment. Another quote from Spinoza, mentioned in Frankl's book, states that we cease to suffer when we form a clear and precise picture of an emotion. This confirmed that my approach over the past six years had been right.

He who has a why to live for can bear with almost any how. This reinforced the concept that when we have something to believe in about ourselves, no matter how small, we have a thread to hang on to when life isn't going as we wish. That thread was what my mother gave me. No matter how much I was punishing myself, there was always that little glimmering thread tempting me to fight in search of what I couldn't recognise within myself.

It's incredible how something so small can still shine through all that darkness that tries to crowd it out. There were times when I interpreted it correctly. Still, those inner forces would distract me with what I thought were more pressing and consequential beliefs, along with the mass of adopted and misaligned labels and beliefs I had accepted and dedicated myself to, as though they were my own.

I still think that the foundations of my personality, narcissistic or otherwise, can be formed at a very young age by repeating specific patterns enough in that child to be mentally locked within that vicious process cycle without a glimmer of realising how abnormal this is. But even this is not as it seems because, as a child, I chose to create that very protection process system based on the limited resources I had in the restricted environment in which I was emotionally involved.

Over the years, that protection system gradually grew into something more of a monster that was still working against all those fictional threats I regularly mentally created and lived with throughout my life. The sad thing is that none of those threats even existed. They were built on the protection process I developed in response to the first of a series of initial threats I had received. They also created a defensive role that I played out daily, thinking I was being resourceful.

The following quote from Frankl's book profoundly impacted me, fundamentally changing my perspective on the purpose of suffering: *To suffer unnecessarily is masochistic rather than heroic.* How true this is. I am no hero, and I am no masochist, so why have I been masochistically punishing myself for all these years? If I am not either, then what am I?

This insight compelled me to reassess my relationship with suffering. I realised that enduring pain without purpose or necessity is not a mark of strength or courage. There is no medal of honour, only an exhausted mental life. It is a form of self-inflicted punishment with no constructive purpose. This revelation encouraged me to let go of the notion that suffering was somehow noble or necessary.

I gradually began to understand that the true purpose of suffering lies in the lessons it can teach us and the growth opportunities it can present. By viewing suffering through this lens, I could shift my focus from enduring pain to seeking meaning and learning from my experiences.

Another point Frankl makes is the use of humour to cope with the most horrific moments we have faced. For most of my life, I have tried to be too humorous to the point that it hurt me more by keeping others away due to its hurtful impact on others. Why? I thought that if I was being funny, I couldn't offend anyone, but I couldn't come across as amusing in a kind way. There was always an undertone to cause hurt. Even if I did say something genuinely funny, I tried to build on it by taking it further beyond the bounds of others, which ultimately drove others away. All I ended up with was disrespect, which, subconsciously, was what I wanted.

Another point is that I have a dark sense of humour because I can relate to its underlying message. Some may not necessarily understand or like it, but it makes sense to me. Once I read Frankl's statement that humour is used in adversity, and upon reflection, I have to agree. Although it pushed many aside, it helped me come to terms with what I was trying to understand about myself. Recognising the tragedies with dark humour around me helped me deal with mine in some way.

Although my sense of humour has evolved, thankfully, it retains a dark side. I wonder whether it has softened because my perspective on what is happening around me has changed. Alternatively, does my dark humour indicate that I still have unresolved issues, or do I appreciate it for what it is? Can I laugh at it because I know what it was, and it no longer controls me?

However, let me clear up one thing: a tragedy is still a tragedy, regardless of its form or intensity, and I completely respect that. Humour can be a coping mechanism, helping us navigate a society that often feels alien. We find comfort and a sense of belonging through such humour, even if it sets us apart from the masses. I'm okay with that.

This shift in my humour reflects a broader change in my outlook. Humour is not about dismissing the seriousness of past experiences but about acknowledging that they no longer have power over me. Humour has become a tool for resilience, allowing me to connect with others who share similar experiences and find solace in shared understanding.

Since I have done everything independently, I decided to undertake this project alone rather than working with an expert. Instead, I used the excellent book *Existential Psychotherapy* by Irvin D. Yalom as my starting point. Although I have briefly touched on my existential experiences earlier, I would like to explore further how the four pillars covered in this book affected me. I will review them in the same order as I read them, which is how they are written.

Life is a journey that must be travelled, no matter how bad the roads and accommodations are.
Oliver Goldsmith

Death

The concepts of death and dying are closely connected, yet they represent distinct aspects of the end-of-life experience. Dying refers to the physical decline, encompassing the emotional, spiritual, and physical changes that occur in the lead-up to the final moment. It is the journey of gradually letting go of life. Death, in contrast, is the definitive point when life comes to an end, a final and irreversible state marked by the cessation of all biological functions. While dying involves the approach towards this conclusion, my focus here is specifically on death itself rather than on the process of dying.

The Taboo of Death

Death is the one inevitable destination we all share, the final chapter that awaits us from the moment we draw our first breath. It is the only goal after birth that is universally guaranteed. Yet, paradoxically, death remains one of the most deeply ingrained taboos in our society. We speak of it in hushed tones, if at all, and it looms large as one of our greatest fears. We often avoid discussions about death, entangled in a web of cultural superstitions and anxieties. Instead of confronting our mortality head-on, we usually relinquish control over our perceptions of death, allowing others to shape our understanding of this most personal of experiences.

Many of us go through life without ever genuinely contemplating death, not just in terms of the practicalities like writing a will, but in a deeper, more existential sense. Considering our mortality can feel like admitting to our vulnerability, a stark reminder that our time here is finite. How unfortunate this is, for in reality, death is an intensely personal journey. When the time comes, no one else can take our place. Regardless of how many loved ones are by our side as we draw our last breath, the journey of dying is one we must undertake alone.

Given this inescapable truth, why do we, as a Western culture, resist preparing for death when practically every other culture embraces it? Why not do the same and accept the reality of our mortality, allowing ourselves to live with a greater sense of peace and acceptance in the days we have left? Wasting time denying the inevitable is a true shame, especially when that time could be used to deepen our understanding of life and its transient beauty.

The way we prepare for death is a profoundly personal matter; there is no one right way to do it. I acknowledge that for some, the idea of confronting death is far easier said than done, especially if there are unresolved issues or lingering regrets that have yet to be addressed. However, by engaging with the reality of our mortality, we might find that our fear of death lessens, allowing us to live more fully in the present.

Personal Preparation and Acceptance

As I have mentioned in my previous writings, I have grappled with the unknown of approaching death, and these reflections have profoundly shaped my perspective. Thanks to the insights gained from psychedelics and extensive introspection, I find that death now occupies no intimidating place in my thoughts. Reading further on the subject has only confirmed my sense of preparedness. While it doesn't mean all questions are answered, I feel equipped to deal with them as they arise. However, I must acknowledge that I cannot definitively know whether my perspective is correct. The ultimate truth of our existence and what lies beyond our last breath remains a mystery until that moment arrives.

Living With Acceptance

The one constant in my life now is the acceptance of my inevitable death, an understanding that has, paradoxically, brought me a more profound sense of peace and fulfilment. Knowing that death is guaranteed at some point in the future has allowed me to approach the remaining phases of life with a newfound curiosity, pleasure, and open-mindedness. This acceptance encourages me to make the most of the present, to savour each moment as it comes, rather than being consumed by fear of the unknown. Ultimately, nothing will matter when I am gone. Is this perspective perverse, depressing, or simply realistic?

I believe it is far better to die amid something we enjoy, to leave this life with a sense of purpose and engagement, rather than sitting idly, waiting for the end to come. Yet, how many of us truly live this way? How often do we see people, even in the prime of their lives, putting off happiness, sitting and waiting for a better day, while the best moment slips by unnoticed?

Ancient Texts on Death

For those of us who grapple with the fear of death, there is a wealth of wisdom in ancient texts that has stood the test of time. Two particularly profound works come to mind: the *Egyptian Book of the Dead* and the *Tibetan Book of the Dead*. These remarkable texts offer comfort and guidance for those preparing to leave this world. Written with deep spiritual insight, they serve as invaluable companions in helping us to navigate the often-overwhelming journey of coming to terms with our mortality.

The book, *Egyptian Book of the Dead*, a collection of spells, prayers, and incantations, was intended to assist the deceased in navigating the afterlife. It is a work steeped in the ancient Egyptian belief system, offering a roadmap for the soul as it transitions from the physical world to the spiritual realm. Similarly, the book, *Tibetan Book of the Dead*, also known as *Bardo Thodol*, provides detailed instructions on navigating the intermediate state between death and rebirth. It teaches us how to understand and accept the dying process, offering a path to liberation from the cycle of suffering.

These ancient texts are not merely historical artefacts but living documents that resonate with readers today. They offer timeless advice on navigating life's challenges and approaching death, guiding us toward acceptance as time draws near. Their teachings remind us that death is not an end but a transition.

Moreover, the influence of these texts extends far beyond their original cultural contexts. Their themes and teachings have permeated other religious and philosophical traditions, leaving an indelible mark on humanity's understanding and approach to the concept of death. This cross-cultural impact underscores the enduring power and relevance of these ancient works. They speak to something universal in the human experience, offering solace and understanding when needed. Through their wisdom, we are reminded that we are not alone in our journey and that death, like life, is a natural part of our existence.

Facing the Past

But what happens when time is running out and we cannot confront the most troubling aspects of our past? What can we do when it seems almost too late to address the shadows that linger from years past? We must undertake this responsibility alone, without expecting intervention or validation from others.

We must acknowledge what we've done, the lives we've irreparably changed, the damage we've caused, the hurt we've inflicted, and the mistakes we've made along the way. This act of ownership helps us reflect on the experiences we've lived through since those events took place, even when the emotions they evoke are ones of deep shame, guilt, anger, confusion, or fear. The journey towards release begins with recognising what we've said and done, no matter how painful that might be.

This process is not about seeking one-way redemption or expecting forgiveness from others. It's about accepting our actions, taking responsibility for our decisions, and acknowledging the consequences for us and those around us. We cannot turn back the clock to undo what has been said and done; these things will stay with us until the very end because we chose to do them, yet we can learn from them. So why not hold onto them for what they were, as reminders of how we've been shaped by events that were, at times, beyond our control?

Responsibility and Reconciliation

The people affected by our potentially damaging actions during our erratic moments will never forget what we once said or did. Nor should they. They have every right to protect themselves against whatever they perceive as a threat.

If we ever cross paths with them again, we should not attempt to convince them that our previous actions were justified or excusable because they weren't. Our behaviour has already spoken volumes, and it has already told those we've hurt that they needed to take steps to protect themselves from further harm. We must accept that what we said and did changed their lives in ways we may never fully understand because, at the time, we did not take responsibility for our thoughts before they became words or actions.

What we can do now is accept and respect their viewpoint. We must allow them to move on without expecting them to drop the opinions they've formed about us or the defences they've built due to our actions. Just because we have changed doesn't mean they should. Their journey is their own, just as ours is ours, and they should decide what is right for them. And perhaps the greatest gift we can give them is the space to live their lives without our interference, allowing them to continue on their chosen path. In return, they do the same for us by keeping their distance and allowing us the space to move forward.

Daily Acceptance of Death

Every night, as we close our eyes and drift into sleep, we experience a small, symbolic death. Each evening, we can set aside the day's burdens and let them go the next morning; we awaken, reborn, free from the weight of the previous day. However, as soon as we wake, we often carry the grudges, problems, opinions, and inherited beliefs from the prior day. These are our choices, though we may not always recognise them as such.

Proximity of Death

Let's consider, for a moment, just how close death is to us all. At any given time, we have only about four to six minutes of life ahead of us—each breath prolongs those precious minutes. It's astonishing how casually we treat this fact, often taking it for granted until something goes wrong with our ability to breathe. But what can we do to prevent such failures if we don't explore different ways of caring for our health and well-being?

We need a new way of thinking that embraces fresh ideas, tools, and resources and cultivates a stronger sense of self. This approach can help us navigate life's challenges, even if our efforts are imperfect or we experience setbacks. This part of my life journey, which spans over six years since I began this project, has been one of constant questioning, testing, adaptation, and learning.

I don't say this to congratulate myself, but to emphasise that straightforward answers exist. However, the noise of inherited beliefs, commercial interests and superficial solutions often obscures them. If we don't find the right path immediately, we must persist, wading through the distractions until we do. This perseverance is crucial for our physical health, as exemplified by the importance of caring for our lungs and every aspect of our lives. Simplicity and focus are essential to maximising our limited time here.

The Journey

I may have taken the long way around to get to where I am today, often stumbling through life's distractions and regularly falling off track, only to pick up where I left off. Yet, that doesn't matter; we're humans, people with lives and emotions, facing new challenges and still trying to discover what is holding us back. It doesn't matter how long it takes.

What matters is that I am now in a place where I can live more freely with a calmer and more observant mind, even as I continue to learn from my past mistakes. I will undoubtedly have something new to learn tomorrow as I continue on my path, and I am perfectly fine with that, as it takes me towards death. Perfection is not the goal; there isn't enough time in my lifespan to achieve it, and I'm at peace with that. With all its twists and turns, my history has shaped who I am today, making me a unique individual. We are all, in our ways, such that every moment, frustrating or otherwise, has been worthwhile in getting me where I am today.

Realising the Present Moment

Who among us hasn't felt the passage of time slip away, leaving us with a sense of helplessness? Perhaps we've realised that the simple life we once dreamed of is slipping through our fingers, but we don't know what to do about it. Maybe we feel lost, unsure where to turn or what steps to take. Perhaps we know that letting go is the key. Still, we resist it because we're comfortable in our current role and familiar with how it unfolds in this stage of life, even though it sometimes tests us to the point of frustration in our created environment. These and other paralysing thoughts can hold us back from taking that first necessary step until we give up trying altogether.

Letting go could mean stepping into an unknown role that might disrupt our relationships with others and alter our place in society. Yet, it could also give us something new that takes us further on a journey of self-discovery.

Working Through Issues

So, what can we do to initiate change and break free from the personality roles we currently choose to play? Sometimes, the most straightforward approach is to start with what bothers us the most. It might not be the most challenging issue, but it's a start. Working through that one issue, no matter how long it takes, can be enough to help us accept, own, and take more responsibility for our actions. This process can also ease some of the fear of death, making the transition a little smoother. In reality, this is the second biggest challenge we face. The first is simply acknowledging there is a problem to begin the work.

Acceptance and Responsibility

But what if we take responsibility for our past actions and still can't let go of what we once said or did? Even then, we must accept that our behaviour is a part of us and commit to doing our best never to repeat those actions. Why? Because everything is allowed in life, meaning nothing in (an ethical) life is forbidden. It's okay to tell ourselves that we won't do something because it goes against our ethics, not because someone else's morals dictate it. We will never return to the same inner consciousness we had before the event, but we can recognise it as a lesson, acknowledge that it's part of us, and move on with the promise not to repeat it. External labels may remain, but we mustn't continue embodying them.

We are the only ones who can take action for ourselves by accepting what we have done without asking for forgiveness from others. We can't expect someone to change their opinion of us just because we've changed our views. Nobody else needs to know what influenced us to behave as we did, as sharing these details can often come across as making excuses. And while we may not see them as excuses, the listener likely will. They aren't there to hear explanations; they want an apology, plain and simple. The justifications are our private burdens to bear and come to terms with.

Moving Forward

Suppose we have questioned our lives enough to recognise our behaviour for what it is. In that case, we can continue our lives more lightly and without any unnecessary intruding thoughts, even if others still hold specific labels against us. Let them entertain those thoughts because what others think of us, justified or not, is ultimately none of our business. We must recognise what happened, declare it to ourselves, and accept that it's part of our history and personality. It's a memory; while it may remain with us, it doesn't have to define us, nor do we have to relive it. We learn from our mistakes, not punish ourselves for them.

Conversely, the events we suffered at the hands of others, especially in our formative years, may have forced us to develop intense defence mechanisms that later caused issues in our lives. These events were not our fault, but we are responsible for facing them, taking ownership of them, and doing what is necessary to change their impact on us. We don't deserve to carry the weight of someone else's unacceptable behaviour to our graves in the hope that it will make their lives easier somehow. We will make enough mistakes without adding theirs to our burden.

The Afterlife and Previous Lives

We don't know what comes next—whether there is an afterlife or not is still a matter of speculation after all these millennia. But what if there is? What if we carry on from where we left off in this life, working through all the unresolved issues before we can enjoy it for what it should be? What if the afterlife is also temporary, just like our current existence, and we must die again to enter yet another stage, still grappling with unresolved issues from this life and the next? What then?

Taking this further, could it be that our life now is the afterlife of a previous existence? Are we dealing with unresolved issues from that past life, along with the challenges of this one? If so, how stressful will the next afterlife be if we don't sort things out now? Could this be why some people experience more severe symptoms? They may not have addressed their issues in previous lives and now face the compounded stress of unfinished business, as well as the ones they have in this one.

Conversely, what if there is no afterlife? What if this is our only life, the one fleeting experience as a speaking ape with a functional thumb, bound by the same universal laws as every other living thing on this planet, and we get only one go at it?

At the end of our molecular life, do we return to stardust, our atoms mingling with those of countless others, forming something new that breathes and reacts according to the same chemical processes that governed our lives? This new life wouldn't be ours; it would just be another iteration in the endless cycle of existence. Isn't that what we are now, a consciousness formed from the remnants of billions of lives that came before?

Acceptance of Universal Laws

Taking this thought one step further, it doesn't matter what we do within the vast system governed by universal laws because it will guide us through two key steps: birth and death. At worst, we could wipe ourselves and all other species off the planet, yet the Earth would continue to spin, changing with each moment as the universe expands, indifferent to whether we are here. In other words, the Universe remains unchanged and continues on its merry journey. If that were the case, would we be an incidental happening on the planet until its next phase begins?

Is this thought process depressing? Have I lost the plot, or does some of this make sense? Ultimately, it doesn't matter what I think or what you think about my feelings. What matters is that life suddenly becomes much simpler once we strip away our non-existent biased thoughts about ourselves, how we perceive ourselves in the eyes of others and even about ourselves. This is a creation of civilisation.

Observing the world with an unbiased perspective clarifies how little we need to understand about ourselves, others, and the universe to make the most of our time here. This realisation can be liberating, opening up a sense of freedom within the natural bounds of our species and environment.

Accepting that we have nothing, we find ourselves surrounded by everything. This realisation is the prize available to all of us once we let go of yearning for things that don't exist. All that truly exists is the present moment and our experience within it. Everything else is a fleeting external experience that vanishes as soon as the moment passes, leaving behind only a temporary memory, which, when remembered, is, at best, a fictional recollection shaped by our perspective of what happened.

Man is born free, and everywhere, he is in chains.
Jean-Jacques Rousseau

Freedom

As I delved into the section on freedom, I found myself mentally doing somersaults with excitement! Why, might you ask? Well, it became clear that throughout my life, without fully realising it, I had formed a connection to what freedom is—a concept I had already touched upon in my reflections on death. However, I had also misunderstood certain aspects of freedom, and this section helped me to align them. This section beautifully clarified my confusion, revealing how easily we can twist or misinterpret the meaning of words to suit our needs, as I had done for decades. It made me wonder how many of us do the same, convincing ourselves that we have attained some elusive goal when, in reality, we may have only been chasing a mirage that doesn't exist.

Misconceptions of Freedom

I've come to understand that freedom isn't simply the ability to do whatever we want whenever we feel like it, without reflection or consideration—that kind of behaviour borders on hedonism and, in more extreme cases, libertinism. True freedom, however, is about taking full responsibility for ourselves and every aspect of our lives, especially keeping our ethics in mind. When we relinquish parts of our lives to someone or something else, we might believe we are handing over responsibility, but we aren't.

Even when we think we've surrendered control, we still make the final decisions and bear the consequences of those decisions, whether we consciously acknowledge them or not. When we allow fate or some external force to guide our choices, we often end up blindly fulfilling others' needs instead of our own, leading us to place blame elsewhere rather than where it rightfully belongs: with ourselves.

Taking responsibility for our lives doesn't mean we won't make mistakes. Mistakes are inevitable. However, I've learned from my past behaviour that coping with my errors is far more manageable when I take full responsibility for them. The mistakes I didn't take proper responsibility for continue to haunt me, even decades later. Some of these unresolved issues will accompany me to the grave, and that is a burden I will have to carry.

The Universe and Ethics

Over the years, one thing has become increasingly clear: we live in a universe without reason or a defined goal other than eventually dying. It follows only the universal and natural laws that govern all things, animate and inanimate. The universe is simply happening, just as we are. Many believe we would be doomed without artificial spiritual guidance or moral codes. I beg to differ. If we cannot trust ourselves to make appropriate decisions and rely on external rules to dictate our behaviour, we may be the problem. This raises a crucial question: Why are we encouraged to follow the whims of others rather than take responsibility for ourselves?

Have we intentionally forgotten how to take responsibility for our own lives? Is it because we want to deflect blame away from ourselves for not taking the appropriate responsibility at the time? Are we so terrified of recognising ourselves in what we are not aware of that we avoid taking responsibility because it is easier to take the time to understand it? Is it the fear of confronting the vastness of our existence and acknowledging that there is no inherent reason for our being here and that the decision to live lies solely with us? And why do we do so little about it? Is it comfort? Conditioning? Fear of success: Are we conditioned not to use it? Or perhaps the fear of failure?

Ultimately, no external force guides our lives. The universe, or any spiritual entity we might believe in, doesn't protect us or have our backs when things go wrong. We are self-governing and responsible for our actions as individuals, and the only harmony we can hope to achieve is with the universe's unwritten laws because we are a part of them, even when we don't fully understand them or try to resist them with our imaginations.

In a sense, we are our spiritual gods, an internal force within our physical bodies. Our bodies are merely vehicles, temporary vessels that carry us through life until they inevitably break down. As these internal gods, we possess the power to create life and to bring new things into the world, both great and small. But we also have the power to destroy, to take life from the environment that sustains us, with or without giving something back in return. Isn't this what it means to be a god in the traditional sense?

Reflecting on Responsibility

My journey began with recognising an issue I had with responsibility, and now, years later, I find myself returning to that starting point. However, there is a significant difference between how I viewed responsibility then and how I view it now. This prompts me to ask whether we still take responsibility for ourselves in a way that truly enhances our lives or if we choose actions that bring us the most pain through educational means, whether through our caregivers, family, teachers, or other forms of media.

Now, I realise I need to take responsibility for what I've avoided or done wrong, based on my ethics, and take it to the next level. This requires a willingness to delve even deeper into the darkest corners of my past, to respect and accept what I find there, and to release as much of it as possible. By doing so, I can find that neutral balance within myself, freeing myself from the restrictive bounds that have held me back. My history remains; however, I must accept that as a condition of taking responsibility for myself.

Relationships and Communication

In relationships, for example, freedom isn't about control or being right. It's about striking a balance between giving and taking, working together while maintaining our thoughts. This doesn't mean blindly following someone else's opinions just because they've told us to. Communication is key. We need to talk, make compromises, and build trust so the other person knows they can rely on us without fear of judgment. The only person I can truly change is myself. Once I've changed, my environment and reality will adjust accordingly. I can't change others, just as others can't change me. We must also recognise that we can't always be aware of everything happening around us or in the lives of others. So, I try to give people the benefit of the doubt when encountering something that causes inner conflict.

I don't always know what drives another person to react in a certain way, but that doesn't mean I need to respond with hostility just because their opinion differs from mine. I can consider their views without necessarily accepting them, and I believe we can all do the same. Maybe they'll say something that helps me adjust my thinking, but that's as far as it goes. We're all entitled to our opinions, even if they differ from what we want to hear. This doesn't mean we have to agree, but we should at least acknowledge the other person's right to their perspective.

This realisation represents a 180-degree turn for me, and I find it incredibly liberating not to get entangled in other people's conflicts. If I'm drawn into a disagreement, I've learned to take a lighter approach, thanking or acknowledging the other person's comments with a smile and then moving forward. However, I'm all in if a genuine debate is possible, where two open minds exchange ideas and thoughts. This is a new experience for me, and I find it exhilarating!

Practicing Discipline

Of course, there are times when we need to exercise discipline and refrain from speaking our minds to avoid offending someone unnecessarily. After all, nobody is perfect. If I can't always meet my expectations or be fully aware of every situation in my life, how can I expect others to do so? We need to give ourselves and others some space, especially when we don't fully understand what the other person is thinking or going through. We aren't in their shoes. Some people won't appreciate or respect my journey, what I've been through, or where I am today, and I respect that.

Unfortunately, we live in an age where more and more people are quick to voice their grievances, often believing that the world is somehow wronging them. We must remember that everyone has opinions and concerns, many of which are unrelated to one another. Some people expect the world to stop and accommodate their vision without considering the broader consequences. They may need to reinforce their stance by raising their voices or attacking others rather than taking the time to understand different perspectives.

It makes me wonder whether these one-way diatribic screamers are grappling with self-doubt, fear of being alone in their stance, or a need to be heard and recognised, regardless of the topic. Perhaps they choose provocative subjects to gain attention or validation, compensating for a lack of recognition or 'love' in other areas of their lives. They might bind themselves to an issue or a like-minded group because they don't know how to process it further within themselves, becoming overly reliant on the egotistical opinions of others. Sadly, most of us haven't learnt how to moderate our egos outside.

We must not forget that shouting and getting angry are often controlled responses people use to communicate their opinions more forcefully. These opinions are deeply rooted in their thoughts and memories, aligning with their inner values and life expectations shaped by their upbringing. I've experienced this myself, and what a relief it was when those inner destructive dialogues were finally silenced, allowing me to live the life I wanted.

The Cycle of Self-Harm

When things aren't going as planned, or when we're unconsciously sabotaging our lives based on our inherited inner beliefs, it can lead to a cycle of self-harm, either mentally or physically. This might manifest as cynicism, bitterness, anger, self-harm or other restrictive emotions and actions, which is often a cry for help. Over time, this behaviour becomes ingrained; we become disillusioned with the lack of help we receive, and others may begin to see it as a part of our personality, eventually avoiding us to protect their fragile understanding of where they are. The problem is that most people we meet don't know what they're doing themselves.

Another problem is when we don't get what we need; we may either intensify these emotions as a desperate cry for help or withdraw from life, resigning ourselves to a pattern of hopelessness until our time ends. This gradual acceptance of labels others place on us leads to a steady decline in our true selves as we subconsciously start using the label as a crutch, becoming what others perceive us to be through that label. No wonder many are lost and disillusioned, are on drugs or play a role so intense it drives others away from us.

Personal Journey and Transformation

A few years before starting this journey, I reached a point where I recognised a pattern of self-destruction in my behaviour. I've always known I was different, a fact I initially disliked. I played it up as a cry for help. Still, I was sending out the wrong message, thus allowing it to become a part of my personality, something I could identify with until I found (or was ready) to change direction and become who I am today.

Naturally, I wish I could have released what held me back thirty or forty years ago, but I can't turn back the clock. Instead, I'm grateful that I've learned what was happening to me and had the chance to work through it, releasing it. The quality of my life today is incomparable to how it used to be, and now I can say that every low I've endured over the past seven years has been worth it. I still embrace my uniqueness with a much more caring and open heart; I don't take myself as seriously anymore and enjoy life as if each day were my last.

There are still things that get me worked up, particularly when innocent children and women are abused. Thankfully, my work as a psychologist, particularly with those who have never had a chance at life due to what happened to them in their childhood, allows me to give back and help those who haven't realised their potential. With them, I use everything I've learned, except psychedelics, to help them neutralise their inner pain so they can find some freedom and have more options in life. It may not seem like much, but seeing the past abuse they suffered that wore them down gradually, losing its grip on them, is incredibly rewarding.

Whenever we face a decision, we have three choices: option A, option B, or to do nothing (option C). Each choice has its own set of advantages and disadvantages. Option A might mean missing out on something in option B, and vice versa. Even doing nothing has its consequences, which are often overlooked. Some might try to get the best of both worlds by choosing neither, but this rarely works. As the old saying goes, by chasing two hares, we catch neither.

It wasn't until I read this book on existential psychotherapy that I realised I had never adequately considered the positive and negative consequences when making decisions. I now understand that for much of my life, I had programmed myself to choose the path that caused me the most pain, a pattern that began in childhood when I acted out to get attention from my parents, regardless of the consequences. The problem was that I forgot to stop doing this when it was no longer relevant.

The greatest thing in the world is to know how to belong to oneself.
Michel de Montaigne

Isolation

Isolation is a profoundly personal experience many of us grapple with at some stage. It has been a constant companion, a feeling I never fully understood until recently. Throughout my journey, I've realised that isolation is not merely a state of being alone but a complex interplay of identity, self-perception, and societal expectations. In this exploration, I delve into the nuances of isolation, reflecting on how it has shaped my relationships, understanding of freedom, and approach to life.

For much of my life, I've felt a profound sense of isolation that lingered without understanding. I was eager to explore this familiar yet enigmatic experience as I delved into this section. This journey taught me to confront, understand, and ultimately embrace isolation. This process has allowed me to appreciate what I have and find peace in solitude.

If you were to ask whether I consider myself an introvert or an extrovert, I'm not entirely sure how I would answer. In my younger years, I desperately sought the spotlight, believing that being the centre of attention was the key to acceptance and fitting in with society. Like many, I managed the initial stages of relationships well, putting on a façade that seemed to work. But once that first hurdle was cleared, those inner doubts began to creep in, whispering that I didn't deserve the recognition, attention, and praise I had sought. Inevitably, I would sabotage the relationship, gradually chipping away at it until it was irreparably damaged.

The most disheartening aspect of this pattern was that I genuinely believed I was doing everything correctly. It took me a long time to realise that my actions were, in fact, a form of self-harm. It wasn't just what I said that mattered, but how I said it, when I said it, and how I reacted to others, oscillating between extremes of kindness and cruelty. Another tactic I frequently employed was taking the opposite stance of whatever someone else said, 'just for the sake of it.' This contrarian approach was a surefire way to provoke others, often leading to unnecessary conflict.

Another perspective on isolation is to recognise that we are all alone fundamentally. We have unique experiences, capabilities, beliefs, and opinions—just like the person next to us. We are neither exceptional nor inferior and certainly not equal in all respects. As individuals, we have strengths and weaknesses that are both similar to and different from those of others. We relate to our friends, family, colleagues, neighbours, and partners correctly. However, no matter how close we get to someone, there is always a gap between us that can never be fully bridged. Even in the most symbiotic relationships, this gap remains.

Our parents or caregivers play a crucial role in shaping our early years, programming us with the tools and resources we'll use for much of our adult lives. While many parents do an admirable job of preparing us for 'the real world' as they know it by providing a broad range of resources to navigate life's challenges, not all are equipped with the necessary skills to develop their children in a balanced way.

In the worst cases, parents or caregivers can have a devastating impact on a child's life. However, as children, we don't believe we are to blame for our upbringing. We make the best of the situation with the limited resources and life experience we have at the time. This resourcefulness often sets up a protection system that, while initially beneficial, can become more complex and less effective as we age.

While we are not responsible for how our parents educated us, we are responsible for addressing any parental misprogrammings once we become adults. Thankfully, this understanding is gradually becoming more widespread, with more people recognising the need to correct past issues they carry daily. There is also a growing interest in alternative therapies, such as psychedelics and self-work, as people seek out ways to heal rather than being sidelined by institutional labels and medications.

Therapy vs. Medication

It can be challenging for those who choose to work through these issues, whether alone or with the help of a therapist. It may take time, but the process is often more rewarding than being numbed by medication that merely hides or dampens the issue, leaving it to resurface later. For me, confronting past pain has been worth the effort. However, I respect that others may choose the medical route, and that's perfectly fine. The industry is designed to cater to specific needs, but every choice involves a sacrifice, and it's essential to consider whether that sacrifice is worth it. For me, the side effects of medication were not an option I wanted to pursue.

A Shift in Career and Life Priorities

There is a growing trend of people opting out of the industrial career game in favour of a simpler life with more free time and less mental stress. Increasingly, individuals are discovering that the simple things in life bring the most pleasure and peace of mind. Caring for the inner self yields the most significant mental and physical benefits, allowing us to respond more harmoniously to our environment and the laws of nature. Whether due to the increasing intensity of our fictional society or the weight of personal history, the reasons for this shift are less important than the outcome: finding peace with oneself, which, in turn, contributes to peace in the world around us.

It's essential to recognise that this lifestyle shift isn't suitable for everyone, and that's perfectly fine. Some people thrive in the rigours of business, competition, and the associated stress, mainly when they are younger. Ultimately, it doesn't matter what path we choose as long as it has meaning. No two people are alike, and we must respect those who choose different paths as long as their choices don't harm others.

Many years ago, I worked briefly at Terry's Chocolate Factory in York, UK, and found the work to be both challenging and mind-numbing. My task was to place chocolates into plastic trays as they moved along a conveyor belt, and the pace was relentless. The experienced workers beside me could do it with their eyes closed, chatting and laughing as they worked, while I struggled to keep up.

I recall asking them why they did this work, and their answers were primarily straightforward: they came to work to earn a living while enjoying the company of their friends, and once they clocked out, their time was their own. For them, the mindless nature of the work was a relief, a chance to switch off from the outside world. Ever since that experience, I have had immense respect for factory workers and the dignity with which they approach their work.

One of the things I love most about my journey towards understanding isolation is how it has changed my interactions with others. I'm more relaxed now, enjoying various conversations, philosophy, and topics I once dismissed as trivial. I enjoy reflecting on what triggers me and observing the world with a more open mind. I also appreciate a good laugh whenever possible. Previously, I was consumed by self-punishment and my perceived lack of self-worth, which prevented me from fully engaging with others. I even believed that any success I achieved needed to be undermined to match the level of self-worth I thought I deserved.

Never in my life did I imagine that discussing interesting things with others would bring me such great pleasure. I once viewed such conversations as a waste of time, believing relationships were built on controlling others and pushing boundaries. I assumed that everyone operated this way to some extent. How wrong I was!

Despite these changes, I sometimes struggle to initiate conversations and find small talk challenging, especially with strangers. However, I've learned to accept this. I have my strategies when needed, but don't need to be a social butterfly, so I'm content with the level of interaction that naturally arises.

Embracing Isolation as a Strength

Realising that we are all inherently isolated from everything and everyone has become a new strength in how I relate to myself and others. I always sensed a gap between myself and others in the past, something I felt I needed to bridge but didn't know how. Now, I understand that this gap exists for everyone, regardless of gender, race, identity, or situation, and it can never be fully bridged. Accepting this has made it much easier for me to connect with others.

How we experience and deal with this gap varies from person to person. Some people seek to be heard, felt, or appreciated, and they choose those around them who can temporarily fill that need, creating the illusion of bridging the gap. For others, this gap may be a source of jealousy, control, and anger, as it was for me. However, the gap is simply a part of our existence; everyone deals with it in their way.

In my more paranoid days, I lived in a fantasy world where I imagined deep, spectacular bonds with others. I tried to project these fantasies onto them, hoping to bring them to life. When, inevitably, things didn't work out as I expected, I intensified my efforts, using words and emotional manipulation to convince them to give me what I wanted. Of course, this approach never worked; it only drove people away.

When someone is deluded, they might resort to a range of manipulative behaviours to gain control over others, from love bombing to verbal aggression and even physical violence. While physical violence was never my thing, I engaged in other forms of manipulation, such as shouting, screaming, and attempting to control others' movements. These behaviours are ultimately destructive and reinforce the sense of isolation.

Today's societal system promotes extroversion, the idea that life should be lived 'to the fullest' by working, playing, and spending hard. We are encouraged to push ourselves physically and mentally to the limit. Unfortunately, this drive can lead to a victim mentality, where individuals become victims of their excessive expectations. Over time, the differences between victim and perpetrator blur, and many of us accept these utopic scenarios as a way of life, keeping our struggles hidden out of guilt or shame.

Consequences of External Expectations

Even those who initially succeed in meeting societal expectations may eventually become disillusioned. The relentless pursuit of external validation can breed discontent, frustration, and bitterness when we inevitably run out of energy. If we're lucky, this dissatisfaction may prompt us to seek something more meaningful before it's too late. However, this shift is more accessible for those with financial security. For those without, the struggle continues to put food on the table and pay the rent. Yet, even in these circumstances, we can find moments of peace by observing and appreciating what's around us. The experiences we have in life are personal and unique, and they remain with us throughout our lives.

We've become enslaved to the gods of currency and hedonism (among others), disguised under the banners of consumerism and capitalism. We chase superficial successes, comparing ourselves to others in a shallow competition. But why? Nobody cares. We spend most of our days chasing someone else's dreams, only to find them unfulfilling once we achieve them. The satisfaction is fleeting, leaving us searching for more.

We live in a world where convenience reigns supreme. We eat and drink without thinking, fulfilling our immediate desires without considering the long-term effects. While I'm not complaining, it's an observation of how our lives have become focused on instant gratification rather than meaningful reflection.

As I reflect on this, I find myself questioning what the baseline of life should be. Should we let others define it for us, dressing it up in a way that only disappoints and robs us of our most valuable asset: time? What does that baseline look like if we take control of our lives? How far back in history do we need to go to find it? Or should we continue sacrificing our inner heritage for fleeting external pleasures? Perhaps the answer lies somewhere in between. But how do we strike the optimal balance between the two in a world with so much to offer?

Take, for example, the decadence of food. Once we exceed the baseline of what we need, we often fall ill from overindulgence. While I enjoy delicious, decadent foods and am just as addicted to processed food-like products as the next person, I can't help but notice that we seem less healthy than we were in the past. We either refuse to recognise this or have lost the knowledge of what to do about it. Our health issues have become the elephant in the room, something we try to hide rather than address. Instead of tackling the root cause, we rely on quick medical fixes that get us back into the hedonistic cycle of spending until the next health issue arises.

Recognising The Societal Game

These medical quick fixes are designed to keep us in the societal game of consumption until our indulgences catch up with us to the point of no return; then, we are committed to the commercial side of the medical game. Those who can afford to participate in this system can continue their decadent lifestyles until it robs them of something precious later in life. Meanwhile, those who can't afford to keep up are pushed to the limits of suffering, warning others not to expect such luxuries. This system creates fear, showing us what could happen if we don't comply with the game designed by a few winners.

I have no complaints about the system people choose to play, as it is their free choice to opt for what is heavily promoted or otherwise. However, other options are less stressful, more affordable, and healthier. I'm not suggesting we change the overall game strategy, as that would be nearly impossible to implement on a large scale. But we can opt out of certain ones, as I have. Playing the game according to societal expectations only caused me physical and mental suffering because no matter how hard I tried, I could never meet those fictional external standards. Very few can. Not only that, but that's also not the life I want to live.

If we're dissatisfied with the mainstream societal model, how aware are we of our ability to step out of it? What alternatives are available? There are as many different societal versions as there are people alive, and we all live slightly varied versions of the main systemic models. We have the power to create philosophical systems that meet our inner needs, allowing us to survive comfortably while enjoying what the world has to offer without excessive cost. Naturally, this isn't what external forces want, but we have as much choice in rejecting their impositions as they do in imposing them.

If we want to uncouple ourselves from the mass-controlled 'eat, work, entertain, sleep' cycle, what do we want to do within the limits that enable us to thrive during our short time here? Am I asking too much? Are we content being led by industry giants and their representatives, or do we seek something more?

Last year, I read a book called *Unscripted* by MJ DeMarco, and it was a revelation. Though somewhat American, the book's message is clear: life has no script. DeMarco advocates for creating our scripts, following our own rules, and living on our terms. He emphasises the importance of financial independence, which can be achieved early in life, allowing us to decide how to spend the rest of our days. It's a far better alternative to having our lives dictated to us by external forces, often leading to a life filled with regrets.

Challenging the Standard-Provided Scripts

If we're not careful, the standard scripts we're provided with can be challenging to escape. Many of us follow the 'nose to the grindstone' routine, struggling to make ends meet without any clear future goals. The problem is that we're not taught about alternative options in school or by our parents, nor are we told why we must bind ourselves to a system that may not suit us. While financial security is often emphasised, we rarely consider the broader implications of security, whether mental, physical, or otherwise.

Security is an elusive concept, as everything can change in an instant. Those who have experienced poverty can become wealthy, while the rich can lose everything in the blink of an eye. The poor often find happiness in simple things, whereas the rich may struggle with dissatisfaction. But why is that?

DeMarco acknowledges that several attempts may be needed before we can achieve freedom. But what if we don't find it? Life is full of risks, regardless of the societal or individual models we follow. We've all experienced setbacks and unfulfilled goals at some point, but it's not the end of the world. Survival may be difficult, but it's part of the human experience. What remains consistent is the need to strive for what truly matters in life.

Working for someone else can provide a sense of perceived security, regularity, and guidance, allowing us to pursue personal interests outside of work. It's up to us to discover what we value and pursue it. There are no universal rules for what is right or wrong for our inner well-being as long as we remain guided by our ethics. It's our current goals that decide what is right or wrong in life.

Am I there yet? I'm on my way. I now have more quality time, which is essential to me than ever before. I still make mistakes and occasionally get caught up in others' games, but I've learned to recognise and correct them, minimising the waste of time that could be better spent on myself.

Our ultimate goal should be to live a peaceful and joyful life, staying true to our ethics and the ideals we wish to commit ourselves to and living them as fully as possible. We always have a choice in how we want to sacrifice our most valuable asset, and that is time for what brings us intentional contentment. Challenges will inevitably arise no matter our strategy or philosophy, so why complicate life more than necessary by adding to the burden?

Perhaps this new way of thinking comes from a growing awareness of the world around me and the impact of the system on my life. With this perspective, I've noticed a trend where people feel entitled to everything without earning it. They go around demanding, expecting, and taking without giving anything in return except for causing problems for others. In reality, we deserve nothing. Everything else is superficial once we have the basics of food, water, shelter, and clothing. Our free time is ours to spend as we wish.

While I've said that life has no absolute rules within our fictitious societal systems, those who choose to shout, scream, or walk away when challenged are entitled to do so. However, they may not receive the moralistic respect they crave.

In another part of this book, I examine how I perceive society as a game and how it is open to interpretation, depending on one's level of engagement. What matters most are the Universal Laws we automatically abide by, which we often try to ignore.

Choosing Our Paths

We can still dedicate our lives to a system activity we've created as a species, whether it's a job, hobby, or something else we enjoy. We could start a business, engage in research, or even redesign the system for personal or overall gain. We can help others, write books, explore nature, relax, and enjoy the things around us. We could also challenge the fictional rules of society and show others that there are alternative paths to follow. Why? Because these experiences are the only things that we take to our deathbed.

Playing the Game

Ultimately, how to play The game is ours. From experience, however, I've learned that we must play the game optimally and with some reflection because it can pull us in if something goes wrong. We may fight against it, but we must also live with the consequences for the rest of our lives. While there are no guarantees, playing the game wisely reduces the chances of being manipulated by others.

Life has no meaning. Each of us has meaning, and we bring it to life. It is a waste to ask the question when you are the answer.
Joseph Campbell

Meaninglessness

The Elusiveness of Meaning

I approached this section with a certain apprehension, more so than with the others, because many of us instinctively search for a sense of meaning that we assume is inherent in our lives. However, this section taught me that life is meaningless unless we imbue it with our chosen significance. In other words, no one will grant us meaning because it simply doesn't exist until we create it ourselves.

This realisation is daunting when we consider that almost all our meaningful beliefs, symbols, and guiding principles are either inherited or externally imposed. If so, what have I been dedicating my life to all these years? Have I been committing myself to meanings and opinions passed down by others rather than discovering my own? It certainly seems that way.

Reflecting on what I've read so far, the section on death provided valuable insights, addressing many questions and affirming that I should not fear death but rather prepare for it by fully living the life I have. Death will come in its own time, beyond my control. On the other hand, freedom is taking responsibility for how we live, guided by our ethics. Isolation is the reality of our existence from birth to death; we are fundamentally alone. All other connections are temporary, no matter how close we think we are to others. Meanwhile, meaninglessness is an absolute void, and any meaning we ascribe to life is simply what we choose to give it. Nothing more.

The more we contemplate this concept, the more we realise that there are no inherent boundaries, rules, expectations, disappointments, successes, failures, or protections. There is nothing, just us alone. Everything we fill our lives with is a combination of beliefs, symbols, and routines that are merely a figment of our imagination, a distraction from the vastness of nothingness. Frightening, isn't it?

We can quickly test this idea. Consider something we do because we believe there is a reason behind it, such as going to work. Why do we work? Is it to earn money, build a career, gain respect, or escape boredom? Or are we enslaved by these concepts without questioning them? And where did these ideas originate? Are they ours, or did we inherit them from our families or society? Let's ask ourselves: Is this career what we genuinely envisioned for ourselves? If the answer is yes, then all is well. But if it's no, why do we continue?

Next, we should ask what we do with our free time. Do we use it to pursue something meaningful, or do we waste it in a repetitive cycle of eating, working, playing, and sleeping? Do we have dreams we neglect for some reason, justifying our inaction? Perhaps we've realised that these lifelong dreams may never be fulfilled, and the opportunity to pursue them has passed.

Ultimately, nothing can tell us what we should do with our lives to create meaning except ourselves. Not even those closest to us can dictate that. They might believe they can, or we might live out their dreams to avoid hurting them, but in the end, we must face the consequences of our choices if we are not putting meaning into our lives.

Another issue is that many of us believe we are just one person, and that needs to be portrayed consistently to everyone; otherwise, we may decide to defend that singular portrayal of ourselves when, in fact, we play numerous roles throughout our lives. We perform these roles so well that we often forget who we are. From the moment we wake up, we begin to assume various roles as we progress through the day—whether it's a work role, a family role, or another functional role, each has its own set of behaviours and expectations. We can make adjustments as necessary, which we already do. Still, most of us don't realise it by preparing ourselves mentally for each of these roles, often interpreting them based on our perceptions and the perceived expectations of ourselves and others.

On certain occasions, we find it beneficial to don various costumes, each selected for specific reasons that enrich our experience. For instance, one might choose to dress as a police officer, a nurse, or a specialist, among other roles, to fully embody them. These uniforms serve not only to enhance the authenticity of the scenario but also to deepen the sense of immersion, allowing us to step into the character more convincingly. Doing so will enable us to explore different perspectives and engage more profoundly with our roles. The act of dressing up adds a tangible element to the experience, bridging the gap between imagination and reality and enabling us to inhabit our chosen personas with greater ease and confidence. Stepping into the roles of others is something we do as children.

The Fluidity of Self

The self is not a fixed entity but a remarkably fluid concept, continuously adapting and evolving in response to our situations. This fluidity becomes particularly apparent when we reflect on moments of transition, such as starting a new job or meeting someone for the first time. Initially, we often present a carefully considered version of ourselves that aligns with social expectations or the perceived demands of the moment. We may be on our best behaviour, striving to make a positive impression and to navigate potential pitfalls.

As time passes and we become more comfortable in our new environment, our behaviour naturally adapts. We become more attuned to the dynamics around us, allowing us to navigate the situation more quickly. This adaptation process may lead us to integrate smoothly into the new setting or make us realise it isn't the right fit. The initial veneer of formality gradually gives way to a more authentic expression of who we are, revealing our true character as we find our place within the new context.

Moreover, the fluidity of self is not just a reaction to our environment; it also reflects our interactions with others. When we encounter someone who makes us feel uncomfortable or uneasy, we instinctively adjust our boundaries and how we communicate with them. This might involve altering our tone, choosing words more carefully, or modifying our body language to safeguard our sense of self. These adjustments are often subtle, yet they reflect the flexibility of our identity and our inherent ability to adapt in response to various social cues and emotional climates.

Essentially, the fluidity of self is a dynamic process of continuous adaptation, where we shape and reshape our identity in response to internal and external influences. Through this fluidity, we navigate the complexities of social interactions and find our place within the ever-changing landscape of human relationships.

Given that we constantly adapt and shed different roles, it leads us to a fundamental question: Who is the real 'me'? Is there a core self beneath the myriad personas we display, or are we merely the sum of these roles, endlessly shaped by the beliefs and attitudes we've accumulated over time? The notion of an 'authentic self' becomes elusive when we consider how fluid our identities appear. Have we ever discovered who we are at our essence, or are we perpetually engaged in a performance dictated by the expectations of others and the narratives we've internalised?

If we were to change our beliefs, would that, in turn, alter who we are? Or is there an unchanging core, a true self that remains fixed, waiting to be recognised amidst the layers of roles and façades we construct? This line of questioning delves into the very nature of identity—whether it is something intrinsic and immutable or a malleable construct shaped by the forces of experience, culture, and personal growth.

Now that I've confronted my past and liberated myself from its imposed constraints, one might wonder if I am any closer to discovering the 'real' me. Have I peeled away the layers of deception to reveal my authentic self, or is this newfound sense of freedom simply another belief, another role I have adopted? Could it be that in our quest for authenticity, we are merely replacing one set of illusions with another, never quite reaching the essence of who we are? Does this mean I have to choose the most essential illusion to me?

These questions challenge us to consider that our true self might not be something to discover but something we continuously create. Perhaps identity is less about uncovering a fixed core and more about embracing the fluidity of our experiences, recognising that we are both the actors and the directors of our lives. In this light, the search for the 'real me' becomes not a destination but an ongoing journey—one where each step brings us closer to understanding yet also reveals how much further there is to go.

The Search for the Natural Self

If our perceived roles do not define us, what is our natural self once we strip away these inherited behaviours and conditioned responses? Who are we at our core, beyond our roles and the masks and costumes we wear? This question prompts us to delve deeper and explore the essence of our being that remains when all the layers of societal expectations and personal history have been peeled away.

When we observe people in an open space, moving through life in their various roles, we see them, like us, drifting through multiple phases of their lives towards their inevitable end, which we know as death. In these moments of reflection, it becomes apparent that each person is engaged in their unique journey, trying to make sense of their existence and the path they tread. Despite the differences in our experiences, we share a commonality in the search for meaning and understanding of what to do while we are here, if we haven't taken on the goals of others.

Many may feel alone in grappling with these profound questions of identity and purpose, believing their struggles are unique. Yet, these questions resonate with countless others. We don't realise it because most of those we come across are putting on an act for us so they can hide their honest thoughts. The search for the natural self is a shared human experience, a universal quest to understand who we are, considering beyond the roles and expectations initially placed upon us.

As we strip away these roles we play, we might be lucky to glimpse the core of our being, that part of us untouched by external influence. But even this core is not easily defined; it may be elusive, shifting, and challenging to grasp. The search for the natural self is not about finding a singular, unchanging identity, but about understanding the fluid and dynamic nature of our existence. It is a journey that compels us to confront the fundamental aspects of our humanity: the inevitability of death, the search for meaning, and the realisation that, while our paths may differ, we are all moving towards the same goal.

The Fear of Meaninglessness

Isn't it deeply unsettling to consider that life might be devoid of inherent meaning? This fear gnaws at the foundation of our existence, perhaps explaining why we so readily judge others by labelling those who seem unmotivated or unfocused as lazy, or who seem to touch our inner fears or insecurities in some way. Yet, could these individuals have grasped the futility of ascribing meaning where none exists and choose to exist within this realisation rather than resist it? The idea that life is inherently meaningless challenges us to confront a void that we often find too overwhelming to accept. To avoid this discomfort, we cling to our illusions, constructing narratives that keep us comfortable within the crowd, safely ensconced in the collective delusion rather than face the terror of existential nothingness.

Accepting Meaninglessness

When we truly accept that life is inherently meaningless, the scope of this realisation can initially be daunting. It forces us to reconsider the fabric of our lives and the perceived meaning attached to our experiences. This acceptance can be terrifying because it strips away the comforting veneer of purpose that we have carefully crafted. The more we think about it, the more we see how deeply this nothingness permeates our existence. However, this understanding also offers a kind of liberation, a realisation that meaning is not inherent in the world but something we create within our minds. This means the world is a blank canvas upon which we project our desires, fears, and values.

Observing Meaninglessness

Consider observing someone on the street, moving through life seemingly without purpose. What remains if we strip away the beliefs, hopes, and dreams that drive their actions? Nothing. This stark reality forces us to confront the truth that there is only emptiness beyond the constructs of our minds. While our basic needs for survival—food, water, security, and shelter—are tangible, everything else is a transient illusion, a temporary construct destined to disappear with our consciousness. This nothingness is the reality that underlies all our human experiences, and recognising it can be both liberating and disorienting.

This realisation of inherent meaninglessness can initially provoke an existential crisis, leading us to question everything we once held dear. But once we move through the initial shock, we can begin to let go of the illusions we have spent our lives building. This detachment allows us to focus on what genuinely matters to us, stripped of the expectations and pressures imposed by others. Life, in this context, becomes much more straightforward, and in this simplicity, we may find a new kind of freedom that is not tied to the pursuit of external validation but rooted in our inner values.

By shedding the distractions of societal expectations and the limiting fantasies we create to navigate life, we can begin to live more freely in accordance with our ethics and values. This process of making our meaning doesn't imply that life will suddenly become devoid of challenges. However, with a clearer perspective, these challenges become more manageable. We are no longer burdened by the need to conform to societal norms but are free to define our path based on what truly resonates with us.

Fictional Society

In many ways, we live in a society that is a carefully constructed fictional system that is designed for the minority and not for us. From a young age, we are conditioned through upbringing and education to fit into predefined roles, each with its own expectations. Many of us strive to modify or enhance these roles, driven by societal norms and rewarded with tokens of success such as certificates, accolades, and recognition. Yet, few of us take the time to question what it would mean to step outside these systemic roles and live authentically, truly. Doing so requires introspection, courage and independence, often lacking in a world where conformity is prized.

For those who manage to break free from societal expectations, the system may respond in one of two ways: with praise or criticism, depending on how their actions impact the system. However, from the perspective of a systemic society, individuals are largely irrelevant. The system requires us to think and behave in specific ways to participate in and sustain it. The more control the system exerts over us, the more we become bound to its mechanisms, often without realising it. Freedom from these roles is not just about escaping societal expectations; it's about reclaiming our autonomy and redefining what it means to live a meaningful life on our terms.

Consider how much of our understanding of the world is shaped by the selective information we receive through the media, which often distracts us from what isn't reported. The media doesn't merely report events; it frames them, usually leaving out vast swathes of what happens worldwide. This selective reporting creates a distorted reality that many of us accept without question. Few take the time to consider what is omitted and how these gaps in our knowledge shape our perceptions. This unquestioning acceptance of mediated reality is another layer of our fiction.

Defining Our Philosophies

What are our philosophies in life? At their core, they are the beliefs, ideals, and principles we hold, articulated into words that shape our thinking and behaviour. We do not adhere to a single overarching philosophy; instead, we embrace several philosophies relevant to respective aspects of our lives. However, many people are unaware of these guiding philosophies, nor do they realise that they are not their own and have been imposed upon them by perceived societal norms, for example. This lack of awareness can lead to a life lived in pursuit of satisfying the desires of others who have successfully sold us their needs to the extent that we adapt our lives to fulfil them.

As I began rethinking my perspective on meaninglessness and the philosophies I've adhered to, I felt a deep sense of unease. It forced me to confront the uncomfortable truth that much of my life had been spent pursuing things that don't exist. But can life be wasted if it has no inherent meaning? Isn't it only wasted if we commit to something that doesn't align with our true selves? Have I done that? Or was this time necessary to discover what genuinely matters to me? These are difficult questions to consider when exploring such thoughts, but they are essential to understanding oneself.

Understanding Life Choices

At the very least, we have chosen to be someone, even if that choice isn't the best reflection of who we indeed are, based on what we think our options are. Our choices place us within a society where we feel we best belong, which concerns our conditioning and upbringing. I don't see this as wasted time in such a deflective society because it has brought me to where I am today, enabling me to change the direction of my life based on my ethics and environment, where I can utilise those strengths to help me.

This shift has led me to a different, more comfortable societal scenario. However, my roots are still in the same place where I was born. In other words, I have revised my understanding of who I am and where I stand to make the most of what I have today. As my thoughts evolve, I find myself increasingly detached from societal expectations and attach myself to my expectations, which I find liberating.

The Fate of Those Unaware

But what about those who never come to this realisation, who remain bound to their inherited and predetermined roles within society until they die? Have they wasted their lives without discovering what was truly important to dedicate themselves to? It's a difficult question to answer. They may have devoted their lives to inherited beliefs, possibly benefiting others or the societal systems, which may have suited them ideally. Or perhaps they haven't benefited anyone, leading some to view their lives as wasted. It could be that they felt safe where they were, had no choice, or that such things don't happen to them, etc. However, I cannot judge, for I do not know their history. What one person sees as a waste of life, another person might view their challenges and responses as a necessary coping mechanism or a defence against past traumas, just so they can get through the inherited system demands they are fighting against, too.

I can only speak for myself. We live as best we can with the resources we have, shaped by our upbringing and experiences. Few people truly know who they are, why they're here, or what life means. Perhaps ignorance is indeed bliss. My current reflections have opened up many possibilities but may also impact me in ways I haven't yet anticipated, and this can be a significant burden for some. Judging someone else's life is ultimately futile; it only reflects our restrictive understanding of our chosen paths.

Self-Commitment

Looking back, although I have made some serious mistakes, I don't think I failed because I was fully committed to self-destruction driven by my inherited beliefs. I excelled at this by giving myself just enough of what I thought I deserved, only to take it away because I didn't believe I was worthy of it. For example, I formed meaningful connections with people who should have remained, only to push them away because I didn't feel deserving. I have even tried to do this with my closest family. This pattern of behaviour was not a failure but a testament to how deeply ingrained my valueless self-beliefs were and how effectively they guided my actions.

I achieved exactly what I was striving for. The hardest part was realising that this person I had become wasn't the real me. I consider myself fortunate to have become aware of this. However, it's possible my life would have been more peaceful if I hadn't realised that my destructive behaviour wasn't fundamental to who I am. Conversely, I think it would have gradually spiralled out of control when I consider the increasing trends and thoughts plaguing my mind before taking this immense step to understand my past. I would have grown more bitter, detached, and intent on hurting others, which may have ultimately pushed me over the edge.

External Reflection

This realisation of who I had become profoundly impacted me, and the reasons behind it answered many questions and concerns while raising new ones I hadn't considered. It gave me a clearer perspective on the vastness of meaninglessness and the emptiness of our external and self-created symbolic world we allow to guide us.

By clinging to these external symbols and beliefs, we allow ourselves to be manipulated and deluded into thinking they offer us something instead of taking the nothingness at face value by being meaningful and responsible in what we believe and do. Don't get me wrong, but symbols can be helpful and powerful if we use them to remember what is within us. All that disturbs us externally comes from within. All that we love externally also comes from within.

I exist within, and within me resides everything: the world we perceive and interact which mirrors what lies inside. Our thoughts, emotions, and deepest fears are reflected in how we see and experience the world around us. The true challenge we face is not external but internal. It is the task of delving into the depths of our minds and confronting the fears and doubts that dwell within us. By looking inward, we begin understanding these fears, unravelling the layers of our subconscious that obscure our vision.

To reflect inwardly is to engage in a profound journey of self-discovery. It requires honesty, courage, and a willingness to confront aspects of ourselves that we might find unsettling or uncomfortable. However, through this process, we can begin to let go of the illusions and delusions that cloud our perception of reality. When we confront and understand what lies within, we liberate ourselves from the distortions we have created.

The world around us then reveals itself more accurately, untainted by the projections of our inner conflicts. We start seeing things as they are, not as we fear them. This clarity of vision allows us to engage with life authentically, free from the weight of our fantastical inner burdens. While the path of inner reflection is undoubtedly challenging, it is essential for anyone seeking to live a life of authenticity and gain a deeper understanding of oneself and the world we inhabit.

Why is it more challenging to accept the inherent meaninglessness of life than to take the disguised meaninglessness presented to us? Is it because we like to attach some non-existent, mind-created value to distract ourselves from the infinite nothingness we inhabit? This attachment to illusion is a way of avoiding the existential terror of confronting the void. And what about those fleeting moments when we glimpse that sense of freedom, a moment so profound it terrifies us to our core? Is this what we genuinely avoid, the possibility that we might find true liberation in embracing nothingness?

Through the fears instilled in me by others, I became a version of myself that wasn't authentic. If our portrayed personalities were real, we would all be the same, wouldn't we? At its core, we are simply a collection of chemically functioning cells capable of walking, thinking, and talking through a series of chemical reactions that we influence and partially control through our five senses. We're simply trying to survive and live the rest of our lives in peace. The identities we adopt are essentially a result of indoctrination and societal, familial, and cultural pressures that shape us into something that may not align with our true nature.

The Freedom of Meaninglessness

These reflections have helped me see how embracing the nothingness and meaninglessness of life can be a liberating experience. Once we accept this, we realise nothing stops us from being who we are. We can get on with life, centred and calm, living in harmony with the Universe according to our ethics and environment. This freedom is not about rejecting life's pleasures or joys but understanding that they do not define us. We can enjoy them without being enslaved by the need for them.

The concept of boundaries is often misunderstood. The only significant boundaries to us are those defined by our ethics, the natural environment, and the immutable laws of the universe. These principles genuinely govern our existence, providing a framework within which life operates. However, beyond these fundamental boundaries lies a complex web of human-made constructs—rules, regulations, and societal norms subject to constant change. While designed to provide order, these constructs frequently end up confounding us, trapping us in a maze of expectations and limitations that may not truly serve our well-being.

To live authentically, we must first recognise that many of the boundaries we accept as immutable are, in fact, artificial. They are products of human imagination, shaped by history, culture, and power dynamics rather than by any intrinsic necessity. Once we become aware of this, we can begin dismantling these imposed limitations. It is a process of questioning and reevaluating the rules we have been taught to follow, understanding which serve our higher purpose and which merely constrain us.

By redefining boundaries in this way, we free ourselves to live in a manner that is more in alignment with our true nature. We start to prioritise those boundaries that matter, the ethical considerations that guide our actions, the respect for the natural world that sustains us, and the adherence to universal principles that maintain harmony in the cosmos. Everything else becomes secondary, a set of guidelines that can be adapted or discarded to reflect better our evolving understanding of what it means to live a meaningful life.

This process of redefining boundaries is not just about breaking free from constraints; it is about consciously choosing the limits that align with our values and the greater good. In doing so, we empower ourselves to live more fully, with a sense of freedom and purpose grounded in reality rather than illusion. It is an invitation to embrace a life that is true to who we are and in harmony with the world around us, guided by enduring and universal principles.

This helped me understand why I felt trapped in a mental cage of my own making. I was still searching for something to give my life meaning, something that wasn't there. I was searching for something in a vast emptiness, surrounded by people drifting meaninglessly, following others without understanding why.

It's easier to convince ourselves that we belong by following the crowd than to take the time to understand ourselves. It's like searching for a non-existent black cat in a darkened room and convincing ourselves we've found it. This search for external meaning often leads to a sense of entrapment as we chase illusions rather than confront the reality of our existence.

The Depths of The Game

What if we've followed our inherited beliefs and been dragged into the depths of The Game, unable to find a way out? What if we think the only option is to wait until our time runs out? Or what if we're in The Game's depths and don't even realise we are being played? Doesn't this force us deeper into a dark hole we don't recognise and thus don't know how to find a way out? Perhaps we're luckier, seeing that The Game isn't so bad, but it still doesn't fulfil us; however, we feel safe, for example. Then what?

Wouldn't it be better to realise what games are going on and play them accordingly by committing myself to an illusion that I can make the most of it? Breaking free from these more complex illusions requires a profound shift in perspective that few are willing or able to undertake, because if we do, it removes the reasons and crutches we use to blame when something goes unplanned. We are still on our own, and our responsibility still lies with us, but this time, we have removed all the distracting symbolism and delusions we have been hiding behind over the past years.

Living Authentically

Does living authentically mean adopting an austere, frugal lifestyle, maximising the benefits of minimalism, or embracing a state of simplicity? I don't think that's the case. Authenticity does not require us to deny ourselves the joys and pleasures life offers, but to enjoy what we have and accept what we don't. If something brings us genuine happiness and aligns with our ethical beliefs, why should we not fully embrace it? There are no universal laws prohibiting us from enjoying life's offerings; indeed, if such restrictions existed, we would be unable to partake in their experiences. Living authentically is about making choices that resonate deeply with our true selves, unencumbered by the expectations, judgments, or opinions of others, and in alignment with our surroundings.

We don't need to emulate figures like Diogenes, who famously chose to live in extreme poverty to demonstrate that material possessions are unnecessary for a fulfilling life. While his approach offers valuable lessons, it is not a template we must follow to live meaningfully, as it was a personal philosophical choice. We all have individual goals and ambitions that carry profound significance for us, even if others may not fully understand or appreciate them. Once we accept this, we realise that the only meaning in our lives is the one we assign to it. No one else can truly walk in our shoes or comprehend our journey as we do, no matter what they say or do.

As Marcus Aurelius suggests, we can enjoy the world's fruits when available yet remain neutral and content when they are not. This philosophy does not advocate for indulgence without restraint but encourages a balanced approach to life. By appreciating what life offers without becoming overly attached to these experiences, we can navigate the highs and lows with equanimity. From my experience, I can attest that this approach makes life much easier to manage, allowing us to cultivate a life rich in experiences and grounded in a deep sense of inner calm and contentment.

The only way to find true happiness is to risk being completely cut open.
Chuck Palahniuk

Happiness

Reflecting on Happiness

I've spent considerable time pondering the concept of happiness, often finding myself deep in thought or engaged in stimulating discussions on the subject. It's a term we all use, yet its meaning can be elusive, shifting depending on our perspectives and experiences. What's particularly intriguing is that 'happiness,' as we understand it today, has evolved significantly from its original connotations.

This evolution in meaning underscores the complexity of the concept of happiness. It's no longer just about fleeting moments of joy or satisfaction but has grown to encompass a more profound and sustained sense of contentment and well-being. As our understanding of happiness has expanded, so has the way we pursue it. We now recognise that true happiness isn't found in the accumulation of wealth or material possessions but in the quality of our relationships, the fulfilment of our values, and the ability to find meaning and purpose in our daily lives.

Embracing Contentment

When things don't go as planned, I find myself more content than before, recognising that I cannot control the things around me. Acceptance becomes key. It is an understanding that even if I struggle to embrace a situation, there is always something valuable to learn about myself. This shift in mindset allows me to approach challenges with a sense of calm and introspection. Mostly.

Does this mean I've become passive? Not at all. If I foresee an issue and can take steps to avoid it, I will. Of course, losing something valuable or someone dear would be devastating. However, I've learnt to process such events, to acknowledge the loss, and then to let go. It's not easy, far from it, but adopting this Stoic approach has significantly eased the impact of life's inevitable problems.

When faced with potential challenges, I now take the time to consider them carefully before taking action. The amount of time I invest in these thoughts correlates with the importance or potential impact of the situation. I've noticed a shift in my approach: today, I spend about 80% of my time understanding the problem and 20% of my time finding a solution. This balance has profoundly changed my relationship with the challenges I face.

Living Life Actively

Living an active, meaningful life, guided by my ethical choices rather than moral obligations, brings me contentment even during moments of stagnation. In the past, the idea of doing nothing drove me to frustration, as I constantly felt the need to plan and think ahead. This led to prolonged procrastination and a reluctance to admit I was doing nothing. I've since realised that allowing myself these moments of inactivity is not a waste but a necessary part of my inner balance.

I've come to understand that all I have is what surrounds me in the present moment. I can't magically create wealth, cars, or ideal houses, but I can appreciate what I do have without fretting over what I lack. Initially, this way of thinking felt foreign to me, but it has significantly impacted my inner tranquillity with practice. Isn't it remarkable how, when we pause to observe without expectation or judgment, we begin to notice and appreciate the abundance already present in our lives?

Frustration is inevitable (I still experience it), but understanding it for what it is enables me to release it more effectively and move forward. Otherwise, it can take control of me. This is easier said than done, especially in the heat of the moment, but I've developed a process that helps me work through these feelings more effectively. It isn't perfect, but it is much better than what I was doing to myself before.

The Concept of Eudaimonia

This reflection naturally leads me to the ancient Greek concept of Eudaimonia, a term often translated as 'happiness' but carrying a much richer and more nuanced meaning. Unlike the fleeting joy or pleasure that 'happiness' might suggest today, eudaimonia encompasses a profound sense of flourishing, a life well-lived in virtue and purpose.

Eudaimonia represents the idea of living fully in the present moment and making choices aligned with my ethical values, all within the constraints of my environment. It's not about chasing after every whim or desire but about finding contentment and fulfilment in the deliberate and thoughtful pursuit of a meaningful life.

Achieving Eudaimonia requires a delicate balance. It involves recognising and accepting the limitations of our circumstances while striving to live in a way that is true to our most profound principles. This balance can be challenging to maintain, especially in a world that often values immediate gratification over long-term fulfilment.

This approach to life encourages a focus on what truly matters: cultivating virtues such as wisdom, courage, justice, and temperance. It's about living with integrity, making choices that reflect our core values, and finding meaning in even the most mundane aspects of daily life. Eudaimonia, therefore, is not just a state of mind but a continuous process of growth and self-improvement.

Moreover, Eudaimonia recognises that our well-being is not isolated from the world around us. It acknowledges the importance of relationships, community, and contributing to the greater good. Living in harmony with our environment and the people within it enhances our happiness and fosters a sense of connection and belonging.

In essence, eudaimonia challenges us to look beyond the superficial trappings of happiness and seek a deeper, more enduring form of fulfilment. It reminds us that true happiness is found not in what we have but in how we live by staying true to our values, embracing the present moment, and striving to become the best versions of ourselves.

The only absolute control we have is over ourselves.
Anonymous

Control

The Illusion of Control

We often like to believe that we can control what happens around us, clinging to the idea that we can dictate the course of events in our lives with enough effort. However, even the most meticulous control enthusiasts eventually realise that actual control is essentially an illusion. At best, we can influence certain aspects of our circumstances, but that's where our power ends. Life, in its essence, is a series of random, unrelated events, each with its trajectory, regardless of our desires or intentions.

No matter how dedicated we are or how frequently we change our minds, the universe carries on with its agenda, indifferent to our plans. The meaning we assign to events is our creation, shaped by what we seek to gain from them, as long as this pursuit doesn't conflict with our ethics or the environment around us. In this sense, control is less about managing external factors and more about navigating our inner world.

From a young age, much of our life's script is written for us and more than we often realise. The roles we are to play in this seemingly meaningless existence are heavily influenced by how we were raised. For example, if we were taught to believe that our lives are guided by fate, karma, or heritage, we internalise these beliefs and allow them to shape our decisions. Our upbringing has laid the foundation for these beliefs, with our parents often playing a significant role in moulding our perceptions.

As children, we absorb and carry these lessons into adulthood, making decisions that often reflect our early education. Only through gradual experience or a solid inner resolve can we chart a different course and take control of our choices, steering our lives in a more authentic direction.

Ultimate Responsibility

Despite our best efforts to delegate responsibility or escape the burden of choice, we can never fully relinquish control over our final decisions. No matter how much we might want to distance ourselves from the consequences of our actions, the ultimate responsibility for that last decisive step always rests with us. This is true whether the outcome is beneficial or detrimental. We are the ones who must live with the results of our choices.

But what about those moments when something fortunate happens, seemingly beyond our control? Is it the work of some invisible spirit or simply a stroke of luck? The answer is relatively mundane: it's just a matter of luck. The real difference lies in how we choose to respond to it. We have control over our reactions, even if we can't control the events themselves. With nearly 8 billion people on this planet, specific patterns in life are rare, but there's just as much chance of something fortuitous happening to us as there is of it happening to someone on the other side of the world.

Cultural Interpretations of Luck

Cultural perspectives also play a significant role in shaping our perception of luck. If a particular event is perceived as lucky within a culture, those who experience it will likely interpret it in a similar manner. Conversely, if the same event is culturally insignificant, it might pass unnoticed, eliciting no reaction. An individual with an eye for opportunity might seem to have more luck, just as someone who anticipates misfortune often finds themselves beset by it. The more we focus on a particular outcome, the more likely we will notice opportunities or pitfalls that align with our expectations.

Another way to exercise control is by focusing on ourselves, particularly our mental and physical well-being, appearance, and the personal messages we convey to others. Observing those around us shows that everyone subconsciously communicates something about their inner thoughts, beliefs, needs, and history.

I've realised that my previous lack of self-belief manifested in how I presented myself. I would dress down, neglect grooming, and consume unhealthy, convenient foods that left me feeling as poorly as they did. My commitment to fitness was sporadic, and my diet, thoughts, and routines changed as often as the British weather—all to meet my low self-expectations.

However, I've committed to a healthier diet and overall lifestyle (though I still don't shave as often as I might!). As a result, I feel healthier, stronger, and, crucially, more accessible. While I still have the occasional lapse, these have become the exception rather than the rule, and I've learned to appreciate and even enjoy these moments for what they are.

There are still many areas of my life where I can improve, as change is rarely instantaneous, and I need to be fully aware of all that still needs altering. Yet, I am conscious of how far I've come to the point where I no longer recognise the person I used to be. I'm grateful for the improved and non-destructive control I now exert over myself.

Being in control also means being honest with oneself, a task far more challenging than many realise. It's easier to manage our self-destructive tendencies, a truth I've only recently fully appreciated. We control our thoughts, words, and actions because they deliver the outcomes we've decided we want or need, whether we deserve them or not.

This brings to mind the hypocrisy often seen in activism. For instance, there was an anti-car demonstration near where I live in Bremen, a cause that, in principle, is a good idea (I'm not anti-car; we don't own one because Bremen is so easy to navigate using public transport). Yet, many demonstrators arrived by car, which increased pollution significantly in those areas that day.

Similarly, I've observed Fridays for Future groups protesting world pollution while drinking complex coffees from plastic or non-recyclable cups, wearing clothes that contribute to environmental degradation, and sometimes even made by unethical labour practices. It's essential to highlight these issues, but it's crucial to lead by example rather than resorting to loud but empty rhetoric. This disconnect is a classic case of 'do as I say, not as I do.'

Facing the Meaninglessness of Control

One could argue that nothing matters because we live in a meaningless world where control is unnecessary, so why not simply do as we please? After all, we know that at some point in the future, the sun will either explode, obliterating us all (assuming it doesn't cook us first), or the rapidly approaching Andromeda galaxy will collide with the Milky Way, disrupting our stability and potentially wiping out any trace of our existence within the blink of a surprised eye. Before either of these cosmic events occurs, Earth may balance itself according to the laws of the universe, as it has done in the past, only to wipe out most of humanity, leaving the following species levels to repopulate it.

Would it be better to ask how long we have before the human species faces extinction? And if we consider this, is it even worth pondering what species might follow us, given that we won't be around to witness or influence it once our extinction is underway? Instead of succumbing to fatalism, wouldn't it be wiser to focus on making the most of our time, ensuring that future generations can do the same before we're inevitably erased in the next phase of the universe?

Questioning Everything

Throughout my life, I've learned the value of questioning as much as possible, and though it felt burdensome in my younger years, I'm grateful for it today, even when it leads me to uncomfortable truths. I am a thinker, and controlling my thoughts helps me maintain some control over my life. It's worth taking control and questioning what we are told or read as much as possible. While science helps us understand our world by reducing errors in specific fields, it remains susceptible to manipulation by those who benefit from the system, often at the expense of those who consume it.

What about our emotions? Are we indeed in control of them? When someone explodes and lashes out with a one-sided opinion, does it mean they are against us? Often, these are controlled emotions (excluding chemical imbalances, for example) used to manipulate or control others. Why do people resort to emotional outbursts to convince us of a one-sided argument? Perhaps they're trying to convince themselves of a belief they're unsure of, or they fear admitting a mistake and letting go of an idea they've invested so much time and effort in.

They may be afraid to acknowledge their hard work was in vain, feeling they've wasted their lives, yet they can't admit this. However, they haven't wasted their lives; they've confirmed their incorrect hypothesis. All they need to do is accept it, let it go, and move forward in a new direction to avoid repeating it. If we do that, there is nothing more we need to do except live and move forward.

It's easy to be wrong today, given the overwhelming amount of conflicting information we are presented with daily. To regain control over our mental and physical lives and find meaning in our existence, we must sift through this information to see what resonates with us. We cannot rely on industries like food and medicine to look out for us; they have financial obligations to their shareholders, and their approach is designed to profit from their control over us. Our health, wealth, and happiness lie in our hands.

Once we realise that we have a choice in everything we think and do within our ethical lives, what others think about us no longer matters because we can't influence it anyway. All we can do is be who we are as we dedicate ourselves to what we believe is right.

If someone thinks I've lost the plot with these thoughts, I ask you to humour me. This way of thinking has helped me reach a new level of freedom, breaking away from the mental constraints I've carried for most of my life. I haven't fully understood or communicated these perspectives as clearly or deeply as I might have liked, but that's part of my learning ahead of me at the time of writing. If I feel comfortable with how I recognise my reality, then that's what matters. Isn't it?

Like everyone else, we must survive these games until the next ones begin. Life goes on. We need to earn money, sleep, and care for ourselves, including enjoying life, because that's how the system was designed. Depending on how well we understand the unwritten rules, some manage effectively, while others require additional support to make fundamental progress. Nevertheless, critics will always exist, regardless of how we play the game.

That's how civilisation has been designed; there are no fixed rules, only ever-changing and conflicting guidelines. Ultimately, it doesn't matter where we are in the game because all perceived winners and losers reach the same target; what matters is how we spend our time until we get there.

I now understand why some people struggle with aspects of the game and seek escapism within or outside it. Looking back, I didn't play the game correctly, which caused me many problems, including some consequences that I still live with today. As I have mentioned, we may not always realise it, but we control our actions, driven by the positive intentions we hope to achieve.

One lesson that took me a long time to learn is that if we have an idea that isn't widely supported or recognised in society, we might lead ourselves to believe we've failed or are wrong. We haven't. We fit into a different societal position for which the game wasn't perfectly designed. At least it's less crowded there, which isn't bad! Yes, I know. What I say might sound fantastical, and perhaps I've crossed the line into insanity. But what if I haven't, and what if this is sanity, while everything in my past life was a hypnotic delusion?

Ultimately, we all have to choose and dedicate ourselves to an illusion, so why not select carefully what gives us the most freedom?

We are the only species capable of creating a fictional system on a speck of dust hurtling through space at an incredible speed in a vast, seemingly meaningless universe. So, what else can we commit to while we wait for our inevitable end? Hedonism, for example? We could indulge in every pleasure until we can't take it anymore. We could dance and participate in orgies until our bodies give out. If that's what we choose to do, and no one suffers or is forced to do something they don't want, that's fine. We could even go to the other end of the spectrum and sit at home, reading a book in peace each day.

We can do whatever we want, like pushing ourselves to the limit as often and intensely as possible. Some of us do just that, but we do it because we think that's what we must do. We can engage in whatever activities we desire, even to the point of excess, because there are no universal rules against them.

Turning to Philosophy

Alternatively, we could turn to philosophy (and psychology) to better understand ourselves and others, mainly how the fictional system affects us differently depending on our roles compared to those outside the system and how we are more in tune with the universe.

Ideas, thoughts, and perceptions can help us view our surroundings differently, understand how we relate to them and appreciate the differences in life for those who aren't caught up in inherited systems. As I've mentioned, I am familiar with the principles of Stoicism, existentialism, and other philosophies because they resonate with me and help clarify my thoughts.

They provide the honesty I need when we are constantly bombarded with other seemingly conflicting philosophies and ideas for the masses. Honesty brings a sense of purpose to my otherwise meaningless life. They allow me to take control of myself, play the game according to my ethics, and make the most of the short time I have left.

And here's where the fun begins.

Suppose life is meaningless, and I choose to make it meaningful to suit my needs rather than conforming to what I was brought up to believe about myself. Should I adopt a mix of Stoic, Sophist, Epicurean, Legalist, Realist, Pantheist, Daoist, Cynic, Aristotelian, Pragmatist, Nietzschean, Objectivist philosophies, and so on for the peace I've found within myself or should I return to the narrow social game that adheres to the endorsed philosophies of today? We all have that choice. It has always been there. The challenge lies in recognising it, making that decision and adhering to it.

If I followed the masses, I would no longer need to think, because the system would provide my thinking, political options, diet, and safety net in case something went wrong. It teaches me how to navigate within the system, including its barriers, what not to cross, what not to say, and how to behave in certain situations. It instructs us to no longer live in a robust community but encourages us to be overly independent, to battle against others, to strive to be better than them, and so on. But what is all this for? Is it better for us if we don't have to decide what to do with life? Is this how we discover our life goals through others, rather than through our own investigation and inner reflection?

Either way, it doesn't matter. If someone doesn't like my viewpoint, they can avoid me and seek out those who share similar thoughts. Phew! And for those who don't want to avoid me, please let me know your disagreement, and we can debate it. I'm open to new opinions because everything has at least two sides. Nobody wants to become a moral sophist.

As I continue on this path of thinking (which I'm sure will evolve), I often ask myself which philosophy is more suitable for my current reflection. What do I want to become in the brief time I have here? How do I want to communicate with myself and others? What meaning do I want to give to my life? When I reach the end, what will it have meant to me, and what purpose will it have served when I can (hopefully) say that I made the most of the nothingness by reconnecting with the universal laws of nature? In other words, how do I want to remain true to myself?

An Experiment

Out of curiosity, I conducted a brief experiment this morning. Just before my wife left for work, I kissed her goodbye, but before doing so, I deliberately told myself that the kiss was meaningless, and I knew it was a peculiar thought to entertain. After all, I love my wife deeply. But isn't our love for another person often a reflection of what we love within ourselves, shaped by our conditioning? Or perhaps it's the natural qualities we recognise within ourselves that we see mirrored in the other person's qualities, we may or may not fully embody. Or could it be something else entirely, I haven't yet considered?

As I kissed her this time, I did so to appreciate her for who she is: her unique understanding of the world, her interpretation of the universe's inherent meaninglessness, and her ability to navigate life's complexities. At that moment, I was struck by a profound realisation.

At that instant, I could only feel an overwhelming love for my wife as a complete entity, her similarities and differences, her outlook on life, her achievements and challenges, her aspirations and dreams. Her countless inner thoughts, ideals, beliefs, and opinions shape her unique perspective on life, making our shared existence richer.

When I kissed her this time, it was infused with such deep meaning that I was surprised by how much it moved me. In that fleeting moment, we were two seemingly insignificant beings striving to create personal meaning in a vast, indifferent universe.

Universal Laws and Systems

Like my wife and I, everyone is trying to make the most of their existence on this seemingly meaningless planet, seeking some sense of what is going on within the intricate system of systems we live in. With or without these systems, our place on Earth is just as uncertain as it is for the same natural laws of survival that bind all living creatures together. Within the framework of these systems, we create temporary and organic rules. Yet, outside the system, nature's laws are immutable and fixed. Although operating within systemic rules, the mind and body are ultimately governed by these natural laws, which we occasionally forget. Everything else is just fiction.

Living within these systems, we are constantly presented with opportunities for creativity and innovation. Everything we create, however, is not inherently a part of the planet but rather a product of our imagination brought into existence by utilising the planet's resources in novel ways. Though powerful, this creativity is temporary, and our creations can be wiped out instantly, leaving no trace of our existence. When the planet is eventually consumed by the sun, collides with another galaxy, or undergoes a natural rebalancing, our history will be reduced to nothing more than space dust waiting for the cycle to repeat itself in some form or another.

Doesn't this stark reality highlight the transient nature of our lives and remind us that everything, including the universe, is temporary?

Given this, have I become a rebel against the system of systems? No, I wouldn't know where to begin even if I wanted to (not that I have any desire to do so). Fortunately, some more qualified individuals are working to restore balance within the system. My current understanding of the world and reality is something I couldn't have acknowledged before, which is a fascinating comparison to how I saw the world just seven years ago. The depth of this change may be more profound than I intended, and I admit that I may have expressed it clumsily, as I'm still grappling with these concepts myself.

This shift in thinking has taken me in an entirely new direction. I once relied heavily on the system of systems we live in, unaware of other options that weren't openly communicated. Now, recognising that this isn't the only way to live, I can choose what I eat and drink, what I think, what I deem essential, and how I spend my time. Within these systems, I decide what to buy, how to invest my most valuable asset, time, and which businesses and creations to support. I can passively accept what the media tells me or seek out my sources and focus on what truly matters to me.

It's remarkable how many people worldwide are starting to think similarly, creating a new kind of inner freedom and independence that's never taught but is discovered through shared and analytical thinking about conflicting ideas.

We all have these choices, though not everyone realises it. I didn't realise it for most of my life. That's not entirely true, however. I knew some aspects, but was too lazy or uncomfortable within the primary system to explore them further. I didn't think certain things affected me back then, but they did, and some still do, meaning I continue to live with the consequences from many years ago.

I know it's impossible to investigate everything within this increasingly complex system, so we must carefully choose our boundaries, selectively bringing into our lives only those things over which we have control and that align with our environment. This doesn't mean I can or should avoid playing the fictional game within these fictional systems. The way I live, I must, and I have no choice if I want to survive. There is no chance of returning to the hunter-gatherer lifestyle. However, I can still play by my own ethical rules and needs, rather than bowing to the demands of anonymous marketing and commercialism. Currency is the number one driving force in this game, and we cannot ignore it. Society is built on the power of currency and commercialism, driven by a few who have become the new gods we mindlessly worship, often without understanding the cost and dedication required for varying levels of devotion.

So, what does it mean to live a meaningful life in a seemingly meaningless world? It can mean anything we want, whatever we actively choose it to be, as long as we remain true to ourselves. We could dedicate ourselves to helping the starving and homeless, educating the underprivileged, tending to our gardens and neighbourhoods, or focusing on our families, cooking, learning musical instruments, reading, writing, and pursuing personal projects.

We might fight against systemic corruption or represent a religious or spiritual group that provides only those who know what they need in a world that can't cope with its emptiness. We might even decide to participate in systemic corruption, but are we being authentic to ourselves, or are we simply playing the rules?

As I mentioned, we could also choose to do nothing, live a hedonistic life, party, and push ourselves to our limits. It doesn't matter. There are no rules, expectations, prizes, or punishments. What matters are the experiences we gather along the way, the only external things (besides our body, which is given) that we can take to the grave. And that's it.

Reflections on the Past

With this profound change in perspective, I've wondered about almost everything I've done in the past. Do those experiences lose their meaning once I have worked through them? Not at all. My childhood was difficult, and I allowed it to shape many of my life choices, which I thought were right at the time. However, I've been fortunate enough to realise I was wrong in many circumstances, swallow my pride and actively change my outlook through these reflections. It's the only way to survive; adapt accordingly. It is better to have a poor plan than no plan at all.

Changing from one life track to another is easier when one is underway than when one hasn't selected one because one gathers experience to determine whether it's appropriate for oneself. It is relatively more straightforward to compare or analyse. When one has no experience waiting for the ideal moment, one has no reference for recognising whether that moment was right. Ultimately, when we don't decide, we may miss other ideal moments we wouldn't have experienced otherwise.

I consider myself fortunate because I've learned more about myself than I initially expected over the last few years. What I'm still learning today continues to evolve my understanding of reality, shifting my perspective slightly with each passing day. There's more to us than many seem to realise. I'm even more fortunate to have discovered that what I thought I was and wanted to be isn't what I truly am or what I truly want to become, and these moments of realisation are worth treasuring. I hold onto my childhood memories, regardless of what happened, because they forced me down the paths that helped shape me into who I am today. I've made decisions and done some foolish things with lasting consequences, and I will carry those with me until the end. I can't change the past, but I can accept it and take responsibility for who I was when I made those choices, just as I do with my daily decisions now. I'm not perfect, and I will never be.

From the start of this part of my journey, I've often said that if I could experience just one day of complete freedom from my past, it would be worth all the tumultuous years it took to get there. Now that I've exceeded those expectations, I see every day as a bonus, an opportunity to continue discovering who I am through my thoughts and actions. For that, I am deeply grateful.

I know that life could still be fraught with disaster, as predicting the future is impossible. At fifty-seven years old, as I write this, I still make mistakes, but whatever happens, I will face them and deal with them to the best of my ability by drawing on everything I've learned over the past seven years. Until I make those mistakes, I will enjoy it as much as possible, fitting my new life goals. Life can't get much better than that, can it?

I must admit that seeing the world the way I do now, compared to how I used to see it, is so radically different that it can sometimes feel overwhelming. My ever-growing existential and philosophical views continue to expand and evolve, adapting to fit my life, experiences, and environment. Although they are still beliefs, they are now the simplest and most practical ones, stripped of symbolism and dogma, making my time here a eudaimonic pleasure that brings me inner peace. I'm repeating myself, I know, but I want to emphasise the profound impact that what I have learnt has had on me.

Why do I consider this way of thinking a collection of beliefs? We all seek the truth, but it remains elusive. What is the truth when each of us perceives and experiences the world uniquely? We don't know. All we can do is reduce the inaccuracy of our perceptions through one skill that other animals lack: the ability to communicate verbally and debate. In other words, everything we think we know is provisional, but that doesn't mean it's correct. This is as close as we can get to the truth, but we can't fully comprehend it because our beliefs continue to filter and distort what we think we should recognise and interpret. All we can do is remain open to new ideas, thoughts, and actions that help us reach what we define as important in our existential lives.

Trust only movement. Life happens at the level of events, not words—trust movement.
Alfred Adler

Adler

Why am I introducing Adler at this stage of the book, after exploring other philosophies and psychologies? I started reading about him afterwards. A significant portion of Adler's work extends the thoughts of existentialism and individualism from a fresh perspective that challenges conventional psychological theories. His approach to psychology, often seen as short-term psychotherapy, emphasises action rather than prolonged discussion—a particularly appealing method.

One key aspect of Adler's work that I want to highlight is his concept of freedom. In existential psychotherapy, freedom is about taking responsibility for everything we think, say, and do throughout our lives, including our fears and anxieties. However, Adler interprets freedom differently. He suggests that freedom involves accepting that some people may dislike or ignore us from the outset for reasons beyond our control. Instead of trying to change this, Adler advocates accepting it.

Personal Reflections on Adler's Theory

This idea resonates deeply with me because it addresses a struggle I still face: the need to be respected and liked by others, sometimes to an excessive degree. While I've learned to accept when someone doesn't want me after meeting me, I still find it challenging during initial encounters. This aspect of Adler's theory is still a work in progress, but I find it easier each time I meet someone new.

Another profound influence on my thinking came from the book *The Courage to Be Disliked* by Ichiro Kishimi, which draws heavily on Adler's theories. The book suggests that life is often more straightforward than we make it and that our past traumas are less significant than our present goals. This notion was a revelation for me, and I now understand that I have approached my issues incorrectly all these years.

For years, I've focused on my past, particularly childhood issues. Adler's perspective challenges this focus by suggesting that our past experiences and what happened to us don't define us; instead, our present goals shape who we are. This idea prompted me to reconsider whether my intense focus on the past was essential. While I understand that my past was crucial, I now realise that my approach needed adjustment, and I gradually realised that Adler was right; those past traumas don't matter as much as I once believed.

Adler's approach also enabled me to reevaluate some fundamental psychological concepts. For instance, I've replaced terms like 'unconscious' and 'ego' with 'lifestyle' and 'gatekeeper,' respectively. These changes, inspired by Adler's work, have simplified my understanding and made it easier to communicate these ideas in the context of this book.

A Full Circle: Returning to the Present

I feel I've come full circle as I delve deeper into Adler's material. I've returned to the point where I began my journey years ago, but this time with a renewed understanding that the past doesn't matter as much as I once thought it did. This resonates with the existential notion that life's absurdity means none truly matters, not even the past.

However, I must defend my earlier approach. Had I encountered Adler's material at the beginning of this journey, by focusing solely on the present, I might not have been able to come to terms with my past as I have because I think it had such a strong hold on me. The intense emotions of anger, guilt, and shame needed to be addressed before I could move forward. I couldn't have let go of those thoughts without first understanding them. From my experience, this is an okay approach if it works. I needed answers to the questions I had been pondering for most of my life. Finding those answers did a lot to release the pain I was suffering. By releasing that pain, I have a clear mind to be who I know I am each day I wake up.

Transforming Relationships: From Enemies to Comrades

Adler's theory encouraged me to reevaluate my approach to relating to people. I used to see everyone as a threat, treating them with immediate distrust. Even those I respected were seen as too good for someone like me. Recently, I've started viewing others neutrally, considering everyone a comrade rather than a friend or enemy. This shift has profoundly impacted my interactions with family, friends, and strangers, for which I am so grateful.

Why do I think of others as comrades rather than friends? The term 'comrade' feels more neutral, allowing me to view people without the intense expectations of friendship. This change has freed me from the need to form deep bonds quickly and has made my interactions with others more genuine and relaxed.

Building Trust: A New Approach

Building trust with others has been another area of growth for me. I used to believe that meaningful conversations were the only way to establish a connection. However, I've learned that small talk, often seen as trivial, is an integral part of building relationships. Adler's suggestion to consider what we can do for others when we meet them has been particularly valuable, as it helps me focus differently on what I will say during small talk. Nevertheless, I still find small talk challenging.

Looking back, I realise my intense need for recognition and acceptance often pushed people away. Today, I'm more comfortable around others and more balanced in my interactions. While old habits die hard, I am aware of them and continually work to improve them, so I control them and not the other way around.

Core and Character

Throughout this journey, I've noticed that while my personality has evolved, my core character has remained the same. My key character has always been there, struggling to overcome the hurdles I faced, which were trying to convince me to portray a different character. Now that those hurdles are gone, it's much easier for me to be my true self.

Adler's theories have provided invaluable tools and insights that have significantly impacted my life. While this book cannot cover everything, nor have I had the chance to read and implement everything Adler has recommended, which is part of my plan, I hope that the ideas shared here offer a glimpse into how Adler's work can help others, as it has helped me. Assessing and working through one's issues is challenging. Still, by being open and honest with ourselves, we can release the outdated strategies that no longer serve us and move forward with clarity and purpose.

The privilege of a lifetime is to become who you truly are.
Carl Jung

Further Work to the End of 2023

Taking a Break and Shifting Focus

In May 2023, I decided to pause my self-assessment journey, stepping back from testing new tools and taking notes. However, I continued reading philosophy and psychology to explore new opinions, perspectives, and ideas that challenged my thinking. During this period, the most significant change I made was altering my diet and fitness routine, which had some of the most impactful effects on my journey of self-discovery and healing.

One of the most profound shifts I made was changing my diet, which became a crucial part of dealing with my past issues. This change didn't just address the lingering narcissism that I still couldn't eliminate through psychology, philosophy or psychedelics; it also resolved several nagging health problems and improved my confidence. Unexpectedly, this process also revealed a binge-eating problem I had been struggling with for years.

Exploring Jung's Archetypes

In addition to dietary changes, I began exploring Carl Jung's Archetypes, a concept that resonated with me. Although I only touched on a small part of his work, it sparked a desire to delve deeper into Jung's theories in the future. My reading list continues to grow, and I hope to explore all these ideas one day.

Interestingly, when reading Adler and Jung, one encounters their psychological insights, but also finds an aspect of philosophy in understanding and relating these ideas to oneself. The process becomes more Socratic, as it involves asking more questions about the material, its impact on me and others, and how other psychological concepts, such as Freud's, pale into some unrelated insignificance.

The first wealth is health.
Ralph Waldo Emerson

Dietary Change: A Radical Shift

Challenging Conventional Wisdom

The next section of this journey addresses a radical shift in my eating habits and mindset towards industrial food-like products and certain types of food groups. As I investigated this topic, I found myself going down another rabbit hole, uncovering information that contradicts almost everything the industry and government advise us about nutrition.

What I discovered about this diet has changed my life in ways that psychedelics, psychology, and philosophy could not. Implementing practices that go against industrial nutritional standard advice brought about significant changes in my life, alleviating ongoing physical and mental issues that had been worsening over the years.

Questioning the High-Carbohydrate Diet

Despite the widespread promotion of a high-carbohydrate diet, I found little non-industry-sponsored research to support its supposed benefits. Given the growing number of illnesses affecting our population, I began to question why these issues persist if a high-carb diet is truly healthy.

Some readers may find this approach radical and choose to skip over this section. However, I encourage readers to keep an open mind and consider my experience further. If this diet could help me with my mental issues, it might also help others.

The information I uncovered while researching this diet was extensive, leading me to delete much of the content I initially planned to include in this book. It took over half of the book; there was so much to use! Yet even that only touched the surface of the information about the complexities our food and health industries have on us. Instead, I've condensed it to primarily my experiences related to this book, with additional references for further reading, allowing those interested to explore these ideas more deeply.

As I often repeat in this book, as we explore these unconventional points, please don't just take my word for it. Question everything, read, test it on yourself, and decide what is best for your health. It's your life; ultimately, you are responsible for what goes into your body, physically and mentally.

You are your psychologist, doctor, and philosopher, and you have the time and incentive to investigate as deeply as possible. Today, we are lucky if we can visit a specialist who has time for us and doesn't prescribe a pharmaceutical solution that hides the symptoms rather than eliminates the cause.

Eliminating the cause remains our responsibility, regardless of whether we receive external assistance. If we consider the meaning of the word 'doctor', the Collins dictionary states that 'if someone doctors something, they change it to deceive people.' That's what a doctor does when providing us with the ability to hide symptoms through treatment. They also treat the symptoms but don't necessarily heal the cause.

The Confusion of Modern Diets

Food and drink are essential for survival, yet they are among the most complex aspects of modern life. They are heavily influenced by industrial pseudoscience, false marketing, and governmental lobbying that attack those who are dependent on the government for clear-cut answers to protect their health. Like many others, I followed government recommendations and various fad diets for years, only to return to a high-carbohydrate diet each time and feel worse for it.

Today, most people follow some variation of the high-carbohydrate Standard American Diet (SAD), which is now prevalent worldwide. Based on agricultural industry recommendations, this diet emphasises cheap, easy-to-grow grains processed into various food-like products.

Comparing sugar to hard drugs, I found that sugar has a more intense effect on the brain and body, often leading to a stronger addiction. The 'sugar crash' that follows consumption is similar to the comedown from hard drugs, leaving us craving more. Why consume something if there is no worthwhile nutrition that leaves us addicted to more than the short-term high it gives us, which leaves us with that craving and potential damage to the body from something we are not designed to consume often and in quantity?

But what other options are there? Focusing on those that affect our bodies and minds optimally are the Diet-like Carnivore, ketogenic, and paleo diets. They all fall into the 'low carbohydrate' category, each with slightly different effects on the body. The critical question is: What do we replace carbohydrates with once we eliminate them as our primary source of energy?

Understanding Macronutrients

Instead of focusing on micro details like vitamins and minerals, which we haven't been able to do for the last several hundred years, I want to keep this approach to exploring macronutrients as simple as possible—protein, fat, and carbohydrates. These three have been central to our diets for thousands of years and are easy to understand and adjust according to our health needs.

Protein is essential for body repair and growth, especially in children. However, eating just protein without fat or carbohydrates can be detrimental, leading to severe issues like headaches, weakness, lethargy, and ultimately death. Fat, conversely, is a nutrient and energy-dense food that sustains us throughout the day. Carbohydrates are only needed when the seasons change due to a lack of food and water sources, as they help us store fat through increased insulin release. For example, consuming fruits once ripe on the plant source can help. Those sugars signal to our body that we are in Autumn and need to prepare for winter survival. Once we have survived this phase, our kidneys can repair themselves from the damaging effects of fructose, and we can resume our everyday activities, such as hunting and gathering in the other seasons.

My Experience

In the past, I had success with the ketogenic diet, getting from around 100kg (220.4lb/15.7St) to a stable 77kg (169.8lb / 12.1St), but I continually struggled with sugar temptations. This time, I approached it with more structure, revisiting research and reading material that helped me stay on track.

After stumbling upon some research, as one does, I realised that I had been struggling with a binge-eating disorder for most of my life. This revelation was crucial in helping me understand my eating habits and make necessary changes.

As I stabilised my eating, I became curious about tweaking my ketogenic diet to help with weight loss. This led me to explore the Carnivore Diet, particularly the steak-and-eggs diet recommended by Vince Gironda.

The Benefits of the Carnivore Diet

Following the Carnivore diet has led to significant physical improvements, resolving several health issues that traditional diets were unable to address. Following this diet has allowed me to achieve health and wellness that I had not experienced before, which has had a profound impact on both my mental and physical health.

Throughout this change in my eating habits, I've realised that mental and physical health are deeply interconnected. Illness markers, whether physical or mental, indicate that we need to take a different approach. Still, we don't know what (it is this helplessness of not knowing what to do, what resources are required and how to go about it is mainly the cause of our perceived mental issues. By paying attention to these markers and making informed choices about our diet, we can take responsibility for our health and well-being by discovering what could be causing them.

While not a universal solution, the Carnivore diet has proven highly effective for many, including myself, depending on the severity of the marker (i.e., illness). It offers a straightforward approach to nutrition that can lead to significant health improvements with minimal knowledge, just like we have had for hundreds of thousands of years. As we continue to lose touch with our ability to interpret our bodies' signals, taking control of what we consume and how we live is more important than ever. We increasingly rely on industries to dictate our health choices, often prioritising their profits over our well-being.

In the two tables shown below, we can see how quickly the Carnivore diet can remove those unhealthy markers with minimal effort. We can also see, for example, that 100% of insulin injectable medicine users no longer need this marker inhibitor to control something previously out of control, possibly due to a high-carbohydrate diet that the industry recommends in the first place. Correlation or causation?

When we consider the second research paper, which was done in just three months instead of six months, like the first one, we can see how quickly our health begins to return to normal if the markers haven't been left unattended too long, especially when we consider it healed or improved 96% of all diseases the participants were suffering from.

When we consider how long some people have been on some form of medication (years) and with no significant improvement, what does this tell us when we cut our intake to the ultimate basics and get their health or most of their health, back within three months?

It's pretty hard to swallow, especially when we consider how much time, money and other resources have been invested in a conventional system when all we needed to do was eat grass-fed beef (or other grass-eating animals with more than one stomach), eggs, bacon, butter (lard, dripping and clarified butter, for example, and clean water to remove all those complex markers the conventional experts have struggled to do (and with medication). Just think of how much time, resources, and pain these people have spared themselves by stripping their consumption of the ultimate basics. Later, I will explain the beneficial effects of the Carnivore diet on my mental and physical health.

Table 1 describes the physical improvements of over 2,000 participants who followed a Carnivore diet for 6 months or more.

Table 2: A summary taken from Kiltz's same page is another study by Revero (https://www.revero.com/), a Carnivore diet coaching service. The overview below presents the results of 12,000 Carnivore participants who followed this diet for only three months.

A Little Further Down the Rabbit Hole and Transitioning to the Carnivore Diet

After discovering that Vince Gironda's dietary approach aligned with the Carnivore, or 'Lion,' diet, I transitioned from the ketogenic diet to the Carnivore diet overnight. The only deviation I maintained was my coffee intake, which technically places me in the Carnivore category rather than strictly following the Lion diet.

Over time, since following this Diet, I've become more relaxed. After some time had elapsed, as I was eating clean, I tested various vegetables individually to observe their effects on my body. This experimentation allowed me to identify which foods work for me and which don't, enabling me to tailor my diet to suit my needs. At fifty-six years old (at the time of doing this experiment), I am now free from aches, pains, neurosis, narcissistic tendencies, doubts, insecurities, tinnitus, dental issues, and a host of other problems that once plagued me. I will delve into these improvements in more detail later.

So, what's the difference between the types of eating I have mentioned? The ketogenic diet emphasises low-carb, high-fat consumption to encourage the body to utilise fat as its primary energy source. The Carnivore diet eliminates plant-based foods, relying solely on animal products for its nutrition. The Lion diet is an even stricter version of the Carnivore diet, typically excluding all non-animal products, including coffee and other plant-based products. Each dietary approach has its benefits and challenges, and the choice ultimately depends on individual goals and responses to different foods.

All great truths begin as blasphemies.
George Bernard Shaw

Exploring Different Diets: From Lion to Carnivore

The Lion Diet: A Strict Approach

The Lion diet, or Lion Diet, is one of the strictest dietary regimens, consisting solely of meat, eggs, salt, and water. That's it. No more, no less. To ensure proper electrolyte balance, it's advisable to supplement with salt, potassium and magnesium, as modern industrial processes often strip these vital nutrients from our food sources. According to experts like Paul Saladino and others, these supplements can be essential for maintaining health on a limited diet.

The Lion diet is known for offering excellent mental and physical health benefits, which I will elaborate on later. It is also considered one of the most effective diets for quickly and effectively eliminating illnesses and harmful markers from the body. Regarding macronutrient composition, protein makes up 20-30% of total consumption, while fat constitutes 70-80% of total intake.

The Carnivore Diet: A Softer Approach

The Carnivore diet, also known as the BBBE (Beef, Bacon, Butter, and Eggs) Diet, is slightly less restrictive than the Lion's Diet. While the focus remains on animal products, it also allows for the inclusion of fish and other meats. However, some meats, like chicken, offer less potential healing power than beef. At this time, my version of the Carnivore diet included coffee. Giving up tea, especially as a Brit, was a tough challenge, but later testing revealed that tea was causing me issues I never even expected.

Why do I continue drinking coffee despite its potential downsides? The addiction is strong, and while I'm aware of the toxins, moulds and mix of chemicals found on and in coffee beans that could affect my health somewhat, I've chosen to address these concerns later once I have stabilised other aspects of my diet.

Regarding macronutrient composition, the Carnivore diet is similar to the Lion Diet, with protein accounting for 20-30% of total consumption and fat making up 70-80%. Carbohydrates remain minimal, never exceeding a few per cent of the total intake, just as in the Lion's diet. Interestingly, the Lion and Carnivore diet completely excludes fibre, which is often considered essential on high-carbohydrate diets but unnecessary in low-carb regimens like these.

The Ketovore Diet: A Balanced Middle Ground

The Ketovore diet offers a middle ground between a Carnivore diet and a more traditional low-carb Diet, like the Ketogenic diet. When following the Ketovore Diet, I include a few vegetables I've tested and found to cause no problems, such as mushrooms and occasionally onions. I also allow myself some cheese, though I have to be mindful of the quantity.

Unfortunately, nuts are off the menu as they cause me severe breathing problems, which has been a long-standing issue for me that even a lung doctor couldn't diagnose. Interestingly, eliminating nuts (wheat also affects my breathing, but in a way that I notice is distinct from when I eat nuts) from my diet resolved this issue, highlighting how individual dietary choices can significantly impact one's health. It's our responsibility to determine what we can and cannot eat, not the government, the food industry, or anyone else, for that matter.

Observations on Weight and Health

During the three months following these dietary changes, my weight remained stable, but I noticed a significant improvement in how my clothes fit. Any initial scepticism about this diet vanished quickly as I observed positive changes, which started within the first 24 hours. As the weeks passed, my health improved dramatically, with long-standing issues like tinnitus disappearing completely.

I consider myself fortunate to have only had minor health issues, which had been worsening over time. However, I'm also aware that I may have more serious underlying conditions that haven't yet manifested or been recognised. Nearly all the other markers of poor health I was experiencing disappeared within the first month, with a few lingering issues resolved shortly after that.

Rethinking Conventional Wisdom

Interestingly, according to many specialists and doctors, my shift to a Carnivore diet should have worsened my health issues, not resolved them. This contradiction led me to question why the conventional wisdom promoting wheat, fruits, vegetables, and processed foods is often considered inherently healthy, especially when these seem to be causing me problems.

If these foods are genuinely beneficial, why do they appear to harm rather than heal? Could it be that our lack of progress in mental and physical health is due to being encouraged to consume substances that might be toxic to us? Are specialists searching for a cure within what might be the very poison causing the problems many of us suffer from? At the very least, it's a lucrative scheme for those at the top of the chain who engage in this practice. If this is the case, which I think it is, it is unfortunately a tragedy for those who trust these specialists and spend their hard-earned money on false hopes and promises. For what?

The food you eat can either be the safest and most powerful form of medicine or the slowest form of poison.
Ann Wigmore

Results After Three Months on the Carnivore Diet

These are the changes I noticed after going on a Carnivore diet:

Physical Health Improvements

Tinnitus: A lifelong issue that disappeared completely after two weeks on the Carnivore diet. My tinnitus indicates whether I'm getting enough salt; if I consume less than 7g daily, the tinnitus returns.

Nail and Hair Growth: After approximately four weeks, I noticed my nails and hair growing faster and healthier. My nails became pinker and less blue, and my hair grew thicker with more colour.

Aches in Joints: Aches and pains were significantly reduced within two weeks and disappeared entirely after three weeks, even after engaging in intense physical activity.

Plaque on Teeth: After nearly two weeks, the plaque on my teeth began to crumble and was completely gone after two months.

Receded and Bleeding Gums: My gums stopped bleeding within a few days and have improved in colour and form. The gums are even growing back around my teeth.

Heel Pain: After two months, I was able to walk barefoot again, with improved balance and reduced sensitivity to pain.

Muscle Tone: Within three weeks, my muscles became more toned and tighter, which improved my performance and sensation during physical activities.

Prostate/Bladder: After about a month, I no longer needed to use the restroom multiple times at night, and my prostate has returned to a size I can't even remember having before.

Digestive Health: Going to the toilet became easier, requiring less time and toilet paper. My bloated stomach disappeared, and I no longer experienced gas or cramps.

Intestinal and Anal Pain: Long-standing intestinal pain disappeared within two weeks, and I no longer suffer from the intense, sporadic anal pain that used to disrupt my sleep.

Kidney Health: A persistent ache in my kidney area vanished after three weeks on the diet, and my urinary problems also resolved.

Heart Rate and Breathing: My heart rate became steadier and stronger, and my breathing improved significantly. I no longer experience the breathing issues that once puzzled my lung doctor.

Left Hand Tremor: A tremor in my left hand that had been worsening for two years stopped after three weeks. The painful sensation in my left arm, which I had experienced for years, also disappeared after five weeks.

Energy Levels: My energy levels increased within three weeks and became my daily standard after two months, allowing me to engage in more physical activities without feeling tired.

Sleep: I now require less sleep, averaging around five hours per night, and I wake up feeling energised and ready to start the day.

Skin Health: Ageing spots have significantly reduced, and my skin looks healthier, more robust, and more elastic.

Flexibility: My physical flexibility improved slightly after three weeks despite not engaging in specific flexibility exercises.

Mental Health Improvements

Thoughts: After about a month on the Carnivore diet, my thoughts became calmer and more focused. Consuming carbohydrates disrupted my thinking and concentration, but abstaining from them restored my mental clarity within three days.

Narcissism: Narcissistic thoughts have disappeared entirely within a couple of weeks and only return if I eat certain vegetables, seeds, carbohydrates, or processed foods.

Confusion: My confusion and forgetfulness, which had been worsening for years, improved dramatically. I can now concentrate on complex tasks for extended periods and remember things in greater detail.

The improvements I've experienced on the Carnivore diet have been nothing short of remarkable, both physically and mentally. This diet has addressed issues that no other diet, medication, or therapy has been able to. While I recognise that these results may not be the same for everyone, they underscore the importance of questioning conventional wisdom and taking control of our health.

The Broader Impact of the Carnivore Diet

Given the rapid mental and physical changes that I've experienced with this diet, I can't help but wonder what impact it could have on others. Are others experiencing the same remarkable health improvements, or am I an isolated case? And what about those with more severe illnesses, like cancer or neurological diseases? Are they noticing other significant changes as well?

This area certainly deserves more research and investigation. As I mentioned earlier, other dietary approaches can be beneficial. However, the Lion and Carnivore diet offer the most promise for reversing or mitigating the potential damage caused by a high-carbohydrate Standard American Diet (SAD).

Take care of your body. It's the only place you have to live.
Jim Rohn

The Bulgarian Clinic: A New Approach to Health

Discovering a Unique Healing Method

This is where things truly start to become fascinating. Bulgaria's clinic specialises in helping people recover from various physical and mental illnesses, primarily through the Carnivore Diet. You can find more information on their webpage: https://www.paleomedicina.com/en.

Initially, I was sceptical about their bold claim that they would support patients through this dietary regimen until their health issues were resolved. However, after experiencing the physical and mental transformations I've undergone in just three months, I now believe they can back up their promises. I initially thought I might be an exception, but this diet could be the rule for those willing to embrace it.

Imagine the possibility of eliminating most or all of those chronic illnesses we have, assuming it's not too late, by shifting our focus from indulging in food to prioritising essential nourishment. While the array of foods on this diet may seem limited, it surely beats sacrificing our health for fleeting moments of pleasure from inferior, chemically laden food products.

The Importance of Professional Guidance

Of course, if you are seriously ill or uncertain about how to proceed, it's crucial to consult with one of the clinic's experts before attending or attempting this at home. Life has no guarantees; even the best dietary options can't prevent every illness. However, taking care of oneself should always be the top priority.

Finding a reliable specialist who understands the low-carb nutritional approach and philosophy is also essential. Although this is nearly impossible, it is becoming gradually easier. Most specialists trained in the Standard American Diet (SAD) are unaware of the conflicting benefits and challenges of these two approaches.

Ultimately, it's not just about living longer while struggling with various mental and physical issues intertwined with our incessant fears and limitations. It's about living a healthy life by caring for our bodies and minds, the portable temples that must be maintained optimally. This approach to health, as demonstrated by the Bulgarian clinic, offers a promising path to achieving that goal.

It isn't easy to get a man to understand something when his salary depends on his not understanding it.
Upton Sinclair

A Diabetic Specialist's Dilemma

The Reality Behind Dietary Advice

While in Germany, I conversed with a diabetes expert doctor in his practice, opening my eyes to a troubling reality. This specialist understood the importance of avoiding carbohydrates and even practised it himself. However, he never advised his clients to follow such a strict regimen. Naturally, I asked him why. His response was both surprising and unsettling: if he advised his clients to avoid bread and other tempting, carbohydrate-rich foods, they would likely seek out another expert who offered a more flexible approach, allowing them to keep their beloved addictions.

He openly explained that losing clients would jeopardise his income and, ultimately, his business. With a family to support, he felt compelled to prioritise their security over the health of his clients. This revelation was alarming—the doctor's advice was influenced more by financial stability than by the best interests of his patients' health.

Is this illegal? No. A doctor has no legal or otherwise obligation to heal us, regardless of their field.

A Broader Issue in the Medical Field

I'm aware that not every doctor behaves this way and that some doctors advocate against the industry's and government's high-carb dietary guidelines in favour of a low-carb approach. While confirming that my nutritional choices benefited my health, this doctor admitted that he didn't always apply this knowledge when paying clients who relied on health insurance.

The more I research this subject, the more disillusioned I become. One of history's most significant industrial scandals is the manipulation of our health for profit. We, the general public, are the losers, while a few industries profit by compromising our well-being. The level of trust we place in those who misuse their positions is astonishing, yet governments worldwide continue to allow this, as they also indirectly benefit from it.

Finding Meaning Amidst Deception

While this dietary deception has shaken me to the core, it has also given me a new purpose: to pursue optimal health and live life to the fullest while I still have the chance. We must ask ourselves whether we're trapped in Plato's allegory of the cave by blindly following shadows that we're told are real. We must understand what makes us ill and seek out what is healthy.

Working through my past and changing my diet has granted me a level of freedom I've had a right to since birth. By disregarding the flawed advice we've been given, my sense of liberty is expanding, allowing me to live life on my terms rather than supporting an industry that doesn't prioritise my well-being.

A Reflection on the Impact of the Standard American Diet (SAD) Diet

My childhood might have been different if we had been adequately informed about what is good for us and what isn't. The chain of mental and physical events that shaped my life could have been less intense, perhaps even less extreme, without the influence of narcissism. Both my father and I may have avoided some of the issues that arose from consuming carbohydrate-rich and processed foods (albeit less so back then), which we are not designed to eat in the way we do.

Even if my father's psychopathic tendencies were unchanged as an adult, perhaps the most painful moments of my life wouldn't have been so intense. I might have functioned better in many situations if the government had provided us with better information about the dangers of these foods.

Okay, if they had done this, then people like me and my father wouldn't be a source of income for other industries, and our country's GDP may be lower because of it, but I would have my life. Conversely, if I had my life over, I might have been more involved in various activities and invested my money in different ventures, potentially further increasing the country's GDP. For our governments and democracy, GDP is prioritised more than our health.

Why? Because if they decide what we eat, it takes our free choice away from what we consume. It isn't the government's responsibility to read our ingredient labels. It's ours. That gives us the freedom to choose what to drink and what not to as 'treats' that could harm our health or essential building blocks for our well-being.

A Question of What Might Have Been

This raises a profound question: had I followed a Carnivore or Ketovore diet from birth, would I have needed so long to work through all those issues? Could I have avoided some of the debilitating problems altogether, such that what did bother me wouldn't have been as intense? How much or how little help would I have needed?

I'll never know the answers to these questions, but the thought lingers, leaving a bitter aftertaste. How many people around the world are struggling with physical and mental issues because they've been consuming added chemicals, food-like processed products, plants and chemically grown produce that their bodies were never designed to handle? It's a sobering realisation if this is the case.

Experiments and Observations

In addition to these reflections, I conducted several experiments to observe how my body reacted to carbohydrate foods, plants, added chemicals, and processed food-like products. The curious results further solidified my understanding of the impact these substances have on our health. Here are a few of those simple experiments...

Every human being is the author of their health or disease.
Buddha

My Food Experiments

When you read this, please consider how doctors or therapists determine our health issues. Are they searching out and treating the root of the illness, or are they addressing the side effects potentially caused by the added chemicals (including medication), food-processed items, or toxins in what we consume orally or through an application? Here are a couple of planned and unplanned experiments I conducted to investigate their potential effects on me.

Experiment One: The Return of Narcissistic Tendencies

After several months on a Carnivore/Ketovore diet and maintaining stable nutritional ketosis, I reintroduced a supposedly safe food: pork scratchings. I've enjoyed pork scratchings throughout my life, often taking the time to make my own. This time, however, I purchased them from a company through Amazon that claimed to use only quality pork skin cooked in pork fat with a dash of pepper, salt, and lemon juice—nothing more.

The product arrived from Italy, and I eagerly dived in. They were delicious, but within an hour, I noticed my head was starting to tingle and create a sensation over my skin, as if goosebumps were forming, with the skin feeling as if it were tightening. Over the next few days, I noticed that my thoughts were becoming increasingly irrational.

Initially, I didn't connect these symptoms to the pork scratchings. However, the situation worsened, which led to arguments with my wife over trivial matters. This was my first narcissistic relapse since adopting the Carnivore diet. When my wife noticed the change in my behaviour, she asked if I was eating anything different. I mentioned the scratchings, and upon closer inspection, we found that the ingredients listed on the package included several chemicals that weren't disclosed on the Amazon website: aroma, E621 (monosodium glutamate), spices, and other unnamed preservatives.

The Chemicals: A Deeper Dive

Monosodium Glutamate (MSG) – E621

I've known for years that MSG causes erratic behaviour and triggers migraine attacks within me, and this was no different. MSG has been linked to various adverse effects on the brain and behaviour. While not life-threatening, these effects can reduce the quality of life. The government acknowledges these side effects as common but acceptable. It is troubling to consider that they allow products that could force us to seek medical treatment for their side effects, especially when neither the patient nor the doctor is aware that this substance has been consumed. For a chemical that can affect people and reduce the quality of life, I believe there should be a sales restriction or, at the very least, a health warning on food-like packages and companies that use it.

Citric Acid – E330

Citric acid, or E330, is another chemical (extracted from mould) that I suspect was in the scratchings. While generally regarded as safe, citric acid can cause stomach aches, diarrhoea, skin irritation, allergies, and other issues. These symptoms may not be life-threatening, but they don't contribute to a high quality of life, which could prompt one to seek medical treatment that would likely involve another combination of chemicals to address the effects of the initial chemical.

When I stopped eating the pork scratchings, my mind cleared, and my narcissistic tendencies disappeared within three days. I experimented by eating the scratchings again a few weeks later to determine whether they were causing the mental issues, and sure enough, the symptoms quickly returned. This confirmed the connection, and I discarded the remaining scratchings, recognising the poor communication in product labelling (Is this allowed in the EU?).

Experiment Two: Reverting to a High-Carbohydrate Diet

In this experiment, I returned to a Standard American Diet (SAD) for a planned seven-day period, reintroducing wheat and sugar as my primary sources of energy while reducing my fat intake. All my food came from standard supermarkets, relying on government-recommended portion sizes and nutritional guidelines to meet my governmental health needs.

Day 1: Immediate Effects

The taste of processed foods was off-putting, and within minutes of consuming them, I felt dizzy, weak, and out of control. My heart pounded, and I felt lethargic. By evening, I was too tired to attend an event I had planned, demonstrating how quickly this diet was negatively affecting me.

Day 2: Returning Symptoms

On the second day, I suffered from stomach aches, bloating, and an intense craving for sweets, which led to overindulgence later in the day. My physical and mental energy plummeted, and I slipped back into old, unproductive habits. My wife's innocent comments irritated me, a red flag indicating a return to unhealthy behavioural patterns.

Day 3: A Painful Conclusion

By the third day, my body was in significant pain; my joints, muscles, and organs all ached. My mind was foggy, and I struggled with concentration. My intestinal issues returned, and the chest pains were so intense by the evening that I feared a heart attack or stroke. This experiment confirmed that returning to a high-carbohydrate diet, combined with the effects of added chemicals and processed foods, had a severe impact on my health.

After the third day, I decided to stop this diet because if I did suffer a stroke or a heart attack, then I would have to live with those life-restricting consequential effects for the rest of my life.

Was the return of my narcissistic tendencies due to the chemicals and high carbohydrate intake? Could these substances be responsible for other mental health issues, such as ADHD, psychopathy, sociopathy, schizophrenia, epilepsy or other severe conditions? If so, could eliminating these chemicals and processed foods reduce or eliminate these symptoms?

Suppose I take this question one step further. Are narcissistic, psychopathic and other personalities created in the mother's womb, where the mother or just the baby (or both) is suffering some form of adverse reaction to the food-like products the mother consumes? Taking this another step further, after birth, the mother continues to feed these foods to the infant, thus continually triggering such behaviour patterns in the child while in their care. If I take this further, could these issues be exacerbated when that child becomes an adult and continues to eat such foods for the rest of their life?

We don't know.

After eliminating those harmful substances from my diet, my irrational behaviour subsided, and my mental clarity improved. This raises questions about the importance of the role of diet in mental health. Are we inadvertently consuming substances that increase the sensitivities of our past triggers, or are they exacerbating mental health conditions? Is this a topic doctors and therapists of all flavours refuse to address? If such foods are causing mental issues, how much, or rather, how little of the behaviour we display is our own, and how much is influenced by the chemicals and processed foods we consume? How different would we become if we eliminated all those chemically processed food-like products from our diets?

Beyond chemicals, certain plant toxins, such as oxalates, histamine, silicates, and lectins, can also contribute to our health problems. While doctors often assure us that we don't consume enough of these toxins to cause harm, growing research suggests otherwise. Polyphenols, frequently touted as beneficial, may also have harmful effects by killing healthy cells alongside cancerous ones. Why would we want to destroy healthy cells with the hope that they get the cancerous ones along the way? But what if we have no cancerous cells? Are we putting our health at immediate risk? Are the polyphenols killing healthy cells because they have to kill something, and what effect does that have on us?

Taking Responsibility for Our Health

We must take responsibility for our health. The medical field excels in emergencies, but it falls short in addressing the everyday mental and physical health issues caused by our diet for the common person. The current nutritional landscape is confusing, with conflicting advice and a food pyramid designed more for profit than health, which appears to be driven more by industry than by independent research backed by governments.

Although conventional medicine perceives the carnivore diet as controversial, it has significantly improved my mental and physical health. I no longer suffer from the health issues I experienced on a high-carbohydrate diet. Living an active and healthy life may require spending more on high-quality food and saving significantly on non-quality food and food-like products. That investment is a small price compared to the medical treatments I would have to invest in for avoidable conditions today and the accumulated ones when I am older.

Ultimately, it's our responsibility to make informed choices about what we consume because if we don't, others will make those decisions for us, often to our detriment.

The choice is ours.

We can't solve problems using the same thinking we used when we created them.
Albert Einstein

The Environmental Impact of Eating Meat

A common concern is whether consuming large amounts of cattle rearing harms the planet and contributes to atmospheric damage; however, the answer isn't as straightforward as we might think. While every action we take has consequences, including our industrial and agricultural practices, the impact of meat consumption may not be as damaging as we've been led to believe. Before we touch the cows, let's sort out the horses and get the count down to less than the cows first, not that either will make much difference. Not only that, but also stop feeding them wheat and soy; they are not designed for cattle consumption in the quantities they are typically fed. This makes them ill and fart a lot.

According to data from a US government source, the environmental impact of agriculture, industry, and lifestyle choices is complex and multifaceted. Surprisingly, the reality of how these factors impact the planet often differs from what the industry or mainstream narratives suggest. The actual environmental consequences of our actions, including meat consumption, may vary significantly from the commonly accepted views.

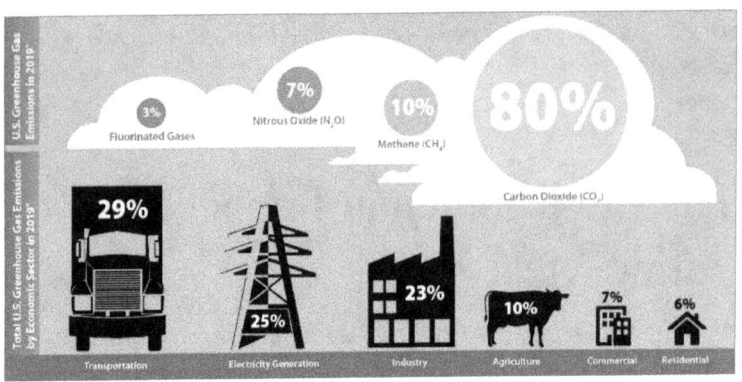

Table 3: Derived from the ERG, showing the sources responsible for overall greenhouse gas emissions in 2019. https://www.erg.com/project/improving-us-greenhouse-gas-emissions-inventory

At first glance, it's evident that agriculture accounts for about 10% of the overall environmental impact. This figure includes animal and crop farming, which is only slightly higher than the impact of our homes. However, the major contributors to greenhouse gas emissions are transportation, electricity generation, and industry (including factory farming practices, where animals are kept in large sheds rather than on pastures), which collectively account for 76% of all emissions. The real issue lies not with agriculture, particularly when livestock are raised on green pastures where they can forage and follow their natural diet.

Our growing reliance on electric vehicles and computerised devices creates a more significant environmental challenge than cattle do. Perhaps opting for traditional, manual modes of transportation, like bikes or scooters that don't require batteries, would benefit the environment and our physical health more than eliminating a food source that can potentially address our mental and physical health issues.

Regarding the added chemicals, I react poorly to MSG, but what about those who have never heard of it or are unaware of its side effects? How can these people improve their health if they don't know what to look for? Ideally, our doctors should be our first line of defence, helping us navigate these issues rather than just prescribing pills to mask symptoms for quick fixes. However, how reliable can these doctors be if they've only been trained in one type of diet, which they are licensed and funded to promote?

Additionally, the average consultancy time is now shorter (around 7 minutes) because the GP has an increased overload that takes valuable time away from each patient; thus, quantity is becoming more important than quality for the doctor.

The internet is flooded with conflicting and confusing advice, and even the books on nutrition are inconsistent, which is disheartening given that other sciences strive for consistency. The media, too, often promotes false information funded by private sponsors, which can also harm our physical and mental well-being.

On the bright side, the widespread availability of media and open communication platforms also enables us to learn from others, which helps us adopt different approaches and achieve positive health outcomes more quickly and cost-effectively. This isn't advice; it's my observation based on my own experiences and those I've read about in the experiences of others. However, I cannot justify their statements and take risks; should I consider something someone else has done? For you, that's your responsibility—no one else's.

Nowadays, we can easily switch between different diets to see how they affect us, compare various theories, and seek out non-industry-sponsored research papers or books by independent specialists to find what works best for us. This process can be slow and frustrating, especially if we don't get it right the first time. A situation that seems to benefit the industry the most is when we have found a doctor who is concerned about their health and has done their homework as well.

We are what we eat.
Ludwig Feuerbach

A Quick Response to Side Effects

Before moving on, I have one final thought. Why did I notice the side effects so quickly after reintroducing certain foods I had previously avoided? Is it because I'm older and more sensitive to cellular inflammation? Does this rapid response also occur in babies who are weaned off breast milk and introduced to fruits and vegetables instead of animal fats and meat? Do they experience the same discomfort when consuming SAD foods as a baby as I did as an adult?

The difference, of course, is that babies can't articulate their discomfort like we can. They can only cry, which we often dismiss as a regular part of infancy. How many parents struggle to get their children to eat vegetables? But how does a baby respond when offered plain, unprocessed meat? They pick it up and suck on it without issue to feed the bacteria in their stomach, which in turn feeds their body. This applies to adults as well.

Another growing concern is the sheer number of unknown added chemicals and artificially produced food-like products to which we are exposed. What I mean here is that if we examine the ingredients, we can't see what chemical concoctions have been used to grow or raise the food, nor do we know what processes have been followed to denature them. As a result, we can't test for the potential side effects. Because of this, it's becoming increasingly difficult to distinguish between the health issues caused by these added substances and those that are simply a part of life and might otherwise be healed naturally with clean foods.

I've often said that life is a game to be played and enjoyed, and I'm learning to do so better each day. But when we participate in the industrial games others set up for their benefit, are we sacrificing our health by becoming bound to their system? Are the choices we make, influenced by these industrial products, leading to a decline in our mental and physical health without us even realising it, or worse, are we just accepting it for reasons we don't fully understand?

Why the Carnivore Diet?

I want to explain why I chose the Carnivore diet over a low-carb, ketogenic or other diet.

The simple answer might seem to be that industrial research suggests eating meat with vegetables can lead to poor health. However, no conclusive research shows that eating unprocessed grass-fed meat alone poses a health risk. It's the opposite. Please let me know if you have found something conclusive to the contrary, and I will rewrite this section accordingly.

Interestingly, the trends suggest that eating grass-fed beef may be one of the healthiest choices when we examine non-industry-sponsored research. While I won't list the specific illnesses that red meat could potentially help heal (as it may sound extreme or unbelievable), I encourage you to explore the results from the Hungarian clinic I mentioned earlier and those of others who have adopted this lifestyle change.

I recommend reading Paul Saladino's book, *The Carnivore Code*, for more detailed information and links to research. Other excellent books are out there, but I haven't read them yet. Moreover, adopting this diet yields the results he mentions. Nothing is contradictory in what he says. It delves deeply into these topics, including the critical role of LDL cholesterol in our health. Contrary to what many doctors suggest, LDL is not directly responsible for forming arterial plaque. We've known this for a long time, but I suppose this has been kept quiet for industrial and financial reasons. Saladino's work highlights the benefits of LDL when carbohydrates are eliminated from the diet, making it a powerful asset to our health.

Because of this Diet, my narcissistic tendencies have wholly disappeared—unless, of course, I reintroduce low-quality factory-farmed meats, eggs, dairy, certain vegetables, fruits, added chemicals, or processed food-like carbohydrate products into my diet. It took some time to realise that eating carbs for health is purely business propaganda. Re-educating myself on the advice to stick strictly to red meat was crucial in helping me achieve the health foundation I need to continue growing stronger and healthier.

The Carnivore Community: A Growing Movement

A rapidly growing international community has been following the Carnivore diet for several years, and their remarkable stories of progress are well worth reading or listening to. Like me, they enjoy excellent health, outstanding blood results, fewer mental issues, and a free life with fewer restrictions. While I can't personally verify every claim made by others in this community, I can compare their similar health transformations with my own experiences.

I consistently say, 'Don't just take my word for it.' Assume that I'm wrong and verify everything for yourself. I'm not here to recommend anything; these notes and other writings document my personal experiences. What worked for me may not necessarily work for someone else.

Nature does nothing in vain.
Aristotle

Famine Foods or Medicine?

First, let's focus on vegetables, often referred to as 'famine foods,' as discussed in Paul Saladino's book. Historically, we turned to these foods when meat sources were scarce because meat and fat remain the most nutrient-dense foods. But what could be so harmful about plants, especially when industry constantly tells them they are healthy? Unlike animals that can flee from predators, plants have developed toxins as a defence mechanism to deter being eaten. Animals that can safely consume these plants often have different digestive systems, such as ruminants and camels, which possess multiple stomachs that humans do not have.

If plants produce toxins to protect themselves, what should we be particularly cautious about? Here, I will focus on four: oxalates, histamine, lectin, and salicylate.

Oxalates

When I first learned about oxalates, I was shocked. For example, if you search online for pineapple oxalates, you'll see that they resemble a collection of sharp, long needles. This explains why eating pineapple can sometimes cause a slimy sensation in the mouth; it's the effect of oxalates dissolving in our skin. These needle-like crystals can become lodged in various parts of our body, including the brain and the kidneys. If consumed in excess, they can cause painful conditions like kidney stones, migraines or other mental issues like Autism, for example.

Research suggests that autistic children tend to have higher levels of oxalates in their brains than non-autistic individuals. While more research is needed, reducing oxalate intake might help alleviate some or all symptoms of autism. Our bodies can handle a small amount of oxalates we produce as waste products. Still, the high intake recommended through plant-heavy diets may exceed what our bodies can handle, thus causing us issues our doctors tend not to consider.

Excess oxalates have been linked to numerous health issues, including gum inflammation, inflammatory bowel disease, leaky gut, skin rashes, joint pain, arthritis, fibromyalgia, and even autism spectrum disorders, for example. The extensive list suggests that too many oxalates in our diet could be causing more harm than we realise.

Histamine

Histamine intolerance can also pose health challenges. While histamine plays a vital role in our immune system, helping us combat allergens, an excess can lead to various issues, including low or high blood pressure, Parkinson's disease, migraines, eczema, asthma, anxiety, and irregular sleep patterns, which can significantly impact our quality of life.

Lectin

Lectins are anti-nutrient proteins that can interfere with our bodies' absorption of nutrients. They bind to the nutrients in our food, preventing their proper absorption, which can lead to a range of nutritional deficiencies, for example. High levels of lectins can cause digestive issues, such as nausea, vomiting, diarrhoea, and a leaky gut. Soaking, fermenting, and cooking foods can reduce lectin content, but excessive consumption can be problematic.

Salicylates

Salicylates are natural plant chemicals that defend against bacteria, fungi, and insects. Overconsumption of salicylates can lead to gastrointestinal issues, skin problems, respiratory difficulties, and behavioural changes. While these issues may not be immediately life-threatening, they can drastically reduce the quality of life, often necessitating medication to manage symptoms.

The Broader Implications

None of the above toxins are typically life-threatening, but they can cause enough discomfort and health problems to require medical intervention that can prevent us from living more freely. These toxins are found in various vegetables, such as nightshades (tomatoes, potatoes, and eggplant) and root vegetables.

While I haven't delved into starches here, it's worth noting that they can also cause issues such as blood sugar spikes, which increase the risk of insulin resistance and weight gain.

After considering the potential harms of these so-called 'survival foods,' it's impressive to see the dedication of vegetarians and vegans who choose this path, often at the expense of their own mental and physical health, to save the lives of farm animals. Their commitment is admirable, but it's not a sacrifice I'm willing to make, especially with the information available today.

While I agree that industrial farming practices need significant improvement for the health and welfare of both animals and humans, we can make more informed choices about where and what we buy, aligning our purchases with our budgets and ethical standards.

The government could implement changes to address these issues, which seems unlikely due to the potential industrial financial losses for specific sectors. Until transparency improves, I'm unwilling to risk my mental and physical health again by following advice that has led to the cognitive problems I suffered in the past. Life was becoming unbearable under such governmental and industrial guidelines. Now that I understand how plants and processed foods can impact my health, I'm committed to finding a balance that aligns with my values and overall well-being.

I know I've only scratched the surface of the low-carb/high-fat diet, and there's much more to explore beyond the scope of this discussion. I've included additional reading materials that I've found valuable for understanding the potential harms of certain foods, products, and strategies. Rather than repeating what experts have already articulated well, I encourage you to seek out their work and continue your journey of discovery. And please remember, when reading scientific reports, even peer-reviewed ones, check first that they are not industry-sponsored.

But what are the benefits of occasionally eating vegetables and fruits that could harm us with overconsumption?

Fruits and Vegetables as Medicine: Occasional Consumption for Health Benefits

While the regular consumption of certain fruits and vegetables may come with risks, they can also offer significant medicinal benefits when used in moderation. Many of these foods have been used in traditional medicine to treat specific ailments or support overall health for thousands of years, and we can continue to do so if we wish. Let's explore some examples, including mushrooms, onions, coffee, garlic, ginger, and herbs.

Mushrooms

Certain mushrooms, such as shiitake, reishi, and maitake, are renowned for their immune-boosting properties. They contain beta-glucans, which help enhance the immune system's response to infections. Occasionally, incorporating these mushrooms into your diet can also support heart health by lowering elevated cholesterol levels and improving circulation. Reishi mushrooms, in particular, have been utilised in traditional medicine for their calming effects, which help reduce stress and enhance sleep quality.

Onions

Onions are packed with quercetin, a powerful antioxidant with anti-inflammatory and antihistamine properties. When used occasionally, onions can help alleviate the symptoms of allergies and respiratory issues, such as asthma. They also support cardiovascular health by improving blood circulation and reducing the risk of clot formation. Including onions occasionally can also help eliminate toxins from our bodies.

Coffee

Due to its high antioxidant content, coffee can offer several health benefits when consumed in moderation (not every day). It has been shown to improve cognitive function, boost metabolism, and enhance physical performance. Additionally, the occasional cup of coffee can aid digestion by stimulating bile production and promoting intestinal motility.

Garlic

Garlic is well-known for its medicinal properties, particularly its ability to support cardiovascular health. It can help lower blood pressure and reduce cholesterol levels when consumed occasionally. Garlic also has natural antibacterial and antiviral properties, making it a valuable food during cold and flu season. It's also beneficial for improving circulation and supporting the immune system.

Ginger

Ginger, a versatile medicinal food, is particularly effective due to its anti-inflammatory and antioxidant properties. It's not just for nausea but can also help relieve pain associated with arthritis and muscle soreness. It's not just for digestion; it can also support heart health by lowering blood sugar levels and improving cholesterol profiles.

Herbs

Various herbs, including rosemary, thyme, and basil, have been utilised for their medicinal properties for centuries. Rosemary, for instance, is recognised for its benefits to memory and cognitive function. Thyme has strong antimicrobial properties, making it helpful in treating respiratory infections and boosting the immune system. Basil is rich in anti-inflammatory compounds, which can help reduce the risk of chronic diseases when consumed occasionally. Although taken in tiny amounts, these herbs can be easily incorporated into your diet, inspiring you to try new flavours while providing health benefits.

While the regular consumption of certain foods may carry risks due to their natural toxins and effects on the body, using them occasionally as a medicinal aid can provide specific health benefits.

Let food be thy medicine and medicine be thy food.
Hippocrates

Further Questions

My observations, along with the simple yet practical and informative research I've read, have raised some intriguing questions. For instance, if I could eliminate my remaining narcissistic tendencies through dietary changes, how many others might achieve the same result by following a similar approach? And if we take this thought beyond narcissism, what about other mental health conditions like psychopathy (anti-social personality disorder as it is known today), OCD, or PTSD, for example? Could the Carnivore's diet at least dampen their effects? Additionally, could this diet potentially benefit those suffering from ADD (and its other variant flavours), autism, autoimmune diseases, Parkinson's, epilepsy, neurosis, schizophrenia, hallucinations, and other neurological conditions?

The Impact of Processed Chemicals on Our Health

If you're interested in exploring the potential impact of processed chemicals in our foods and food-like products, consider researching other substances like E-numbers, phthalates, bisphenols (BPA), perchlorate, artificial food colourings, high fructose corn syrup, artificial sweeteners, soy, sodium benzoate, hydrogenated oils (trans-fats), table salt, fluoride, and seed oils (sunflower, cotton, rapeseed, etc.). If this interests you, it's also worth considering the chemicals and plants used in crop production, animal feed, and fish farming, as well as their potential effects on human health.

When did we begin shifting away from meat and fat as primary food sources in favour of easy-to-gather carbohydrates for emergencies? In addition to the farming revolutions, the key modern turning point appears to be the publication of Ancel Keys's Seven Countries Study, which selectively presented data suggesting that high-carbohydrate diets were beneficial.

Still, it has brought us a mass of illnesses and problems the medical industry does not want to acknowledge. I won't delve into the details of his misleading research here, as there is already plenty of information available online and in research papers that discuss the flaws and essential omissions in the data he gathered in his work.

Another significant moment came when Earl 'Rusty' Butz, the USDA Secretary under President Nixon, decided to transform farming from a quality-driven endeavour into a profit-focused industry, prioritising soy and wheat over other crops. This shift led to declining food quality and the reduced range of proper food choices we experience today.

One often-overlooked figure in the fight to protect our health is Dr. Harvey Wiley, whose work led to the banning of specific harmful processes and chemicals in the food industry. His efforts saved countless lives by ensuring that dangerous foods were no longer sold to the public. If you want to learn more about his work, I recommend watching *The Poison Squad*, a documentary initially aired on PBS and now available online.

I haven't covered every aspect of diet and health in this discussion, but one thing seems clear: like all animals, humans have a fine line that defines good health based on what we consume. The more we complicate our diet with various foodstuffs, the harder it becomes to maintain optimal health. Our bodies are designed to provide us with markers or signals that indicate what to eat and avoid to live a healthy life.

Ignoring such markers can lead to chronic health problems and, in some cases, even death. We can take responsibility for our health or let others do it for us, but we have no guarantee that they have our best interests at heart. Given the confusion surrounding what is healthy and what isn't, we must take responsibility for our well-being, as others may be motivated by profit rather than our health.

Since we haven't been widely educated to recognise potential health markers recently, how do we know what to look for? How can we make it easier to prioritise our health over the financial interests of industries? I approach health with the assumption that our healthcare system is deeply flawed, with doctors often having too little time to fully understand our issues. They can't help us effectively if we can't tell them exactly what we've consumed, especially when we aren't fully informed about what we're eating. While certain medications can be life-saving in extreme cases, they shouldn't be seen as a cure-all. They are a last resort, not a first port of call.

Every minute spent in a waiting room or hospital bed lessens our freedom to live as we choose. That's why I believe it's my responsibility to understand the markers that could indicate a problem, whether related to diet, stress, or other factors, so that I can take steps to manage my regular issues and help doctors help me when necessary.

Macros

Our foods can often be categorised into three fundamental groups: carbohydrates, protein, and fat. These macronutrients are essential for sustaining life and play distinct and interconnected roles in our diet and overall health. By understanding their contributions, we can make more informed choices to support a balanced lifestyle.

Carbohydrates are conventionally considered the primary energy source for the body, often consumed in large quantities due to their widespread availability and promotion within modern food industries. While they provide a quick and efficient energy supply, it is crucial to recognise that carbohydrates are not an essential nutrient; the body can function perfectly well without them. Instead, our bodies can derive energy from fats and proteins, making excessive carbohydrate consumption unnecessary and potentially harmful.

Protein is crucial for the growth, repair, and maintenance of our body's tissues. It is the building block of muscles, organs, enzymes, and even our immune system. Ensuring adequate protein intake from high-quality sources, such as lean meats, eggs, and fish, is essential for long-term health. Protein becomes even more crucial for individuals with specific health goals, such as building muscle or recovering from illness. Balancing protein with other macronutrients ensures that its benefits are fully realised.

Fat, often misunderstood and unfairly vilified, is an essential macronutrient that provides long-lasting energy and supports various bodily functions. It plays a vital role in brain health, hormonal balance, and the absorption of fat-soluble vitamins (A, D, E, and K). However, the quality of fat in our diet is of great importance. Healthy fats, such as those found in butter, tallow, lard and oily fish, can protect against heart disease and aid in regulating metabolism. Conversely, trans fats, commonly found in processed and fried foods, can increase the risk of chronic health problems.

Recommended Reading and Resources

This part of my journey began with the ketogenic Diet before transitioning to the Carnivore Diet. According to Dr. Mark Hyman in the film *Fat Fiction*, the ketogenic diet can heal damage caused by a high-carb, Standard American Diet (SAD).

Other dietary approaches are worth exploring. For instance, the chapter on *Blue Zones in The Longevity Solution* by Dr. James DiNicolantonio is an excellent resource. It highlights how the healthiest people in these zones didn't consume processed, factory-farmed foods or added chemicals.

I also recommend two other books: *Trick or Treat* by Barry Groves, one of the first books I read on the subject, which discusses the dangers of carbohydrates and how hospitals use patients to generate profits, and *The Diet Delusion* by Gary Taubes, a great introduction to understanding the food and health industry.

For those interested in documentaries, *Fat Fiction* and *FAT: A Documentary 1 & 2* are eye-opening films that challenge the high-carb diet and explore the benefits of low-carb eating.

They are beneficial for endurance athletes, such as marathon runners, who use ketogenic or Carnivore diets to avoid 'hitting the wall' during long-distance events. Phinney and Volek cover these diets in *The Art and Science of Low-Carbohydrate Living* and *The Art and Science of Low-Carbohydrate Performance*.

I highly recommend *The Carnivore Code* by Dr. Paul Saladino for a comprehensive understanding of the Carnivore diet and the potential harm caused by vegetable toxins. The book includes numerous research papers for those who wish to delve deeper into the subject. Even though Saladino later added wild, non-commercially grown fruit and berries to his diet, the book remains a respected resource within the Carnivore community. I continue to follow this diet, occasionally shifting from the Lion (no coffee, either!) to Ketovore when I need to reset or add variety to my Diet.

Regarding oxalates, Sally K. Norton's book, *Toxic Superfoods,* is an excellent guide to understanding the damage these substances can cause and how to avoid them. Norton is a leading expert in this field.

Investigating the impact of commercial foods, added chemicals, and food-like products on our mental and physical health can be a revelation. It opens up new avenues of understanding how we are often misled by industries primarily focused on generating profits.

This book primarily explores the factors that have contributed to my improved mental and physical well-being. However, these subjects are covered in much greater depth elsewhere in other reading sources than I can cover here.

Two essential research papers, later published as books, remain as relevant today as they were when first released. They reinforce the importance of high-fat eating through a ketogenic, Carnivore, or Lion diet. The parallels between the illnesses discussed in these works and the health issues we face today are striking. The difference is that today, we consume more carbohydrates, toxins, added chemicals, and manufactured food-like products than ever before, and our mental and physical health has never been worse.

Nutrition and Physical Degeneration

One of the most influential books in understanding the link between diet and health is Nutrition and Physical Degeneration by Dr. Weston A. Price. He travelled to numerous indigenous tribes worldwide long before many of these communities were exposed to Western dietary practices. These tribes, which had existed for thousands of years, maintained their traditional diets, often rich in meat, milk, blood, or high-fat sources like whale blubber. Dr. Price discovered that these tribes had no long-term health issues.

For instance, the Pygmies, who followed a more plant-based diet, had effects that starkly contrasted with those of the meat-eating tribes. The health of these vegetarian tribes differed markedly from that of those who consumed more animal products. Yet, even in these traditional communities, just as in meat-eating communities, heart disease was unheard of, and obesity and other illnesses as we know them didn't exist.

Additionally, dental issues we have today were non-existent, today's neurological disorders were unknown, and traumatic experiences from hunting or warfare were addressed quickly and effectively without the need for prescription medicines.

Something we don't do. This isn't to say that these tribes never fell ill, but when they did, they turned to herbs and plants for medicinal purposes, using them sparingly and effectively due to their potential toxicity. We eat them as though they are going out of fashion.

An especially intriguing aspect of Dr Price's findings was the universal practice among these tribes to enhance fertility and reduce the risk of mental or physical congenital disabilities. The solution was simple: they added more animal fat to the diet of women trying to conceive. This practice, deeply rooted in tradition, had no modern equivalents, such as IVF or chemical treatments. Instead, it relied entirely on consuming authentic, locally sourced animal products. Dr Price's book also sheds light on the adverse health effects that tribes experienced after being introduced to a Western diet high in processed and carbohydrate-rich foods, issues that are now considered commonplace and inevitable and for which there is no hope of eliminating them in our modern society.

The Weston A. Price Foundation's website (https://www.westonaprice.org) is an excellent resource for those interested in exploring Dr. Price's work further.

Pottinger's Cats

Another significant book worth reading is Pottinger's Cats by Dr. Francis M. Pottenger, Jr. His research involved feeding cats a Western diet high in processed and carbohydrate-rich foods to observe the long-term effects on their health and that of their offspring. Although the study was conducted many years ago, it remains relevant today, particularly given that our carbohydrate consumption has increased.

Without revealing too much, Dr Pottenger discovered that a Western SAD diet caused significant health issues in cats, such that the third generation could no longer reproduce. This raises an important question: even though our health issues are similar to those of cats, are we humans starting to face challenges similar to those of cats due to our Western diet?

Dr. Pottenger's research suggested that the excessive carbohydrate intake damaged the cats' DNA, but he also found hope in reversing these effects. If the cats were returned to their natural diet, it would take only two generations for the damaged DNA to be corrected, allowing the third generation to live without the health problems of their ancestors. Today, we often consider certain illnesses hereditary, but what if they aren't hereditary in the traditional sense we are taught? And what if we can reverse such issues within our family generations that we have taken for granted by returning to a simpler Diet? Okay, the next two or three generations would still need to suffer the consequences of our nutritional mistakes, but...

These books provide critical insights into how diet affects our health in the short term and across generations. They challenge the modern perception of what constitutes a 'normal' diet and encourage us to reconsider the long-term consequences of our food choices.

Further Reading

It is a great starting point for further reading on subjects I haven't covered in this book. As usual, please decide whether these subjects interest you. This is a snippet of the books I have read. There are many more sources available that are equally informative. In no particular order, these are:

- *The Art and Science of Low Carbohydrate Living* by Jeff Volek and Stephen Phinney
- The Art and Science of Low-Carbohydrate Performance by Jeff Volek and Stephen Phinney
- *Low Carb 101* by Jeff Volek
- *Fat Fast* by Dana Carpender
- *The Fluoride Deception* by Christopher Bryson

- *Caffeine Blues* by Stephen Cherniske
- *The Obesity Epidemic* by Zoe Harcombe
- *Crazy Makers* by Carol Simontacchi
- *Not On the Label* by Felicity Lawrence
- *Fast Food Nation* by Eric Schlosser
- *The End of Overeating* by David A Kessler
- *The Great Cholesterol Con* by Malcolm Kendrick
- *Supplements Exposed* by Brian Clement
- *Devil in the Milk* by Keith Woodford
- *Cure Tooth Decay* by Ramel Nagel
- *The Untold Story of Milk* by Ron Schmid
- *Food Politics* by Marion Nestle
- *Big Fat Lies* by Hannah Sutter
- *Salt Sugar Fat* by Michael Moss
- *Wheat Belly* by William Davis
- *Pure, White and Deadly* by John Yudkin
- *The Diet Delusion* by Gary Taubes
- *Natural Health and Weight Loss* by Barry Groves
- *Trick and Treat* by Barry Groves
- *Bad Pharma* by Ben Goldacre
- *Coconut Cures* by Bruce Fife
- *Primal Body, Primal Mind* by Nora Gedgaudas
- *Confessions of a Medical Heretic* by Robert Mendelsohn
- *The Whistleblower* by Peter Rost
- *Food Inc.* by Peter Pringle
- *Homo Optimus* by Jan Kwasniewski
- *Sugar Shock!* by Connie Bennett
- *The Primal Blueprint* by Mark Sisson
- *The Carnivore Code* by Paul Saladino
- *The Complete Ketogenic Diet for Beginners* by Amy Ramos
- *The Ketogenic Diet for Epilepsy and Other Conditions* by Kossof, Turner, Cervenka & Barron
- *Low Carb for Beginners* by Sylvia Haper
- *The Complete Guide to Fasting* by Jimmy Moore and Jason Fung
- *The Obesity Code* by Jason Fung

- *The Cancer Code* by Jason Fung
- *The Diabetes Code* by Jason Fung
- *The Longevity Solution* by Jason Fung and James DiNicolantonio
- *The Collagen Cure* by James DiNicolantino
- *The Salt Fix* by James DiNicolantonio
- by Jayne Buxton
- *Super Fuel* by James DiNicolantino and Joseph Mercola
- *Target Keto* by Sim Land
- *Keto Cycle* by Siim Land
- *Fat for Fuel* by Joseph Mercola
- *The Truth About Seed Oils and their Impact on our Health* by Olivia Phillips
- *On the Dangers of Seed Oils* by Paul Saladino
- *The Plant Paradox* by Steven Gundry
- *Toxic Superfoods* by Sally Norton
- *Food Triggers* by Food Heroes
- *The Hidden Dangers of Soy* by Dianne Gregg
- *Ultra Processed People* by Chris Van Tulleken

Instead of using medicine, better fast today.
— Plutarch

Fasting: A Powerful Tool for Health

I've included fasting in this discussion because it's one of the most effective ways to cleanse the body of excess food and carbohydrates, as well as the lingering effects of added chemicals, processed, and factory-farmed foods. Even for those who don't follow a low-carb diet, fasting provides a valuable break for the body, allowing it to repair itself. For example, excess sugars are typically burned off within about twenty-four hours. Some experts suggest that specific insulin issues can stabilise within seven days of clean fasting.

In its simplest form, fasting means consuming only water and taking some electrolytes. This is what's known as pure fasting. A slightly more flexible version allows drinking water, tea, and coffee without additives such as milk and sugar. Regardless of the fasting method, electrolytes are crucial for maintaining the body's electrolyte balance.

There are variations of what some call 'dirty fasting,' where, for example, small amounts of food, such as broth, are allowed, typically around 300 to 600 calories per day. However, I don't consider this true fasting because the digestive system is still engaged. Fasting can vary in duration, from skipping a meal to fasting for several days, depending on what you want to achieve for your body and mind.

There is a documented case of a man fasting for over a year without experiencing any adverse effects. Angus Barbieri, a Scot, undertook this prolonged fast under medical supervision, beginning with a significant amount of body fat to sustain him. After he resumed eating, he experienced no adverse effects and was able to maintain the weight loss. While this is an extreme case, it illustrates the body's remarkable ability to survive without food for extended periods of time. However, without supervision, I wouldn't recommend fasting for such an extended duration, regardless of body size.

Fasting and starvation are not the same. Fasting is a voluntary act, often undertaken to replicate the health benefits of periods of not eating. On the other hand, starvation is an involuntary process that occurs when food is unavailable, leading to other stresses over time.

When we fast, our bodies generate extra energy, which, in ancient times, helped us hunt, gather, and find food. Today, this function is less about survival and more about giving our bodies and minds the clarity and energy needed for daily tasks. Interestingly, I find fasting more challenging if I'm not in ketosis beforehand. After a few days of fasting, the body resumes burning ketones, albeit inefficiently.

During a fast, our bodies burn off the glucose stored in the liver (usually within 24-36 hours) and shed the excess water from carbohydrate consumption. Fasting also gives our digestive, circulatory, and other organs a chance to repair themselves. Longer fasts can lead to more profound ketosis, promote the breakdown of dead cells (autophagy), and even stimulate the production of stem cells for cellular repair and regeneration. A seven-day clean fast can help restore insulin resistance to normal functional levels.

Like any other activity, fasting has potential risks that must be taken into consideration. One common mistake is overeating immediately after breaking a fast, which can undo many of the health benefits gained from the fast. Discipline and control are essential, especially when tempted by modern food-like products often laden with chemicals and sugars.

Fasting isn't for everyone. For example, those who are underweight, anorexic, pregnant, or suffering from certain illnesses should avoid fasting. If you're considering fasting, it's essential to research this further and consult with a doctor who specialises in nutrition and fasting before starting. They can provide guidance and support to ensure the process is safe and effective.

One exciting aspect of various traditional diets, such as the Mediterranean diet, is the inclusion of fasting, which is often overlooked in modern interpretations of these diets. Countries like Greece and Italy have historically incorporated fasting into their routines, observing a fast of approximately 120 days a year, typically lasting 24 to 36 hours twice a week. This regular fasting helped them maintain high energy levels, clear minds, and excellent physical health, even while performing manual labour.

Unfortunately, today's society encourages frequent eating, up to five to seven times a day, and a heavy reliance on processed food-like products. This constant consumption doesn't allow our bodies the necessary time to rest, recover, and eliminate toxins, which could be contributing to the widespread health issues we see today.

In ancient Greece, scholars such as Aristotle, Plato, and Epictetus were known to fast before lectures or debates to sharpen their mental thinking and processing abilities. This practice highlights that fasting offers physical benefits and enhances mental acuity. Today, it's well-known that eating can make us feel groggy and less focused, which is why fasting might be a valuable tool for improving cognitive function.

Fasting offers a powerful means to improve physical and mental health while being a cost-effective practice. Many high achievers incorporate fasting into their routines to help them achieve their goals and gain physical and mental clarity. I've found that exercising in a fasted state is more intense and leaves me feeling fitter and more energised. Additionally, my food bill has decreased significantly, saving me money, which is a bonus.

If you're considering fasting, especially transitioning from a diet high in glucose, be aware that the initial switch to burning ketones can leave you feeling weak and exhausted. It's a challenging mental and physical process, but the rewards are worth it. Once you're in ketosis, fasting becomes more accessible, with fewer hunger pangs and a more relaxed mindset, even when breaking the fast.

I regularly practice 36-hour fasts once a week. While fasting can be challenging, it dramatically boosts my energy and emotional well-being and helps me naturally regulate my weight.

As always, what I've shared here is based on my experiences and may not be complete. If fasting interests you, I encourage you to research, consult with experts, and plan carefully, especially when breaking the fast, as this is a crucial aspect of maintaining the benefits.

Recommended Reading and Resources

I recommend starting with Jason Fung. He has written several books, and I started with *The Complete Guide to Fasting*. It is brilliant and explains much more effectively than I can here. This is my reference book when I need to refresh on some theory or consider other fasting options.

Other excellent fasting books and sources are available, and it is worth reviewing various media to hear what some experts and experienced individuals say about fasting, including options, challenges, lessons learned, and the process of carrying out longer fasts, for example. As with any subject, there are a few red herrings, so please be careful.

Non-specialists or non-doctors write some books, and one that comes to mind is Jimmy Moore's *Livin' La Vida Low-Carb: My Journey from Flabby Fat to Sensationally Skinny in One Year.*

Sorry if this reference section is a bit slim, but I aim to recommend only beneficial reading material rather than list books covering a subject. Because I haven't read them, I can't verify them, and I don't want to recommend something here that I have not reviewed myself.

What we eat is a matter of life and death.
Lailah Gifty Akita

Insulin: The Double-Edged Sword of Health

I'm not entirely sure why I've saved this topic for last, yet it probably should have been at the forefront of the discussion on the Carnivore diet. However, it's crucial to address the role of insulin in our health, particularly the potential harm that can arise when we produce too much of it on a regular basis.

Insulin is a peptide hormone produced by the beta cells in the pancreas. While we often hear negative things about insulin, such as its association with insulin resistance and diabetes, it's essential to recognise that insulin plays a vital role in our health. Its primary function is to regulate glucose levels in the body by facilitating the uptake of glucose into cells for energy. However, the problems begin when we produce too much insulin, often due to a diet high in carbohydrates or chronic stress.

The more carbohydrates we consume, the more glucose enters our bloodstream, which requires more insulin to help push that glucose into our cells. If this process occurs too frequently, our cells can become insulin-resistant, leading to a condition in which the body produces high insulin levels but struggles to lower blood glucose effectively. This is where the catch-22 comes into play: our bodies store excess glucose as fat, but when there is too much glucose, it can't be effectively utilised by the cells, exacerbating cellular inflammation and leading to various health issues.

Insulin resistance is linked to a wide range of health issues. These include obesity, cardiovascular diseases, non-alcoholic fatty liver disease, polycystic ovary syndrome, frequent colds and flu, viral infections, bladder problems, various cancers, eye and vision issues, headaches, skin infections, slow healing, skin tags, darkened skin patches, persistent hunger, cravings for sweets and wheat products, lethargy, neurological conditions like Alzheimer's and Parkinson's, autoimmune diseases, epilepsy, brain tumours, digestive issues, joint and muscle pain, and even sickle cell anaemia. The list is long and alarming, highlighting the extensive impact that insulin resistance can have on our health.

The Concept of 'Diabetes III'

A specialist once suggested that a helpful way to conceptualise many interconnected illnesses is to categorise them under 'Diabetes III.' This notion highlights the connection between these conditions and the inflammation triggered by excessive insulin levels. The implications of this are indeed alarming. Furthermore, there is a troubling potential for insulin resistance to damage our DNA, damage that future generations could inherit. This idea echoes the findings in Pottinger's Cats, where the health of subsequent generations was directly influenced by the conditions experienced by their ancestors.

Not only that, but I seem to read that more and more house pets are starting to suffer illnesses similar to ours. I am not surprised when I observe how many pet owners feed their pets only dried or tinned food. Rarely do I see the dog give a good chunk of fresh meat. Tinned and dried food are processed products. It isn't food. Tinned food was once considered a novelty food for humans. In my eyes, it still is so.

Reflecting on this journey, I wonder if I've managed to keep your attention or lost you along the way. Either way, I don't want you to believe what I have written. Instead, I encourage you to question everything, to doubt me, and to explore these ideas for yourself. Read further, consult experts, and seek out others who have embarked on similar journeys. No two stories are alike, and your path to health will differ from mine.

For me, this journey has been life-transformative. I've confronted and dealt with my past, eliminated narcissistic and other harmful behaviours, and regained both my mental and physical health. Every day, I feel overwhelmed by how far I've come. I've found peace in my life and meaning in my actions, and I'm surrounded by the people I value most: my wife, family, and friends. I'm content with what I have and with what I'm able to give back to the world.

I'm also acutely aware that I still have much to learn. The more I read and explore, the more I realise how little I know. Socrates once said that the only true wisdom is knowing you know nothing, and I'm beginning to understand the depth of that statement. I don't strive for perfection; I accept that I will make mistakes, face uncomfortable situations, and sometimes say the wrong thing. But I'm grateful for these experiences because they remind me that I'm human and have given me qualities I would have never discovered otherwise.

Please do not wait to strike until the iron is hot; make it hot by striking.
William Butler Yeats

Sport and Fitness

Until recently, my journey in sport and fitness followed a frustratingly familiar pattern: consistent weight gain with little to no progress. Each time I embarked on a new fitness programme, I was filled with enthusiasm and passion, armed with ambitious plans to get super fit and toned. However, my initial fervour would fizzle out within a few short weeks. Eventually, I found myself lucky if I managed to make it to the gym once a month while still dutifully paying my membership fees.

When I did manage to attend, my dedication was a shadow of what it once was. I would go through the motions, pretending to train, just enough to convince myself that I was making an effort without actually putting in the work. This charade would continue until I could no longer ignore the reality: I was fooling myself. I wasn't going to recapture that short-lived motivation. Inevitably, I would cancel my membership, take a break, and then, after some time, join another gym and repeat the cycle. Those fitness companies certainly made a tidy profit from my sporadic attendance!

Each time, I found excuses for my lack of progress, excuses that conveniently avoided admitting the real reason: my laziness. I would tell myself to do things differently next time, but nothing changed.

So, what was going wrong, and how have I managed to gain better control now?

After some honest reflection, I realised that my behaviour stemmed from a profound lack of self-respect. Whenever I started to progress, I would find a way to sabotage it, unconsciously ensuring that I remained at the level of self-worth I had convinced myself I deserved. This pattern is familiar to many, including professional performers who often seem to hit a career plateau that aligns with their self-perceived worth. Unfortunately, once we reach this perceived limit, we frequently struggle to push beyond it despite our efforts to convince ourselves otherwise.

This mindset profoundly impacts our lives because the level of success we achieve in society often reflects the value we place on our internal goals. This principle isn't limited to the sports field, either.

I was determined to reach my internal benchmark of low self-worth, and I did so with remarkable success. I even went so far as to create a persona that convinced others and myself that I couldn't be relied upon. I became so committed to this narrative that I stopped trusting myself. It's sad, isn't it?

A New Approach to Fitness

Today, at the end of 2023, I'm following several routines with a level of physical and mental commitment that surpasses anything I've managed before, especially considering my age. I complement this with regular Pilates sessions to maintain good posture, as I've previously mentioned how vital Pilates is in my routine.

In the past, missing a training day bothered me, and my enthusiasm would quickly wane. If I miss a session due to time constraints or fatigue, I take a break and return to it the next day or as soon as possible. I'm comfortable with this approach, and it motivates me to stay focused on the journey rather than obsess over the goal.

I've finally come to understand that there's no race I need to win, especially not against myself, because, in truth, there is no such thing as a race. There never has been, and there never will be.

This realisation has allowed me to enjoy sports for what they are and appreciate how they enhance the quality of my life. This understanding is crucial as I aspire to make the most of the unknown time I have left. Fitness, for me, is no longer about meeting some external standard or impressing others; it's about living in a way that aligns with my values and taking care of the only body I have.

I might have been driven by the need to impress others in the past, but I've come to see that it was never worth it. The truth is, they weren't interested then and aren't interested now—no one is. I was projecting my insecurities onto others, hoping to gain their interest, only to be rejected in return.

With this shift in how I perceive myself, I've found a renewed appreciation for my body, especially now in the second half of my fifties. The walking stick I purchased a few years ago, anticipating that I would soon need it, remains untouched in the cupboard. I'm aware that, due to my leg, I will likely need it someday, but that's a different scenario. What matters now is that I'm not prematurely dependent on it simply because I wasn't willing to care for what I have.

This change in mindset has given me a new level of freedom to live on my terms, without the pressure of a non-existent race. It's not about competing or proving anything to anyone; it's about enjoying the journey and maintaining a body that serves me well in the life I choose to lead.

Our body is our only portable temple, and proper care is the key to maximising our brief time on this earth. When we lose part of our health, we lose part of our life.

The Role of Technology

Technology has made remarkable advances in helping us maintain and restore our health. However, while it provides significant support, there are no guarantees. Technology allows us to shift responsibility onto something external rather than taking full ownership of our well-being.

Despite the progress, there are still limits to what technology can achieve. We must care for any replacements or modifications made to our bodies just as diligently as we would our natural selves. Only by doing so can we ensure that we continue leading rich and fulfilling lives, protecting our precious time.

Our Only Guaranteed Goal in Life: Death

Death arrives in its own time and on its terms without reiterating too much from before. While it took me some time to adopt this perspective, I've realised that I would much rather die while doing something I love than sit idly, waiting for the Grim Reaper to collect me for my final activity. Some may find this way of thinking extreme, but I've wasted time waiting for something that never arrived simply because I believed it was 'due' for some reason. Why wait? That's just dead time. We have plenty of that ahead of us once we are six feet under.

It has now become clear that I need to create those 'due' moments rather than wait for them to be handed to me or not by some external force. I have years of living to catch up on and must decide what truly matters to me. Perhaps my experiences have shaped this focus on personal significance, but after what I've been through, I am biased towards what matters most.

As I mentioned earlier, who cares what others think? The journey towards death only holds meaning when we have given it meaning through the experiences we've chosen, fought for, or been forced to accept as part of our self-reinvention. Ultimately, it's my life and my choice. Right?

When you're happy, you enjoy the music. When you're sad, you understand the lyrics.

Frank Ocean

An Overview of My Highs and Lows

In this section, I would like to share my experiences of the highs and lows I've encountered over the past six years. By reflecting on them, I aim to understand their comprehensive impact on me.

The Highs

We all experience highs in life; some fade from memory. That's why it's been wonderful to recall specific moments when I know I did something right. Some of the most straightforward yet meaningful moments were when I made someone laugh, helped someone out, or achieved something I once thought was beyond my capabilities. I also recall the fleeting moments of peace, those brief escapes from the inner turmoil that once consumed me.

I think of my past and present friends and the things we did together, whether tackling a challenge or just being silly. I remember the love my mother gave me and how pleased she was when I could do something to make her proud. I also cherish the simple joys, such as playing hours of board games like Backgammon and Newmarket or double patience with my family. My sister and I were close despite the usual sibling rivalry, and we still are.

I look back fondly on my relationships, recalling when we were free to enjoy each other before I started making a mess of things. I also remember the first day I no longer had to wear a calliper on my leg as a teenager: the freedom, both mental and physical, was overwhelming. Wearing trainers as everyday shoes for the first time, I felt like I was walking on air!

There's joy in remembering the freedom I felt playing badminton, regardless of whether I won or lost. Then, there's the pride I still feel at being accepted to university without A-levels, having attended a pre-prep course that brought me up to the required standard. I recall partying so hard that I had to retake exams during the summer holiday to start my degree, and how I fought to earn a second chance at university after failing my first year due to a significant mistake. But I stuck to my commitment and finished that degree.

Afterwards, I took pride in my first job, where I progressed from being a technician, which I enjoyed, to an engineer, although I wasn't exceptionally skilled in the role. This was still a significant milestone for me.

I recall the self-discovery journey that began as a teenager and continued until I found answers in my fifties. Despite my doubts and frequent missteps, I persevered. That seed, planted twenty-six years ago, grew into the incredible journey I've documented in this book. Psychedelics gave me my first taste of mental freedom, and today, that inner freedom is becoming a reality. Sometimes, we must listen to ourselves, rather than the system, to determine what is best for us.

I've exceeded my hopes, dreams, and expectations of what I deserved. I am enjoying life again, now working as a psychologist and giving something back. For all of this, I am deeply grateful.

The Lows

We all face lows at some point, and I've come to value mine by accepting and learning from them. It's exhausting to treat past mistakes as lessons to learn from constantly. Still, after years of reflection, I've realised that once the pieces begin to fit together and the painful memory surfaces, it becomes more manageable to handle and release.

Of course, I still make mistakes, sometimes spectacularly, but they are genuine errors, not deliberate acts of self-sabotage. I've accepted that I'm human and prepared to live with the consequences if someone takes offence. What I can do, once I recognise my mistake, is to apologise sincerely and leave it to the other person whether they wish to trust me again.

When difficult memories arise, I accept that these were parts of my personality designed to protect me from further harm. Though it can take time, I try to find alternative solutions. This isn't an excuse but a way to reflect on who I was and why I acted the way I did.

In the past, I created manipulative scenarios of forgiveness to gain attention or control. This gave me a fleeting sense of superiority, but in the long run, it caused more harm. Seeing it as a sign of weakness, I couldn't ask for help. If I need help today, it's still not easy, but I do ask for it. If the answer is no, I will respect that and move on.

Learning to talk about things that bother me, even minor issues, has been transformative. Whether it's complaining about a hot day or discussing deeper concerns, sharing has had a profound impact on me. I now realise that conversations don't need to be exhaustive; we can change subjects and move from the trivial to the serious, and that's perfectly fine.

I used to think that talking about emotional issues required staying with them until every angle was explored. Thankfully, I've learned that's not the case. We can change topics, keep things light, and share experiences without delving into every detail. I love this freedom to engage in a more balanced, conversational flow.

I haven't forgotten my old communication style, but I choose not to use it. The ability to speak to someone neutrally, without anger or emotional outbursts, feels like a revelation. It still amazes me that people are willing to share their opinions and offer help without gathering ammunition against me.

The Fine Line of No Return

The lowest moments in my life felt like standing on the line of no return. Thankfully, I never crossed it, although I came close to it. When I realised how I had hurt others and myself, the emotions were overwhelming. I couldn't look at myself in the mirror, repulsed by the reflection of the person I had become.

The essential tool that helped me in these dark moments was acceptance. Accepting what I had done and understanding that it was a part of me at that time allowed me to come to terms with my actions. This isn't an easy process, but it's necessary to prevent past mistakes from continuing to erode your self-worth.

Living in Bedford and struggling to secure work, I reached a financial low during a challenging time. My mother stepped in, offering financial support and practical advice. She suggested I rent out my home to alleviate the pressure. Although I had initially resisted the idea, feeling that it would be an admission of failure, I took her advice. Within a week, I had a tenant, and soon after, I secured a new work contract.

Her support helped me regain my footing, and I've carried that lesson forward.

Over the last few years, my words and actions have hurt others and myself. I lost friends and relationships, not because they didn't care, but because I didn't think I deserved their love or friendship. In my lowest moments, I felt like I was on the brink of giving up. But each time, I found the strength to step back.

What's kept me going is the belief that I need to see how my story ends. That desire to know has been a powerful motivator, even through the darkest times. Why let the past dictate my future? I can't control how I'll die, but I can control how I live up until that moment.

Each low point has been a building block towards a better understanding of myself. It hasn't been easy, and I'm not proud of everything I've done, but I've learned from my mistakes. The key is not to give up, to keep working through the pain, and to recognise that this journey is worth it.

We all have histories we're not proud of, and we must live with the consequences of our actions. But no one is perfect. Acceptance isn't about excusing our behaviour; it's about recognising it, learning from it, and choosing to do better. Through this acceptance, I've found a way to rebuild myself, one step at a time.

I hope this makes sense.

Understanding Luck

For many years, the concept of luck confused me deeply. I spent a long time believing that luck was something I was entitled to and that it would eventually fall into my lap. I felt frustrated when things didn't go my way, and I often saw myself as a victim, thinking life wasn't fair because I wasn't getting what I believed I deserved.

Looking back, I'm not sure whether this mindset stemmed from some underlying narcissism or if there was another reason behind it. It was almost like a superstition: this idea that luck was always just around the corner, waiting for me and that the world owed me a few favours. When things went wrong, I couldn't shake the feeling that I had been cheated out of something I was entitled to.

In time, I realised that luck isn't something you can rely on, nor is it something you're owed. It's just luck and nothing more. If you sit around waiting for it to come to you without effort, the chances of being lucky are exceedingly slim, considering there are around 8 billion people on the planet. Statistically, someone has to obtain the correct numbers or find the item they are looking for.

I eventually learned that we could influence the likelihood of luck by being active and working hard. While luck may seem random, it's often a combination of being in the right place at the right time and doing the necessary groundwork. Dedication and hard work are essential ingredients, but success can sometimes come down to a bit of chance.

Some people might not call this luck at all; they might attribute it entirely to effort. However, I view it as a type of luck that can be increased by stacking the odds in your favour through preparation and persistence.

The only ordinary people are the ones you don't know very well.
Alfred Adler

The Rest of 2023: Discovering Alfred Adler

Alfred Adler's work is truly remarkable! I recently started reading *The Courage to Be Happy* by Ichiro Kishimi and Fumitake Koga, a book grounded in Adler's psychological theories. It was a revelation, and several of Adler's concepts made powerful mental 'clicks' for me, helping me tackle some of the lingering psychological issues I've been working through.

Adler's Five Stages of Problem Behaviour in Children

One concept that stood out to me was Adler's five stages of problem behaviour in children. These stages describe how a child progressively reacts to unmet needs for attention. If a child doesn't succeed at the first stage, they tend to move down the list until they find something that works for them. The five stages are as follows:

Demand for admiration: The child works hard to be praised for their abilities and achievements.

Attention-seeking: The child seeks recognition, often through humour or similar tactics.

Power struggle: The child (or even adults, in some cases) competes to assert authority over others.

Revenge: The child seeks retribution against adults or peers for perceived wrongs.

Proof of incompetence: The child chooses to appear incompetent to gain attention.

In my previous book, I wrote about my childhood decision to adopt the 'proof of incompetence' stage to gain my parents' attention. My mother loved and praised me, while my father focused only on my faults. I consciously decided that if I couldn't earn their attention through achievement, I would gain it by being incompetent and doing everything wrong.

This realisation goes even deeper. I distinctly remember where I was when I made that decision as a child. The power of that memory is striking because it shaped my behaviour as a child and throughout my life. I can see how this pattern influenced many of my choices today.

What did these five stages reveal to me? I understood that at some point in my life, I had considered each stage, escalating my responses until I landed on the most intense one, which was proof of incompetence. Although I don't recall consciously moving through the earlier stages, I remember settling on that final one.

My parents became my primary models for attention despite their conflicting styles. This model didn't just stay confined to childhood; I carried it with me throughout my life, applying it to almost every relationship and interaction I had as I grew older.

One of the most astonishing realisations was my commitment to that childhood decision. I stayed loyal to it, no matter how much harm it caused me. I began to understand that whenever I achieved something brilliant on the first try, I would slowly sabotage it over time. The first attempt would succeed because there were no expectations. Still, as soon as I recognised my capability, I would undermine myself until I reached the incompetence that I thought I deserved.

This, in turn, led others to adjust their perception of me until their views aligned with what I thought they should be. Looking back, it's heartbreaking to realise how much of my life I undermined because of the insecurities instilled in me by my father.

This realisation also confirmed another truth: there are no accidents in who we become if we don't learn how to deal with the misleading information our parents provide us about playing The Game of Life. The way we internalise their guidance, or lack thereof, can shape the entire course of our lives.

Binge Eating: A Surprising Discovery

Isn't it amazing what we can discover about ourselves when we least expect it? I recently realised that I have an eating disorder: I am a binge eater. This wasn't something I had been actively looking for, but rather something I stumbled upon after recognising specific patterns in my life. Most notably, my eating problem emerged in the evenings, which I later realised was the active part of the binge-eating cycle. But the routine had started much earlier in the day.

Thinking that something from my past was still bothering me, I followed a powerful technique I had learned in NLP. After completing this routine, my thoughts stabilised, but after a few weeks, I lost track again. After several months of trying to get back on track, I decided to consult with a psychologist who follows a similar approach. Again, it helped briefly, but eventually, I drifted back. The addiction was too strong.

Or was it?

It was when someone mentioned that I had some symptoms that I could have parasites and worms that I changed my direction altogether. Instead of taking medication like Ivermectin, which has an excellent reputation against parasites and many types of cancer (worms are now being found within the core of cancer cells), it is possible that if we kill the worm and remove its source of food (carbohydrates), the worm dies, and so does cancer. Although this research is still in its early stages and appears promising, I decided to try the natural approach using Diatomaceous Earth, Zeolite, and a combination of Black Walnut oil, Wormwood oil, and Clove oil.

The first month was uncomfortable, and getting into a routine took a few days. However, after the first week, my appetite calmed, and I gradually managed to bring my eating under control without bingeing on carbs.

So, this wasn't a mental issue I was suffering from, but it was a physical one!

After some reading, I realised how many people have. Maybe it's because nobody does a worm cleanse anymore. At least once a year seems like a good idea, which I now do.

Now, I feel stable. My eating habits are mostly under control, and I no longer crave sugar or similar products. My weight has also stabilised, and I now have better control over what I eat, which pleases me greatly. Do I occasionally stray from my Carnivore/Ketovore diet? Yes, every so often. For example, when I have a curry, I might indulge in some rice or naan bread, but the next day, I reset with a 36-hour fast.

That's a great place to close this chapter and move on to the next.

A New Part of My Philosophy

Over the years, I have come to understand that philosophy influences us from the very moment we are born (maybe even before through the behaviour of our mother carrying us). However, I only recently realised I had been following several philosophies for my entire life without even knowing it. Now that I know them, as you will have gathered from earlier, they significantly influence me and continue to evolve as I deepen my understanding of philosophy, myself, the world, and the system in which we live.

The following section explores a key perspective that has simplified and enriched my life. I also reflect on how these newfound insights might have shaped my approach to the past six years had I embraced them sooner.

The Game of Life

I've mentioned several times that I now view life as a game where I play a role on this immense theatrical stage, which shouldn't be taken too seriously. If we do, we risk becoming part of The Game, and others will define our roles, allowing them to manipulate and use us as they see fit. Whether they follow our created societal and social rules doesn't matter; nothing stops them from doing what they want. We've already chosen or inherited our roles, but many are unaware that we can change these roles at any time. No role is permanent, except for the fact that we are human. While we can take breaks within the game, we can never completely escape it.

How old is The Game? Perhaps it dates back to the beginning of the Universe as we know it, maybe even earlier. Some say it began with the dawn of civilisation. Regardless, The Game starts for each of us the moment we are born. Some even believe it begins at conception or maybe even as we travel towards birth, depending on what we believe.

How the Universe started doesn't matter to those of us playing The Game. Speculation about these and other things is simply part of the fun. Once introduced into The Game, it operates within fixed boundaries called the Universal Laws of Nature. These oft-chaotic laws are our constants.

Rules, Roles, and Participants

The Game has no written rules, goals, or objectives. There are no winners or losers. Every living and inanimate thing is part of The Game, where inanimate objects form the stage, and living things are the participants. Participants can do as they wish, provided it aligns with their chosen ethics.

There's no hierarchy here, and we're not necessarily the highest species on the planet. As players, we face risks and red herrings, and as we become aware of them, we make decisions to keep playing and ensure the survival of future generations; otherwise, it's game over. Every decision impacts not only ourselves but also the environment and other participants.

Some players may believe they play The Game across several levels or lifetimes, while others claim this is the only chance to play; however, we will never truly know if there is another level to play. Are we humans playing on a higher or lower level than other creatures? Is our population rising because fewer participants are achieving the level's demands?

Do we have to repeat this level before moving on, or do we progress automatically? Is this the first or last level, or are there more levels ahead? If we do get another life after this one, and if so, will we play a similar game in the role of someone or something we treated well or poorly, or is it all random?

If there is a goal we must fulfil as participants, how do we know if we're achieving it? And what happens if we don't? Is doing more or less the better approach, and what does 'doing more' or 'doing less' entail? With so many unknowns, the questions can feel overwhelming. But does it even matter? The important thing is to make the most of what we have now. And how do we define that? That's up to each of us.

I've finally learned to keep life simple. As long as I live now, I'm not concerned about missing any 'Universal goal.' If, at some point, I need to repeat a level or start The Game again for something I did or didn't do, I'll deal with that when the time comes. Until then, I can do little to influence it, so I choose to enjoy the ride and leave my mark on this fictional societal system.

Within The Game, we can choose which mini-games we want to play and how. We can stumble through, follow the systemic rules, or make up our own to fit around them if we so wish. We can even create mini-games for others to play, making our lives easier or more challenging within the current system.

We must decide what ethics to follow and how we wish to play. Morals and the expectations of others make The Game unnecessarily complicated. Instead, we should focus on playing according to our ethics.

Here's what I believe are the basic guidelines for The Game:

- There are no absolutes in The Game, except for this one.
- The Game has no rules (except the Universal laws of nature).
- Every action has a consequence in The Game.
- You are alone in The Game.
- You have nothing to achieve in The Game.
- In The Game, you are responsible only for yourself (and the next generation, if you choose to be).
- You have only your ethics and experience to guide you.
- You have an unknown time limit within The Game.
- There is no inherent meaning to The Game, except what you give it; even then, it still lacks meaning.
- Ignore these guidelines, and you become part of someone else's game, serving at their beck and call.

Many participants face the problem of relying too heavily on others to make decisions for them, forgetting these guidelines and becoming trapped in conflicting roles. This occurs when we allow the morals of others to dictate our lives, leading us to live according to their fictitious rules rather than our own ethics.

Once trapped in another participant's game, whether in work, family, finances, or beliefs, we relinquish our freedom of choice, allowing them to dictate how we should play for their benefit. Some participants even suffer for causes that don't exist.

Ultimately, it doesn't matter because the only goal, if there is one, will be achieved when the Universe and our short-term lives end. Our solar system, galaxy, and everything we know will eventually cease to exist except as space dust. It's not something we'll ever witness directly.

We play various roles throughout our lives, constantly changing in response to our needs and surroundings. Those who struggle with The Game may feel ostracised by society, but we're all participants in different societal groups. How we play our roles determines how we perceive our value within society.

From birth, we begin to play roles, starting with the essential functions of a baby; pooping, crying, gurgling and eating/drinking. As we grow, these roles become more complex, and we assume different masks depending on our interactions with others, including parents, friends, partners, colleagues, and even strangers.

But these masks and roles are temporary. They don't represent who we are. We wear them to make situations, and others perceive us differently. The closest we come to understanding ourselves is when we reach a state of neutrality, free from life's dualities, and momentarily lose our awareness of everything around us.

Life is a series of mini-games, and it's up to us to decide how many, what kind, and how intensely we want to play them. Whether it's relationships, careers, hobbies, or friendships, each mini-game offers its own set of challenges. We can play to progress, to find stability, or even to lose. It's entirely up to us.

Reflections on What I Did and Didn't Do Through These Last Years

Looking back with the benefit of hindsight offers a valuable opportunity for growth. Reflecting on what I might have done differently is not about dwelling on regrets but recognising the lessons these experiences provide. It allows me to acknowledge how I've grown, consider pivotal moments that shaped me, and explore how I might approach similar challenges. In this section, I'll delve into the decisions and outcomes that, with the clarity of experience, I might have navigated differently—and how these reflections continue to inform my journey.

Prioritising Diet Change

If I could do it again, I would first change my diet and make a concerted effort to stick to it. Switching to a Carnivore diet had a profound impact on both my mental and physical health, which would have saved me lots of time and effort. By eliminating plant toxins and processed foods, I resolved many of what I thought were core mental problems, but were related to what I ate instead. Had I started with this dietary change, I believe the rest of the journey would have been much smoother, and the changes would have come more quickly. Giving up coffee simultaneously would have accelerated this progress even further.

Doing the Background Reading

Reading as much as possible before embarking on any significant self-improvement journey, especially involving dietary, psychological, or philosophical changes, is essential. I spent a lot of time studying the experiences of others who had gone through similar journeys. Interpreting their insights is challenging, as language often struggles to convey profound personal experiences. However, I could gradually filter out unreliable information by reading widely and noting consistent themes.

Approaching Psychedelic Therapy with Respect

The use of psychedelic therapy is rapidly growing now that it's legal in many countries. However, I chose not to seek a guru or guide, as not everyone who offers these services truly knows what they are doing. If there were to be a mistake on my part, I wanted to be the one to take responsibility for it. That said, I listened carefully to others and did thorough research before making decisions. The same applies to reading up on professionals; having a certificate doesn't always mean they know what they're doing. Ultimately, whatever path you choose, the decision is yours.

Be Prepared for Difficult Days

There will be times when the journey gets tough. Seeing ourselves for who we are or realising that our hopes and expectations are illusions can be overwhelming. While I've always tried to remain analytical, there were moments when this self-realisation became too much. However, it's crucial to keep reflecting and working through these moments. We are who we are, and we've all made poor choices at some time. Now is the time to accept those choices and let our true selves emerge.

Have Support During Psychedelic Experiences

One of my psychedelic sessions was particularly frightening, and although I didn't need emergency help, it would have been comforting to have someone nearby. If you decide to explore psychedelics, ensure that someone is with you. Even if they aren't experienced, it is vital to have someone there to help if things go wrong. I cover this topic more in my first book, *How I Changed My Mind*, where I explain what a support person needs to do during such experiences.

Be Patient

One key lesson I've learned is the importance of patience because the slower we go, the faster everything comes together. After my first psychedelic session, I thought I had dealt with all my issues. I had only scratched the surface, and more unresolved problems soon emerged. Even today, I have a slowly shrinking list of situations I want to test out. The key is to take the time to reflect and keep moving forward. It's the journey that's important, not the goal.

Embracing My Old and New Personalities

I know my personality has changed, although I don't concern myself too much with how it's perceived. I'm more relaxed now and enjoy life in ways I only used to dream about. If someone disagrees with me or wants to distance themselves, that's fine.

I'm respectful and courteous, but I have my boundaries and uphold them. I now approach debates with respect, listen to others, and accept their views for what they are—something I couldn't do before.

Expect a Philosophical Shift

Your life philosophy may change as you delve deeper into your self-discovery. We all have philosophies shaped by our upbringing, education, media, and environment. Some people aren't even aware they have them. Be prepared to reassess these philosophies and adjust them as you grow and develop.

Redefine Happiness and What Matters

Your understanding of happiness and what's important to you will change as you grow. Be ready to redefine these concepts when the time comes. I began this journey thinking I knew what I wanted, but quickly realised I was wrong. I wanted to belong to the masses and be part of a group without realising that there are countless different groups. Now, I enjoy my company, am content with who I am, and actively participate in various groups on my terms.

Be Selective About Connections

We are wired to connect with others, but being selective about the people we let into our lives is okay. I now take my time before accepting new connections and am happy with the people around me. They provide a sense of relaxation and openness, which I need.

Reject Labels

Labels are just generalised descriptions created by someone else. We aren't the labels we've inherited, and it may be best to live without them. Ignore the labels others give you. Reflect on them; ultimately, you are who you are, not the labels others have for you. If you don't like who you are, work to change it and express that change outwardly.

Understanding Who You Are

Who we think we are is not necessarily who we are. I haven't yet discovered who I am, but I've certainly found out who I am *not*, and that list is long! Am I concerned about not realising who I truly am? Not really. The more I let go of caring, the more I enjoy life, and in those moments, I'm being my true self. We aren't just one person; we are a multitude of personalities, each emerging at different times. That understanding is enough for me.

Memories Are Not Facts

Our memories aren't exact recollections of what happened. They are memories of memories, reshaped each time we recall them. Over time, they become a collage of images and emotions. While they once served a purpose in protecting us, they can become a hindrance if we cling to them. We aren't stuck in karma; we've just been punishing ourselves, thinking it's a form of karma.

Take Responsibility for Your Emotions

No matter how much pain we endure, it's our responsibility to manage our emotions. If someone offends us, we can't control whether it was intentional, but we can control our reaction. Walking away is often the best course of action. If we respond, we give others the satisfaction of provoking us, which feeds their inner needs.

Releasing the Past

We release a burden each time we let go of something from the past. Some people can release their past in a single session, while others may require more work. If you need more time, embrace it. This is your journey, so don't compare it to anyone else's.

Life's Journey

Even after we've dealt with the past, life will still present challenges. The key is to take them in stride, to pick ourselves up and keep moving forward. Dwelling on the past keeps us from living in the moment.

Embrace Death

Death is the only certainty in life, so why not embrace it? The fear of death only makes life more painful. Instead, find peace with its inevitability and live your life to the fullest. We can't control it when the time comes, but we can welcome it with open arms.

Live on Your Terms

Get on with life; nobody cares what you do. Some may be jealous, others may be offended, but that's their problem. Don't hold yourself back because others don't know how to move forward with their own lives.

Choose What's Right for You

I chose to revert to eating, which reflects how we lived over 12,000 years ago. It has significantly improved both my mental and physical life. Modern food and medical interventions often complicate our health, but our digestive systems have remained unchanged for approximately 12,000 years. I'm not perfect, but I've taken control of my health in a way that suits me rather than letting an anonymous modern system dictate it.

Final Thoughts

Life is worth living, and once we truly start living it, it becomes worth dying for. These insights have been invaluable to me, and while you may agree or disagree, they've helped me tremendously. One interesting aspect is that reflecting on how I am now allows me to remember how much control we have given to others and that we are, and have always been, in control of becoming who we are by being what we are. Being the person I am today, which is constantly evolving, sometimes feels surreal because I am transforming from a person who harbours a lot of hate, frustration, and confusion to a relaxed individual who accepts life for what it is, making life much easier to live and enjoy.

In the next chapter, I'll share my summary from 2024 and some discoveries that have influenced my life and work as a psychologist.

Only once we are at the end are we back at the beginning.
Neil Holmes

Finally, The End

This is the final section of this book. Initially, I considered updating you on the changes I've experienced. However, since our journeys are unique to each of us, I decided against it. Instead, I want to offer a different summary: a reflection on what I believe is essential when addressing trauma and other mental health challenges I've encountered.

Drawing on my experiences, I would like to briefly share how I support my clients in regaining their footing as quickly as possible. The only aspect I don't explore with my clients is the use of psychedelics, as this is a deeply personal decision whether someone wants to go down this path. Those interested need to seek qualified guidance, as I don't assist in this area.

The four key areas I wish to touch upon are psychedelics, psychology, philosophy, and nutrition. These elements are deeply interconnected and vital to fostering meaningful change for individuals grappling with historical challenges that complicate their lives more than they should.

In this discussion, I will focus on how we approached life in the past rather than increasing our reliance on technology, such as apps or other digital tools. For most of human history, we have lived in a world devoid of the modern society we know today. We faced the raw wild and survived. If we could endure those conditions without advanced medical technology, why do we struggle so much now?

As technology becomes increasingly advanced and integrated into our lives, it often fosters a sense of dependence. In many cases, this dependence seems to harm our mental and physical well-being more than it helps. Instead, we should leverage the tools and wisdom that've sustained us for millennia, combining them with the knowledge gained through modern advancements. This approach enables us to enhance the natural resources available, including our innate ability to support one another during mental and physical hardship.

This philosophy could be described as de-transhumanism, a return to nature and human-centric holistic solutions, as opposed to transhumanism, which focuses on integrating technology into every aspect of our existence.

Psychedelics

Psychedelics have been used throughout history, from the early discovery of psychoactive plants by medicine men and witches to their use in Greek and Abrahamic ceremonies and now, in modern psychedelic-assisted psychotherapy.

Today, an increasing number of people are confronting various forms of trauma (unanswered questions and problems of varying difficulties), ranging from recent experiences to events buried deep in the past. These traumas can weigh heavily on us, affecting our physical and mental health and sometimes leading to social withdrawal. As social beings, withdrawing from society can amplify the pain, creating a more complex escape cycle.

One of the challenges of addressing trauma, especially after years of avoidance, is the exhaustion that can follow. Such therapy can help dismantle the psychological defences we've built over time, but the process can leave us feeling too drained to embrace the life we long to return to fully. Yet, once we reclaim our lives, the relief can be overwhelming.

This newfound mental peace and emotional balance may initially feel unfamiliar, even unsettling. Adjusting to a calmer, more neutral state where thoughts are clear, challenges are handled with composure, and inner silence is comforting can take time. However, this state often becomes profoundly appealing. As we shift into this healthier mindset, our behaviour may change in ways loved ones might not immediately recognise or understand.

Initially, these changes can cause concern among those close to us. They may misinterpret our transformation, believing we're still struggling. However, this evolution often leads us to connect with others who share similar perspectives and experiences, offering a sense of belonging and mutual understanding that can be deeply rewarding.

To release the past, we must confront the darkest parts of ourselves: those demons, haunting memories, and unresolved pains we've buried within. Facing these truths head-on can be overwhelming, forcing us to confront our authentic selves. The key lies in embracing self-love and acceptance, acknowledging that, like everyone, we are capable of both good and harm. What matters most is owning our mistakes, committing to never repeating them, and supporting those whom others have hurt.

When we reach this level of self-acceptance, the sense of release is transformative. We carry our history with us, not as a burden but as a testament to the resilience and understanding it has given us. These experiences provide insights and qualities that those who haven't faced similar challenges may never fully comprehend.

Psychedelics, when approached with proper preparation, can sometimes offer breakthroughs that might take years of traditional therapy to achieve. Over the next eight to twelve hours, they can unveil parts of ourselves that no other method can penetrate so deeply. However, it's crucial to understand that psychedelics are not a cure-all. They can lay a foundation for confronting repressed thoughts, but the real work lies in integrating these revelations into daily life.

Adapting to this new understanding requires ongoing effort, ethical reflection, and a commitment to personal growth. It's a lifelong journey, one that each of us must undertake individually.

Yet, even on this solitary path, our journeys intersect with others. These connections offer opportunities for learning, companionship, and mutual support as we navigate life's complexities.

That said, I do not advocate or promote the use of psychedelics. I strongly recommend thorough research and consultation with experts before considering such experiences. Moreover, in many countries, including my own, the use of mind-altering substances is illegal. Taking unnecessary risks could lead to complications far beyond the original intent, and I urge you to approach this topic with caution and responsibility.

Nutrition

As I mentioned earlier, I wish I had started with this change, as I found that eliminating certain foods from my diet had the most significant impact on the core issues that psychedelics, psychology, and philosophy could not address. Whenever I reintroduce those foods into my diet, the associated mental problems return with a vengeance.

I've previously shared my thoughts on the benefits of a Carnivore diet, which involves eliminating all fruits, vegetables, processed foods, and artificial chemicals in food-like products. Interestingly, mental health issues related to diet are not yet listed in the DSM-5, but I wouldn't be surprised if this changes shortly.

In 2024, I discovered two brilliant books that profoundly shaped my understanding of the world. The first, *Change Your Diet, Change Your Mind,* by Dr Georgia Ede, reinforced my belief that the foods we eat can profoundly influence how we think and behave. It confirmed that I was heading in the right direction. The second, by renowned psychotherapist Thomas Szasz, argued that mental illness doesn't exist in the traditional sense. Instead, for those without brain damage, it often stems from intentional behaviours or a type of psychological delirium, serving as a self-protective mechanism. Szasz's work resonates deeply with my approach, where I help clients uncover their inner resources to confront and resolve longstanding issues.

One critical aspect of modern diets is the presence of addictive chemicals in processed foods. These substances encourage overeating, often triggering more severe mental and physical health issues. If this topic interests you, I recommend reading the books I mentioned or seeking additional resources. We are ultimately our own best advocates for health, capable of experimenting with what works for us, especially when specialists may prioritise profit over genuine healing. Sometimes, a simple dietary change can resolve issues that even science hasn't fully understood yet, and that's perfectly okay.

Your health belongs to you. Doctors often don't have the time to thoroughly investigate individual cases, instead prescribing medication as a one-size-fits-all solution. While this approach may work for some, we are all unique, and what works for one person might not work for another. Adding chemicals to counteract issues caused by other chemicals is irresponsible, as it amplifies both the effects and side effects of the mixed concoction. Deciding how much responsibility you want to take for your health and how much to delegate to others is critical to achieving the best outcomes.

Finding a doctor specialising in my dietary approach has been transformative. Keeping my diet focused and straightforward has allowed me to address health concerns quickly, effectively, and affordably. Reflecting on my journey, I wish I had adopted the Carnivore diet earlier; it would have cleared toxins from my body much faster.

If you're curious about your susceptibility to certain substances, try giving up caffeinated drinks for a week. Alternatively, consider giving up your mobile phone for a week if that feels too daunting. Every time you think about reaching for it, you'll get a glimpse of what addiction feels like. The difficulty of withdrawal varies, but the challenge highlights how deeply ingrained specific dependencies are in our lives.

This raises an important question: If we struggle to give up something mild, such as coffee (or caffeine) or a mobile phone, how can we expect to tackle more substantial dependencies, like those on alcohol, tobacco, sugar, processed food additives, or even prescription medications? For me, quitting coffee was a game-changer. After transitioning to the Carnivore diet, I felt more relaxed and in control of my life. However, once I gave up coffee, my stress levels decreased, my energy increased, my sleep improved, and a minor health issue (dry skin) that had been lingering for weeks was resolved.

Quitting coffee required both physical and mental adjustments, but it also eliminated my sugar cravings. Now, I can enjoy small indulgences, like a chip or a piece of chocolate, without succumbing to further cravings. I've realised that coffee has triggered my desire for sugary products, particularly chocolate, which contains caffeine. Fasting has also become more manageable, and my weight is finally moving in the direction I want after hitting previous plateaus.

For those interested in the potential downsides of caffeine, I recommend Caffeine Blues by Stephen Cherniske. This book offers an eye-opening exploration of its effects. I suspect one reason doctors rarely suggest quitting coffee is that many of them are addicted to it themselves.

From personal experience and research, I've learned that eliminating foods and food-like products not designed for our consumption has dramatically improved my mental and physical health. While the foods I now eat are less exciting than my previous Diet, I view food as functional rather than indulgent. Food is not merely an addition to our well-being. It's central.

Philosophy

In ancient Greece, philosophy was considered the medicine of the mind. Today, many people are unaware of the philosophies they follow or how they shape their lives. Philosophies like Stoicism, Epicureanism, and Pythagoreanism were once actively lived, debated, and woven into the fabric of daily life. They provided structure, ethics, direction, and insight, helping individuals recognise and appreciate diverse perspectives on the world.

Actively embracing a chosen philosophy, such as Stoicism or Epicureanism, can have a profound impact on our lives. In contrast, passively adhering to philosophies we aren't even aware of can leave us feeling unmoored. Reading and practising philosophy has helped me organise and tame many of my thoughts, offering clarity and understanding about myself and others, particularly in questions like who we are, why we exist, and what we aim to become.

Stoicism, for instance, is a practical philosophy that is seeing a resurgence today. Introducing profound yet straightforward concepts into our lives provides us with tools to navigate challenges with greater resilience and composure. Once we become aware of these ideas, we can adopt them or, as in ancient Greece, create our philosophies to align with our unique needs and values.

One of the most rewarding aspects of philosophy is the awareness it cultivates. The more we question our lives and thinking patterns, the more options we discover for growth and self-improvement. Even now, I continue to refine my philosophical outlook. Whenever I encounter an idea that resonates with me, it enhances the 'illusion' I follow (and we all follow some illusion) to make life simpler and more fulfilling in ways that suit my needs.

Philosophy is a lifelong pursuit. The more I realise how little I know, the more eager I am to learn. There is still so much to explore in the history of philosophy, including how others' interpretations can expand my perspective. Philosophy reminds us that there is rarely a single 'right' answer, only opinions shaped by education, experience, and context.

If you're wondering where to start, Stoicism is a good entry point, as it continues to gain momentum for its practical and timeless teachings. Another excellent philosophy to explore is Humanism, which complements Stoicism and Epicureanism beautifully, offering a structure to bring order to life's chaos.

For those new to philosophy, there are many accessible books worth exploring. One standout recommendation for beginners is *Sophie's World* by Jostein Gaarder. This book provides a beautiful overview of key philosophical ideas, sparking reflection and prompting new questions. It introduces the reader to the most significant aspects of philosophy in an engaging and approachable way, helping them identify areas of interest for further exploration, whether that's Stoicism, Humanism, or something entirely different.

Psychology

I have saved this section for last for several reasons.

Firstly, suppose our foods and food-like processed products are affecting us mentally, such as the side effects of these processes that cause people to think something is mentally or physically wrong with them and lead them to visit an expert. In that case, we may have unnecessarily been diagnosed with some mental or physical issue that could have been eliminated by avoiding certain foods and food-like products, and we have to unnecessarily carry a mislabelling for, perhaps, the rest of our lives.

As with myself, if we take our nutrition to the absolute basics, how many mental health issues would we overcome to think more rationally again? Since wheat had an impact on my mental health, is this one of the reasons why religions focus on bread as a staple that causes some level of irrational thoughts in such followers?

Secondly, what effect would this have on the medical industry if this were the case? Would they suffer financially, along with the doctors, encouraged by their patients to help them find the cause of the problem rather than treat the symptom? This is one reason why taking control of our health and researching what suits us is essential. We don't fit into a one-size-fits-all approach, so why do we allow others to treat us that way?

Even if I take this thought too far, how many people follow industrial philosophies without choosing their own? Each philosophy benefits someone on different levels, so instead of our benefits going to someone else, why not find out who, what, and when they, and we, benefit from such ways of thinking?

As a psychologist, one of my concerns is that we focus too strongly on emotions rather than helping clients tap into their inner resources to find and implement the solutions they have sought since that incident. Emotions are not worthless; they are significant indicators that something bothers us while searching for what we seek.

With every patient I have sat with, there has always been at least one key theme to their issues, and their problem is that they don't know what to do with what it, that may well keep them mentally tied up as they project various outcomes into their future and onto others which locks them into a time and threat that doesn't exist.

Examples of such are whether it is something as simple as an argument that hasn't been resolved, a death in the family or someone near to them, a problematic situation like bullying, family or societal oppression, leading up to the worst forms of neglect and abuse.

Even daily issues, such as affording food and rent, can have mental health impacts that can be alleviated quickly once the problem is resolved. However, no matter what type of stress or experience we have learned from, whether minor or significant, we can never be the same as we were before it happened, and that is good because it leads to inner growth.

While working out what is bothering us (regardless of what it is), we develop certain qualities that we carry for the rest of our lives. It doesn't mean what happened to us wasn't terrible; it was, but at least we can look at the past as an emotional and solution-building exercise for those moments we had no control over and accept what happened enough to move forward with the new qualities we find within ourselves without the past bothering us anymore.

We need practical solutions to help us navigate the part of life that was forced upon us and the fictional effects that spiralled out of control within our minds. We must understand and accept what happened, letting it go, which would help us move forward. Once we understand what happened and how it should have happened differently, we implement that solution in our past enough to release the burden, allowing the emotions to subside and leaving us free to move on with life as we wish. Our experiences are still there, should we need them sometime in the future, which allows us to remain more present.

Our job as psychologists or therapists is to help our clients learn how to release the past once they understand what has happened to them (we don't need to know every detail). Hence, they control the situation and tap into new inner resources, allowing them to live freely in the moment. We can show them how to let go, where to find their inner resources and how to respond differently the next time, should there be a next time, for example. We can help them learn how to change their beliefs and manage emotions such as pain, confusion, anger, shame, guilt, doubt, conflicts, and other complicated feelings quickly and effectively. They know what they want. As therapists, we often have no idea what our clients want. All we can do is show them how to release that burden by providing the answers they wanted to implement but didn't know how. That is the key part of our job: to show them how to do it and move forward with life thereafter.

Why am I not talking about understanding their emotions? In most cases, indirectly, they are by releasing the past cause with a practical solution rather than focusing on the symptoms. The symptoms disappear or are significantly reduced if we help them change their understanding of the cause. The client wants to move forward with life without being bothered by the past, rather than focusing on managing the emotional symptoms on a daily basis.

Why don't we, as psychologists, need to know the details of what happened? It's less traumatic for the client, quicker (if money earning isn't the primary goal of becoming a psychologist or psychotherapist), and more structured. We are showing them how the process works so they can release the past themselves, even when we are no longer available, should a new issue arrive unexpectedly.

If we, as psychologists or therapists, can't show them how to work through these issues quickly, are we doing our job correctly? Nothing is worse for a client than ending a session without finding a resource for a problem being worked on. Secondly, I am not doing my job correctly if a client doesn't leave with at least one new resource or solution that allows them to release their past issues within that session.

Naturally, this works only with those who want to release the past and work through our processes to live a new life. As the old saying goes, those who think they can achieve something will, and those who believe they can't, won't.'

This sounds like quite a statement. Yet, it has worked for the hundreds I have worked with (excluding the use of psychedelics) in finding their inner resources to release the past.

And that's it, other than to say that the world-renowned therapist Thomas Szasz is correct. Generally, there is no mental illness. We are seeking solutions to the problems that have been lingering from the past. All we have done is build a mentally defensive system to protect us from it ever happening again until we find a solution. Once we have that solution, we know how to react should it ever happen again, and we can dismantle that defensive system to allow us to get on with our lives.

Where Am I Today?

In May 2025, I worked through my past and am living as I ethically choose to, with new projects planned once I have released this book. I proudly stand outside society because I don't like what it offers, and I only enter it when it provides me with what I want without the risk of it pulling me in. I prefer to choose philosophies and goals that suit my needs and curiosity rather than following an inferior yet well-functioning system that benefits the instigators more than me.

I still wear my appropriate masks and play the stage game accordingly each day. I am still learning, but my game rules are different and more suitable to me, making life more enjoyable, simpler, and stress-free. That doesn't mean things don't go wrong and that I don't make mistakes; I do, but I deal with those moments accordingly, which frees me up to be in the moment that stops me from being pulled into the system that can sap my limited time and energy.

This change in thinking impacts our life choices regarding how we earn money, how we spend it, how we make the most of our time here, and ultimately, how we care for ourselves because the only resource we sacrifice for all these choices is time, with the unknown lifespan we have on this beautiful planet.

We have many choices of how we want to spend our time here. We can dedicate our lives to someone else's dream, work on our inspirations, or mix the two. It doesn't matter as long as we live according to what we believe is best for us rather than what others think is best for us. Others don't care what happens to us because they have learnt to take and not give.

A reassuring thought I have to remind myself of is that what we do with our time here is unknown; what we do with our time is our choice, rather than mindlessly following something we have been convinced is the only way. Additionally, how we interact externally reflects how we perceive ourselves internally. For example, we treat the external world as a disposable commodity, and we often treat ourselves in the same manner. We treat ourselves with love and respect, and do the same with the wonderful people around us. It can be so wonderfully simple when we want it to be.

Lastly, throughout our entire time here, nothing belongs to us, not even the resources on earth and what we take from them; we must also return the remains to future generations. This isn't just for future humans but for the universal system as a whole. As a species, and unlike other living things, this is the one thing we have forgotten in exchange for a world of fantasy.

Ultimately, nothing guides or pushes us, and nothing is demanded of us other than survival and reproduction. We have no place on this planet that sets us apart from different species, and we all have a right to be here. In the millennia, once we had food and safety, the rest was our free time, yet today, we use our free time to justify these two essentials. Also, those essentials have been downgraded to prioritise the non-essentials first. In other words, free time comes first, and survival comes second, although today's societal system and philosophies often disguise this order.

How? We sit in our temporary home, surrounded by the things we have collected, engaging in temporary activities such as work and hobbies, believing that this is all our existence is. Yet we are homeless, we are insignificant, we own nothing, and when we die, we take nothing with us. Still, we focus on what we can externally collect along the way, what we can identify with, and how we can control the uncontrollable chaos to achieve some form of order, perceived stability, and external recognition.

Yet, our lives can change instantly, and if we choose to, we can return to our generational roots just as quickly, leaving the system where we have been trained to be ashamed of and criticise others for some temporary and superficial systemic chemical rush. We focus on the outer world stage games that don't exist except within our minds, and we try to live up to them based on other people's unique moral expectations instead of finding our roots, what is essential to ourselves, and being content with them. Other than food, water and security, everything we need lies within.

Only when we have achieved internal peace and harmony can we enjoy and integrate with the external world through our internally reprogrammed ego rather than being told what is right and wrong by others. Sure, it's wild and dangerous out there, and there are only the Universal rules of survival to abide by (even within the system, the Universal rules have the last say about our health, well-being and how long we remain alive).

Still, no matter how wild, crazy, or dangerous life becomes, our ethics determine what and how we interact with others around us. We already operate within a dual system: the universal system of survival and procreation, and the current substandard moralistic system of external identification and pleasure, which has additional fictional risks. We are not designed to fully comprehend this one-sided system, nor are we encouraged to do so.

We have no control over anything except what we think, say (or, in other words, grunt eloquently), and do. Let's start there and live by our ethics, making our time an experience that empowers us to give rather than take, and which of these temporary memories we are willing to add to the ether.

Thank you for reading this book of ideas, changes, challenges and rants. I hope that somewhere, I have helped someone understand something within themselves, because externally, there's nothing to understand; that's just circumstantial. Additionally, I have taken my thoughts further than I thought I was capable, and I am sure that, on occasion, I have misunderstood myself or not yet fully grasped a particular concept.

However, that is the fantastic experience of listening to others to consider how I can apply their thoughts to mine in helping me understand who I am, what I am, what gives me my value and how I can help provide value to others who think (not necessarily the same as me) in understanding how little I know and how integrated all our lives, regardless of what living creature we are, that we all have the same goal until we die, survival and once we have that, then it is our free time to do with what we want.

Okay, I am waffling and repeating myself. There is something else I want to say, but I'm having trouble formulating it. Maybe one day, I will understand what it is. Yet, I know that when I appreciate my interpretation of what I want to say here, there will be something else I am trying to understand, and so on. I could wait until I know what it is, but if I constantly wait until I understand everything, this book will never be complete.

My final thought on this book is that whoever you are, regardless of your background, upbringing, race, or any disability you may have, you are worth it, irrespective of your experiences. Love yourself for who you are and grow from your experiences. The most remarkable people get on with it without crying and shouting about whatever they think they miss out on and how unfair the world is. They are a victim of their delusions. Just get on with it, wherever you are, even if life has dealt you a horrendous start with even bleaker prospects. Please try, fail, fall, pick yourself up, learn from it, and do it again until you can achieve the standard you wish to reach. And once you have done that, keep to your ethics and expand on your personal goal(s) in life.

These individuals earn my respect because they operate within universal rules, not systemic ones. Without realising it, you may help someone understand something about themselves that could be passed on to someone else, and that is one of the most remarkable side effects of living authentically. No matter how hard that start was, the quality, skill, inner strength, and resources you gathered from that unwanted experience make you unique.

Neil

November 2024

Thank You

This book has always aimed to show how I approached it, what I went through, and, more importantly, how my thinking and personality evolved as my beliefs and opinions changed. It may not have been the best way I went about this; we don't know. Then again, maybe it was.

Neil

www.ingramcontent.com/pod-product-compliance
Lightning Source LLC
Chambersburg PA
CBHW052014070526
44584CB00016B/1741